# The Family Fund

International Library of Social Policy

General Editor   Kathleen Jones
*Professor of Social Administration*
*University of York*

Arbor Scientiæ
Arbor Vitæ

A catalogue of the books available in the **International Library of Social Policy** and other series of Social Science books published by Routledge & Kegan Paul will be found at the end of this volume

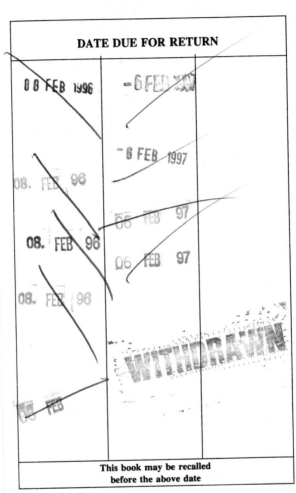

# The Family Fund

## An initiative in social policy

Jonathan Bradshaw
*Department of Social Administration*
*University of York*

Routledge & Kegan Paul
London, Boston and Henley

First published in 1980
by Routledge & Kegan Paul Ltd
39 Store Street,
London WC1E 7DD
9 Park Street,
Boston, Mass. 02108, USA and
Broadway House,
Newtown Road,
Henley-on-Thames,
Oxon RG9 1EN
Set in Press Roman by                        cc
Hope Services, Abingdon
and printed in Great Britain by
Thomson Litho Ltd
East Kilbride, Scotland

British Library Cataloguing in Publication Data

Bradshaw, Jonathan
The Family Fund. – (International
library of social policy).
1. Handicapped children – Services for –
Great Britain
2. Economic assistance, Domestic – Great
Britain
I. Title        II. Series
362.8'2        HV890.G7        80-40003

ISBN 0 7100 0520 2

# Contents

# Figures

# Tables

# Acknowledgments

The research on the Family Fund was essentially a matter of team work, and without the collaboration of other members of the team, this book would not have been possible. Sally Baldwin and Caroline Glendinning joined me as research fellows. Dorothy Lawton started work as a coder and became a part-time research fellow responsible for the data bank; she has been of particular help in the computation and statistical analyses. Margaret Joyce has diligently coded the details of over 42,000 applicants for the computer, and Jane Weale, Edwina Goodwin, Christopher Hood, and David Phillips collaborated in parts of the analysis. Jeanne Horsfield has played a key role as project secretary throughout. I am also grateful to Liz Wilson and Sue Medd who have typed and retyped drafts, and to John Cook who helped to prepare the manuscript for publication.

Without the co-operation of the staff of the Joseph Rowntree Memorial Trust and the Family Fund, this research would not have been possible. I am most grateful to all the staff, particularly Lewis Waddilove, Robin Huws Jones, and Ralph Connelly from the Trust and Dennis Hitch and Eleanor Barnes from the Family Fund, for their willing co-operation at all times.

The Trust established an advisory committee on the research consisting of Peter Barclay, Lewis Waddilove, Robin Huws Jones, Gerrard Bebb, Elspeth Hope Murray, Walter Henderson, Andrew Dunsire, and Kathleen Jones; I am most grateful for the work they put into reading and commenting on working papers.

I am particularly grateful to Kathleen Jones who encouraged and supported the research project within the department and in the University.

Finally, I am also grateful to the many thousands of families caring for severely handicapped children who have helped in this research. I hope that they more than anyone agree with the conclusions.

# Introduction

On 29 November 1972, Sir Keith Joseph, Secretary of State for the Social Services, announced in Parliament that he would establish a fund of £3 million, 'to ease the burden of living on those households containing very severely congenitally disabled children.'[1] This unexpected announcement was the result of a public campaign on behalf of children damaged by the Thalidomide drug. To administer the Fund, the government bypassed all existing statutory agencies and sought the help of an independent charitable trust – the Joseph Rowntree Memorial Trust, based at York. The Trust had no experience of the type of work that would be required, nor any special expertise in the field of child handicap, but with some misgivings it agreed to take on the task of administering the Fund for three years in the first instance.

The Fund was named the Family Fund and began operations in March 1973. In December 1974 its terms of reference were extended to include the non-congenitally disabled and by April 1976, the date on which this study ends, the Fund had received applications from 31,788 families and distributed grants in cash or kind worth £6,827,679. The Fund was established for three years in the first instance, subsequently refinanced until the end of 1978, and is now operating on an open-ended contract.

The Family Fund is a small policy innovation in terms of resources, yet it is nevertheless a particularly interesting subject for research. The manner in which it developed is unusual; it was announced suddenly in response to a crisis; it was devised and established with great rapidity; and the administrative form it took was unprecedented in British social policy. Never before have such large amounts of public money been given to an independent body to distribute directly to the public.

The Joseph Rowntree Memorial Trust recognised the research opportunities presented by the Fund and decided to establish an independent research project at the University of York in order to monitor and evaluate the work of the Fund. In doing this, they gave research workers a most unusual opportunity of observing and evaluating an agency developing from its inception. This opportunity presented by the Trust could not have been brought to a successful conclusion without the active support of the Trust's director, Lewis Waddilove, and the very open way in which the staff of the Trust and the Family Fund responded to the research.

The Family Fund has presented many research opportunities. The information available from the large number of families who applied to the Fund has supported studies of a range of subjects, including the needs of families with handicapped children; the operation of existing health and personal social services; and aspects of the social security system. Features of this research have been reported elsewhere; this book is focused on the Family Fund itself, and provides an over-all evaluation of its work during the first three years of its operation.

# 1    Methods

There is no one method available to evaluate the effectiveness of a social policy initiative.[1] In this study a variety of social research techniques have been employed to collect relevant data – including sample surveys, statistical analysis of records, interviewing, and observation. However, the over-all strategy adopted is 'action research'. This term has been used to describe a wide variety of approaches to social investigation.[2] Broadly speaking, action research ranges from action informed by a measure of social investigation – the model adopted by many of the Community Development Projects – to action directed to research purposes, such as the field trial or quasi-social experiment which was adopted in the national pre-school experiment that formed part of the Educational Priority Area study.[3]

The action research approach adopted in this study falls somewhere between these extremes. The Family Fund was certainly not the handmaid of the research project and the research project endeavoured to be as independent as possible of the Family Fund. This approach was determined more by circumstance than by the choice of the participants in the project. Given a choice, the ideal research design to evaluate, at least, the substantive goal of the Family Fund would have been an experimental one. Cochrane has advocated the increased use of such techniques in evaluation studies of the social services[4] and some attempts have been made to use experimental studies in social policy.[5] An experimental design would have been the only means of demonstrating beyond reasonable doubt whether a change has occurred as a result of the help given by the Fund, and that that change would not have taken place without its help. Although one part of the evaluation reported in this study has involved at least a quasi-experimental method, the main characteristics of an experiment could not be adhered to. For example, it was not possible to obtain measurements before the intervention of the Family Fund because, as with many action research projects, the research began some months after the Fund had begun issuing grants. Also it would have been unethical to have withheld help from some families in order to obtain the necessary control data. Furthermore, an experimental design by itself would not have elicited the kind of

1

multi-level data necessary for an over-all evaluation of a social pro-gramme, particularly on the administrative processes of the Fund.

As Caro has pointed out, the principal difficulty in action research concerns the relationship between action and research and that relation-ship depends on the position of research in the organisation.[6] There is a dilemma between 'inside' and 'outside'. The advantages of research remaining outside or independent of the organisation being evaluated are that the research worker can maintain greater objectivity and can avoid non-research tasks. He is not regarded as part of the organisation hierarchy and therefore he has freedom to publish. However, there are obvious advantages in being inside an organisation – in being able to observe in detail the processes at work, having access to administrative data, and having the opportunity to discuss developments with person-nel involved. Striking the right balance between involvement and independence is perhaps the most difficult task for action and research personnel in an action research project.

How was this tension resolved in this investigation? The project was formally independent of the Family Fund. It was financed by grants from the Department of Health and Social Security (DHSS) and the Joseph Rowntree Memorial Trust, and it was employed by and housed at the University of York. The research team was given complete freedom to decide what research was to be carried out and by what method, subject to limitations of available resources and the under-standing that research activity should not interfere too much with the work of the Fund. The research team was guided in its work by an advisory committee consisting of academics and members of the Trust and Family Fund management. Research workers were given completely free access to the Fund: they could attend meetings of the Panel, the Management Committee, and the Consultative Committee, as well as staff meetings; they were given free access to case files, administrative files and other records; and were afforded every opportunity to inter-view those involved in the work of the Fund.

In all its involvement with the Fund the research team endeavoured to maintain a neutral position, its members sitting as silent observers in meetings in order to minimise their impact on the policy of the Fund.

This was the formal position; but in a number of informal ways, the relationship between research and action was less clear-cut – the research workers were neither as independent as the formal arrangements suggest, nor was the Fund unaffected by the activities of the research. For example, because administrative statistics were vital for research purposes and because the team possessed the necessary technical skills, the research project took responsibility for providing the Fund with them. For research purposes this had two advantages; it gave the research project direct access to the statistical data necessary for monitoring the work of the Fund, and it also meant that the exchange of information between the Fund and the research project was not entirely one-sided.

However, the task of producing administrative statistics necessarily involved the research team to some extent in the administration of the Fund. In addition, the statistics that the research team produced, over and above those that would have been produced for normal administrative purposes, may have influenced the decisions of the Fund. For instance, the information that the grants from the Fund varied by social class would not have been available but for the associated research, and the finding might have been a factor in the Fund's decision, for example, to replace grants for second-hand cars by car hire. The information produced on area variations in application rates was certainly used in implementing the publicity programme.

The published and unpublished papers prepared by the research team during the course of its work were made available to the Fund and the Department of Health and Social Security. It is impossible to gauge the impact, direct or indirect, that these papers had on the policies of the Fund, the DHSS, or the general climate of opinion about the Fund.

In a number of simple ways, the research operation influenced the work of the Fund. For instance, if an error or oversight was identified when cases passed through the coding process, they were referred back to the Family Fund staff. In relationships with the staff over a three-year period, it was impossible to remain completely neutral in the views expressed about the Fund's policies and procedures.

In contrast, the Fund's staff also influenced the research. As well as the requests for particular studies, the actual research carried out was influenced by the views of the staff, either in conversation or through their attendance at the research advisory meetings. The principal audience for the research during the project was the staff, and disagreements about the implications of the findings inevitably influenced future research.

One of the original intentions of the research team was, in fact, abandoned partly because of the difficulties in remaining neutral. An attempt was made to maintain day-to-day observations of the organisation in order to analyse its behaviour at a micro level. This attempt was abandoned, partly because other research opportunities presented themselves which were of more interest to the team members involved, and also because it became impossible to observe the organisation closely without becoming embroiled in internal conflicts of opinion. To sum up, the research unit had some influence on the work of the Fund, which in turn certainly influenced the focus of the research. Research, however, was not part of the Fund; it ran alongside it, providing assistance where it could, but maintaining a critical if sympathetic independence. As George Smith has said about another context: 'The dilemma for research is whether to watch the race, setting up elaborate machinery to record exactly who wins or whether to study and inevitably be drawn into the jostling and argument . . . the wheeling and dealing.'[7] This research tried as far as possible to adopt the first alternative.

Five methods were used to collect data for this study.

## 1  Interviews

Interviews were conducted with all the participants in the Fund. These ranged from single interviews with, for example, key civil servants, the chairman of the Trust, and selected Family Fund agents, to regular interviews with, for example, the director of the Trust and the secretary and staff of the Fund. The interviews tended to be informal but were focused around specific subject areas. They were recorded in note form and subsequently fully written up. Interviews with the social work staff of the Fund were tape-recorded and the tapes transcribed in full.

## 2  Observation

The research workers were given access to the principal committees of the Fund. Most of the early Panel meetings and all the Management and Consultative Committees were observed. At these meetings the research worker did not participate unless asked to comment on the progress of the research or on the administrative statistics. Notes were taken during the meetings and these were supplemented by the official minutes where they were available. The research team also attended staff meetings, Fund agents' briefings, meetings with the public relations firm, public meetings about the Fund and press conferences, and they also sat in the open-plan office observing the work of the social work staff.

## 3 Documents

The research team had access to all the files concerned with the Fund and all correspondence relating to applicants to it. A collection was made of the important letters and documents covering the origins of the Fund, as well as copies of other documents such as forms, instructions, leaflets, standard letters, and internal memoranda. Statistical data on every case were collected, and the staff of the Fund and the research coder who worked in the Fund's offices were asked to direct the team's attention to any interesting cases. In this way, a collection was made of copies of letters from families, doctors, social service departments, and other agencies.

Two further methods provided the principal source of information for the evaluation of the Fund.

## 4 The data bank

As soon as the research project began work in August 1973, it was decided to establish a system designed to provide a statistical summary of the circumstances of each family applying to the Fund, thus creating a source of administrative and research data on the Fund's work. The system had to be designed quickly, as applications began to pour in; not all the data that were collected proved of use; and some data that would have been useful were not collected. A coder was employed to extract information from each family file and transfer it to a punching document; it was then put, via punch cards, on to a data file on the University of York computer. When families re-applied, the data on the file were updated. Analyses of this data file provided regular, up-to-date statistics on the Fund's operation and became a rich source of information in monitoring its work. However, for use beyond the analysis of the Family Fund, it has limitations because it is self-selecting and probably not representative of the population as a whole.[8]

## 5 Sample surveys

The information from the data bank was supplemented by a number of sample surveys. These were of four types:

The follow-up survey of 303 families who had been helped by the Fund up to December 1974. The families surveyed came from seven local authority areas: Nottingham, Nottinghamshire, the North and East Ridings of Yorkshire, Newcastle, Leeds and Sheffield. A random sample of about half the families who had been helped by the Fund in those areas was selected from the data bank. Each family was approached by the Fund and asked to co-operate and, with their agreement, they were interviewed by a trained interviewer using a structured interview schedule. The response rate for the survey was 96 per cent. The interview schedule, which had been piloted using families in York who had applied, covered the social characteristics of the families; the nature of the child's handicap and the problems presented; the help that they had received from statutory and other agencies; and the help that had been received from the Fund, and their assessment of its usefulness. The sample represented the characteristics of the population from which it was drawn – the families who had been helped by the Fund in those five areas at that time. However, the interviewing was carried out between January and March 1975 and all the families had been helped in the earlier and more generous stage of the Fund's existence. They may, therefore, have been less critical of the Fund's help than were the families interviewed at a later date.

The questionnaires from the survey were coded, punched on to cards, and analysed using the package SPSS. The results of the survey are used selectively throughout the following chapters.

Seventeen families from the follow-up survey were selected for further interviewing. Caroline Glendinning carried out this study, using focused interviewing techniques and a tape-recorder, and visiting each family three times over a six-month period in 1975. She is writing up this study separately, but some material from the transcripts of her interviews that has a bearing on the Family Fund is used in this study – particularly in chapter 7.

Three postal surveys of families who had applied to the Fund were carried out. Two of these concerned issues other than the Fund – the attendance allowance[9] and voluntary organisations[10] – and are not referred to directly in this study. The third postal survey was of 300 applicants to the Family Fund during February and March 1976; they were surveyed twice before and after they had received help from the Fund. Response rates were 86.3 per cent and 94.5 per cent. One of the notable features of the surveys carried out on the people helped by the Fund was the very high response rates.

The final type of survey carried out was of small samples of files at the Fund's offices. These studies involved locating certain types of cases and extracting information from them.

# 2     The origins of the Family Fund

In their major work on the development of social policy, Hall *et al.* have pointed out the scant attention given to the complexity of the process by which needs emerge and are accepted as priorities for government action at any given time, and a new policy formulated to tackle them.[1] Concepts such as 'social pity', 'national unity', 'public enlightenment', and so forth have often been the only explanation for policy developments adduced by the writers of early social administration textbooks.

The study of the origins of the Family Fund that follows in this chapter is, therefore, presented as not only an essential feature of any report on the work of the Fund, but also a contribution to the literature on policy development. We are concerned to try and answer the questions: why did the needs of families with handicapped children gain precedence over other needs in November 1972, and why and how was the Family Fund established to meet those needs?

To do this, it is necessary to reduce a myriad of variables into a simple and coherent whole which may in itself lead to gross distortion of the true process. It is also necessary to assess the role of those who frame policy; but here there is very little information available. In particular, no research workers in this field have ever been given access to information that may help them assess adequately the role of the civil service in social policy formation. Civil servants were only prepared to talk in the most general terms about the development of the Family Fund and it was not possible to obtain access to the departmental files which contain essential records of the meetings and the discussion papers that led up to the establishment of the Fund. The two principal civil servants from the social services and social security sections of DHSS involved in the origins of the Family Fund did, however, comment fully on a draft of this chapter, correcting a number of points of detail and confirming that the over-all interpretation of events is fair and accurate. Apart from the failure to get access to information held by the civil service, the other major blow to this analysis was Sir Keith Joseph's decision that he did not want to be interviewed about the origins of the Family Fund:[2]

I have a relatively poor memory and do not keep records of what lay behind policies or decisions when in office.

As will be seen, Sir Keith, as Secretary of State for Social Services, may have played a key role, not only in originating the Family Fund but in developing it in the form that it took. These imperfections in the data mean that from time to time in the analysis of the development of the Fund, one has to rely on more or less informed conjecture.

## Developments up to September 1972

Before the outburst of feeling about the attitude of the Distillers Company to Thalidomide children, the problems of the families of handicapped children were not a public issue, nor was there an articulated demand for a fresh policy initiative to help parents 'shouldering the various burdens which caring for these children entails'.[3] In public policy things were settling down after a spate of new social legislation which was just beginning to benefit these families. Just before the general election in 1970, Parliament had passed the Social Services Act which had implemented the main recommendation of the Seebohm Report - the establishment of integrated local authority social services departments. The new departments, preoccupied with establishing themselves and already preparing for local government reorganisation, were not pressing for new responsibilities, particularly as they were struggling to implement two other pieces of legislation - the Health Services and Public Health Act 1968, which had given wider powers to local authorities to help the disabled and elderly; and the Chronically Sick and Disabled Persons Act 1970, based on a private member's bill which had been rushed through Parliament before the dissolution in 1970, and which placed new duties on local authorities to identify all the disabled in their areas and provide aids and adaptations to those in need of them.

The other major new measure to benefit handicapped children and their families - the attendance allowance - had been introduced by the Labour government in 1970 as part of a bill, and was subsequently enacted by the new Conservative government in 1971. The allowance became payable to children in 1972 and was extended, at a lower rate, to the less severely disabled in October 1973. Both the attendance allowance and the Chronically Sick and Disabled Persons Act were the focus of public discussion during the period up to the summer of 1972. Sir Keith Joseph was pressed first to implement Sections 1 and

2 of the Chronically Sick and Disabled Persons Act and then to persuade local authorities to administer it more generously and more speedily. But this public interest was not focused on the additional needs of handicapped children, and was more concerned with the proper implementation of existing legislation than with the development of new initiatives.

A search of government and academic papers published in the years before 1972 does not indicate that child handicap was a developing issue of public concern. The only state paper published during the office of the previous two governments which paid any attention to the problems of families with handicapped children was the Seebohm Report.[4] The committee that drew up that Report devoted two chapters to the physically and mentally handicapped, and while it recommended the development, integration, and co-ordination of services for both groups within the new social services department, it did not single out the needs of children as a priority for extra resources.

In 1971 the in-coming Conservative government published a White Paper,[5] and although the needs of parents caring for handicapped children at home for counselling and practical assistance (see paras 14-20 and 139-45) were recognised, it made no mention of a new fund to assist them. In the same year the Government Social Survey Division published the first volume of Amelia Harris's large national sample survey.[6] This study, which had begun in 1967, presented an unprecedented amount of data about the number and condition of the impaired and was followed up in 1971 and 1972 by two further volumes on the housing and income of the disabled.[7] Although these studies reinforced concern and led to further public discussion of the needs of the handicapped, they did not deal with children and most of the attention which they generated was directed to adults.

During the 1960s and early 1970s, a number of independent research studies appeared.[8] While stressing the great physical and emotional burdens that many families had to cope with, they did not recommend any fresh tranche of money to alleviate their difficulties. This was also true of the other studies that were published in this period.

Perhaps the nearest thing to an official statement on the plight of handicapped children published during this period was the report of a National Children's Bureau working party on children with special needs.[9] Parents' letters received by the working party had stressed the need for financial help and described the extra cost of clothing, transport, and aids for incontinence. The report summed up the feeling of many parents with the following quotation from a mother with a six-year-old mentally handicapped son:[10]

> The easiest way as a first step towards helping to relieve the burden
> of increased costs a handicapped child causes would be to make an
> increase in his/her allowance on income tax or, in the case of
> parents of very limited means, a direct grant. But for dignity's sake
> don't make the parents be inundated with red tape, just a simple
> application, quick conferment and payment.

This plea for a Family Fund was not taken up elsewhere in the report
and in a short section on practical supportive services, the working party
merely welcomed the attendance allowance.

Therefore, a search of official and unofficial publications suggests
that there was no growth of special concern for the burdens which
parents faced in caring for a handicapped child and certainly no call
for fresh support for these families.[11] This view is confirmed if we
examine some of the other principal participants in the policy-making
process. None of the political parties mentioned child handicap in
their manifestos for the 1970 general election, nor was there any
interest in the subject shown by the policy-making bodies of the
parties, such as the Fabian Society, the Labour Party Research Department, the Conservative Central Office, the Bow Group, or the Monday
Club. The same was true of Parliament itself. In the late 1960s and
early 1970s, an increasing amount of interest in the problems of the
handicapped was shown by members but this concern did not extend
to handicapped children. During this period, there were no Commons
debates on this subject and in the Lords the only debate on handicapped
children concentrated on educational facilities. Only six questions were
tabled on families with severely handicapped children living at home.
Activity in Parliament cannot, therefore, be described as sustained
pressure for reform.

Nor is there any evidence that pressure groups were active in pressing
for improvements in benefits. None of the large voluntary organisations
representing handicapped children and their families has ever taken up
a radical pressure-group role on their behalf. Indeed, it was because of
the lack of such pressure from the older, established, traditional voluntary organisations that Megan du Boisson and Berit Thornberry founded
the Disablement Income Group (DIG) in 1966 to 'secure the provision
for all disabled people of a national disability income and an allowance
for the extra expense of disablement'.[12] DIG was a pressure group
with a more abrasive campaigning style than the other groups. It
developed close links with the parliamentary group on disability, and

Peter Large, one of its officers, became the semi-official lobbyist for the disabled. DIG used the press, lobbied ministers, and pressed for reform with some vigour, but by 1972 they had campaigned only for a disability pension scheme for adults.[13]

There is no conclusive evidence, but it is clear from the course of events that *government ministers* were not proposing any new benefit for disabled children. The Conservative government came to power in 1970, committed to cuts in public expenditure and taxation. In its first two years in office, the sections of the DHSS that were subsequently to have some hand in the Family Fund, were preoccupied, on the social security side, with the legislation relating to, and later the provision of, the attendance allowance and invalidity benefit; and in the social services field, with implementing the Social Services Act and the Chronically Sick and Disabled Persons Act, and with the reorganisation of local government and the health service.

Busy as the Department was, though, further possibilities were not entirely ignored. When the House of Commons Paper on future social security provision for the disabled was published, it was based on some of the thinking that had gone on in the Department since 1970.[14] This Paper admitted (para. 6) that 'Where disabled children are concerned we lack adequate information about their numbers and about the precise character of their needs.'

It seems reasonable to conclude that the Family Fund was not a premeditated innovation in social policy. It was not part of a long-term strategy, consistent with other measures and carefully planned and organised.

## The Thalidomide affair

Earlier in this chapter it was suggested that writers who have ascribed the development of new social policies to 'public outrage', 'the national conscience', and so forth were taking too simplistic a view. But in the case of the furore over the Thalidomide affair, these ascriptions bear more closely on the truth.

In the 1950s a German drug company called Chemie Gruenenthal manufactured a derivative of glutamic acid which they called 'Thalidomide'. It was sold as a totally safe, non-toxic sedative and sleeping pill, especially suitable for the tensions that occur in pregnancy. It was manufactured and marketed in the UK by Distillers Company (Biochemicals) Limited. In December 1961, after reports in Germany and Australia that women who had taken the drug between the fourth and sixth week of pregnancy were producing abnormal children, it was withdrawn from the British market. Subsequent investigation pointed to the conclusion that about 400 women in the UK who had taken the drug in pregnancy produced children with terrible deformities.

During the next ten years there was little public discussion about the 'Thalidomide affair'; the *sub judice* rule restricted press coverage to reporting the successive attempts by parents to obtain compensation for their damaged children through the courts. In September 1972, the *Sunday Times*, which had been investigating the Thalidomide affair since 1967, decided to campaign more forcefully in a series of investigative and leading articles. On 24 September 1972, it published the first of a series of special articles 'Our Thalidomide Children. Cause for National Shame'. These articles led to a massive upsurge of public concern about Thalidomide children which involved the courts, Parliament, the government, shareholders, the rest of the press, trade unions, local authorities, the large city institutions, retailers, consumers, and many other organisations, institutions and individuals. The public furore over Thalidomide resulted in a number of developments in policy, including compensation for the children at least six times more than the sum originally offered by Distillers; a Royal Commission on Civil Liability and Compensation for Personal Injury;[15] changes in the legal interpretation of contempt in civil cases; a Law Commission report on civil liability in ante-natal injuries;[16] and an Act that changed the law on that subject.[17] It also led the government to establish the Family Fund.

It is worth reflecting briefly on why the Thalidomide campaign produced these results. The public conscience was awakened suddenly and without warning. The *sub judice* rule had stifled public comment and people generally had not become inured to the damage caused by Thalidomide. The numbers of children involved were small enough to identify with; their disablement was visible and was not associated with any kind of mental disability. They were, therefore, a group with which the public could easily sympathise. By contrast, Distillers was one of the largest, richest and most successful public companies in the UK and it was not at any risk if it paid the compensation. In these circumstances, as soon as the campaign became a public issue, it had a good chance of success. The decision of the *Sunday Times* to mount it was critical, and the matter would certainly not have developed without the newspaper articles. However, there were other important factors that influenced the outcome. The Attorney-General's intervention to suppress an article in the *Sunday Times* meant that the campaign became not just the cause of one newspaper but an issue concerning the whole of Fleet Street. Parliament played an important part in keeping it alive during November and December, reflecting a developing public interest; and through the coverage given to debates and questions, MPs were also responsible for setting the tone of that interest. The actions of individual Distillers' shareholders were sparked off by the *Sunday Times* and eventually led to the intervention of the large City institutions, no doubt motivated partly by self-interest but also by the very strong wave of public concern. It was their intervention that finally decided Distillers to make a new and more generous settlement. One of the major participants in most social policies, the government, played a relatively dormant role. From time to time during the campaign, both press and Parliament attempted to involve the government: to get it to use its authority to persuade Distillers to settle or to provide a settlement itself, or to make special tax concessions to the company. Considering the extent of press, public, and parliamentary activity, it is remarkable how successful the government was in remaining aloof from the issue. One reason for this success was the Family Fund.

## The announcement and establishment of the Family Fund

A government fund was not one of the original objectives of the *Sunday Times* campaign. The only action it demanded from the government was the reform of the law relating to compensation and the establishment of a state insurance scheme. However, on 29 October 1972 the *Sunday Times* reported that the Shadow Cabinet was to press for an early debate on Thalidomide with two aims:[18]

> Firstly, to press the government to make immediate *ex gratia* payments under an urgent *ad hoc* scheme to help all known and outstanding cases, and secondly, to have the law of compensation amended.

The motion already tabled by the all-party Committee for the Disabled still said nothing about a fund, but during the following week it was announced that the German government and Chemie Gruenenthal had established a joint fund for the German victims. Jack Ashley followed this up by writing to the Prime Minister to suggest that the government should take a similar initiative. Then, in the adjournment debate on 16 November, Mr Ashley urged the government 'to establish a fund for the children immediately without prejudice to present negotiations' and Mr Astor supported him, saying:[19]

that the government should consider setting up a national fund
for these children and their families . . . . In the meantime [they
should] consider the possibility of . . . giving financial support
to one of the charities, such as the Lady Hoare Trust.

Mr Dean answering for the government said:[20]

As for the special fund I am sure that the Hon. gentleman
appreciates that I cannot on such an occasion as this add to
what the Prime Minister said to the House on Tuesday.

The Prime Minister had said that he would agree to consider carefully
the setting up of a special fund or the support of existing funds. On 19
November, a leader in the *Sunday Times* took up the idea of a fund,
saying:[21]

The case for the government establishing a foundation is twofold:
first common humanity, secondly the responsibility the state has
for their part in distributing a damaging drug.

On 25 November, the Sunday before the debate and the announcement
of the creation of the Family Fund, the *Sunday Times* reported that[22]

when the Commons debates the plight of the Thalidomide
children this week the government will say that a national
foundation cannot be set up until pending legal negotiations
are complete.

By the time the matter came to be debated on 29 November, the
Opposition motion clearly called for[23]

immediate legislation to deal with the problems of such
Thalidomide children including the establishment of a trust
fund to provide for the Thalidomide children.

In his speech Sir Keith Joseph gave two reasons why he considered the
recommendation for legislation was unsuitable:[24]

First it might prejudice negotiations . . . a company that wishes
to avoid responsibility might welcome the responsibility being
taken by the taxpayer. Secondly, desperate though the plight of
the Thalidomide children is, there are many other children equally
disabled.

The announcement about the Fund came towards the end of his speech
and it is worth quoting in full:[25]

No, I will not give way. I have something to say which the House will want to hear before I sit down. I must say again, so that I do not lose the thread of the argument, that compensation is for the company and that the new offer indicates active negotiation.

The government must recognise that there are others born with desperate congenital disabilities which gravely burden their families and which are as severe as the loss of limbs due to Thalidomide. Such families are inevitably involved in all manner of special needs. Many of these needs are the responsibility of statutory authorities but there are other forms of help outside these responsibilities which could improve the life of a child and reduce the burden on its family. The government accept that more needs to be done for children with very severe congenital disability whether or not caused by the taking of Thalidomide.

In many cases the parents need more help in shouldering the various burdens which caring for these children entails. I have already paid tribute to the remarkable achievements of many of the parents concerned. The government have therefore decided to make the sum of £3 million available for this purpose, virtually at once. It is not intended that this money should be by way of compensation for being disabled, but rather that it should serve to complement the services already being provided by statutory and voluntary bodies to help the families concerned.

With this in mind the government will begin at once to consider, in consultation with the statutory and voluntary bodies likely to be concerned, what arrangements they can set up so that the money can best be used for the benefit of the children and their parents. The House can be assured that this will be carried out as quickly as possible. Further, in the light of experience with this operation and as soon as the cases are no longer *sub judice* the government will consider whether to provide a similar further amount of money in trust.

He concluded this speech with the following:[26]

I come now to the motion and the amendment. Because we do not believe, as the Opposition motion presses, that we should legislate at once, or that we should weaken the pressure on the parties to reach a satisfactory settlement, I ask the House not to approve the motion. The motion as amended, in the light of what I have been able to announce today, does meet the three tests which I believe all Hon. Members should set. The amended motion does not prejudice the settlement; it does not wholly and in the light of what I have announced leave out the other very severely congenitally disabled. It provides help now for Thalidomide families, those who need help complementary to that provided by the local authorities in their noble effort to bring up these children. I hope that the House will not accept the motion. I hope that if it is pressed my Hon. Friends will vote against it and support the amendment.

The announcement of the Fund was generally welcomed in the debate, though one or two Labour speakers said that it was too little and others argued that if the government was to establish a proper trust fund, it could do so without prejudicing present negotiations and that Thalidomide children could be selected for special treatment, because their condition was man-made. Alfred Morris, summing up for the Opposition, asked a number of questions about how the Fund would be administered and in his reply Sir Keith Joseph gave the following information:[27]

> The House has generally welcomed the government's decision to make available virtually at once, as soon as we can make the necessary arrangements, a fund of £3 million. I emphasise again that this is not compensation. Its purpose is to ease the burden of living on those households containing very severely congenitally disabled children.
>
> These children and these households look, above all, to the local authorities and the statutory services for the help they need. We intend to help from this fund to complement the statutory services available.
>
> We have it in mind – this answers a question asked by my Hon. Friend the Member for Clapham (Mr William Shelton) – to try to find a set of trustees of an existing trust with responsibilities sufficiently wide to cover beyond Thalidomide the other very severely congenitally disabled cases. We hope that we shall be able to put this into action very soon. We believe that the trustees should have power to spend income and, where they judge fit, capital.
>
> I do not wish to overstate this case, but I suggest that those households which are under particular strain and about which we are, above all, worried during the period of waiting for a satisfactory settlement will be able to be helped to some extent by the trustees of this new sum.

Hon. Members asked me about the second £3 million to which
I referred. I emphasise again that this also is not for compensation.
It is intended to benefit, via the same channel, if our experience
of handling the first £3 million is satisfactory, the same limited
but rather wider than Thalidomide group, by the same means;
namely, the use of income plus capital as the trustees judge fit.

My Hon. Friend the Member for Clapham pressed me hard to
give a time by which this second tranche of money would be paid.
I only wish that I could satisfy my Hon. Friend, but I must stand
on the words of the amendment. This second tranche will be paid
when the cases are no longer *sub judice*.

Outside Parliament the announcement of the Family Fund was
received with a confused welcome. On 1 December both *The Times*
and the *Daily Telegraph* reported any clarification of the details of the
Fund which they had been able to obtain from the DHSS officials and
from the reactions of voluntary bodies representing disabled children.
*The Times* also carried a leader welcoming the announcement 'even if
that approval must be tempered by the uncertainty surrounding the
proposals and the limited assistance that can be provided with such a
sum'. The leader went on to speculate about how the Fund should be
administered and whether an independent trust should or could be
given discretion:[28]

> The administrative arrangements therefore need to be capable of
> carrying a heavier responsibility later on . . . the government should
> act on the assumption that they are establishing a framework for
> a more ambitious system of help for disabled children in the
> future. What is really no more than a small step now could then
> become of more lasting benefit.

The following day the *Guardian* also carried a leader questioning the
adequacy of £3 million but congratulating Sir Keith Joseph for establishing the Fund. The leader concluded:[29]

> It is already devastatingly plain that it has needed the campaign
> to relieve the suffering from Thalidomide to bring forward action
> to help both kinds of victims. Even that must be regarded as only
> a small beginning to what must be a national reappraisal of
> responsibility to such people.

The *Sunday Times*, on 3 December, under the headline '£3 Million
Question: Where Will Mercy Money Go?' posed four questions:[30]

What did Sir Keith Joseph mean by 'very severely congenitally disabled'?
How many children need the money?
Who will qualify?
Who will administer the Fund?

On 30 November, the day after the debate, a professional social work official in the DHSS telephoned Robin Huws Jones, the associate director of the Joseph Rowntree Memorial Trust, and asked him which of the larger trusts (including the Joseph Rowntree Memorial Trust) might be likely to consider running a Fund of this kind. With the agreement of the trustees, Lewis Waddilove, director of the Trust, and Robin Huws Jones met officials at the DHSS on 6 December to assess the possibility of the Joseph Rowntree Memorial Trust's assuming responsibility for administering the Fund. At that meeting, the under-secretary of the DHSS said that he was anxious to entrust the task of administering the Fund to an organisation that was reliable, efficient, and discreet; and which was not one of the voluntary bodies concerned with specific aspects of disability. The Department would lay down broad guide-lines relating to the use of the money but the duties of the Trust would be to decide which parents of very severely handi-capped children needed help, what kind of help they needed, and to make available that help by way of payments to parents. The Trust representatives said that if they were formally asked to administer the Fund, agreement by their trustees would be dependent on the proposed guide-lines being acceptable to them and then, subject to these guide-lines, disbursement would be at the complete discretion of the Trust. The resulting discussions were minuted and the points made became the basis of the subsequent guide-lines. In the light of this meeting, Lewis Waddilove prepared a document explaining the background of the DHSS proposal and the matters that had been settled at the meeting on 6 December. This document was the first to state that the purpose of the Fund was to relieve stress.

At its meeting on 11 December, the Trust agreed to take on the Fund but, as one trustee pointed out, never before can six people have taken so long to accept £3 million. The chairman, Lord Seebohm, was initially against the Trust's taking on the job. He expressed concern about the impact that such an administrative task would make on the rest of the Trust's work. He feared that some of the acrimony sur-rounding Thalidomide would transfer itself to the Trust and to himself as its chairman, and as a vice-chairman of a very large international bank, he had natural reservations about associating himself with an issue that was already involving other City institutions. He also wondered whether this was the best way to help families. Were they merely bailing out the government who had gone out on a limb? The trustees were, however, persuaded by the arguments of Charles Carter, vice-chancellor of the University of Lancaster. He pointed out that if the Trust was capable of taking it on, they must find very good reasons for not doing so. It would benefit children and there were few other trusts to which the government could turn. It was something they ought to do; it would benefit the Trust, it was an honour to be asked; and it would enable the Trust to expand its interests. Above all, the Fund represented an opportunity for the Trust to be involved in a unique social policy experiment.

So the Trust agreed to take on the administration of the Fund, subject to a number of conditions, the more important of which were that they should do so for three years in the first instance and that the introduction of the scheme should be phased. These points, and the general terms of the Fund, were agreed at a meeting between Sir Keith Joseph, Lewis Waddilove, and Lord Seebohm at the House of Commons on the evening of 12 December. The announcement that the Trust had agreed to administer the Fund was made through the medium of an agreed answer to a parliamentary question on Friday, 15 December. After further discussions the Department wrote to the Trust's directors on 21 December, setting out the agreed principles which were to apply in the administration of the Fund.

## Reasons for the Fund

It has been shown that the demands for a fund for any sort of families with handicapped children had not been articulated before the Thalidomide campaign, and the concept of a trust distributing public money directly to families is unprecedented in British social policy. The following section attempts to explain the reasons for both these developments.

Part of the explanation must be in the political background. There was general outrage at the plight of the Thalidomide children. The government was being pressed by MPs and by the press to take various initiatives to provide immediate assistance. The German government had established a fund, the Opposition motion called for one. Although there had been no public threat, the government must have taken account of the fact that some of their own supporters might fail to vote for their amendment. In *Thalidomide: My Fight*, David Mason claims there was considerable background political activity. After Dr Tom Stuttaford had dropped a hint at a dinner party at 10 Downing Street that the government would be defeated over Thalidomide by its own back-bench MPs, Mr Heath sent his parliamentary private secretary, Timothy Kitson, to a meeting of the parliamentary party to ask what would persuade them to support the government. 'We won't take a penny less than £6 million', Stuttaford replied.[31]

The decision to establish the Fund was taken only the day before the debate in Parliament in which it was announced. It is likely that Sir Keith Joseph, having decided that it was necessary to provide some sort of assistance to Thalidomide-damaged children, turned to his officials to work out speedily, without prejudicing the court case and without discriminating against other families with equally handicapped children, the form that help should take. He may himself have hit upon the idea of using an independent trust. Such a scheme accords with Conservative philosophy, which inclines to voluntary rather than government action. The Conservative government was also interested in controlling the growth of the civil service. There was, and is, also a tendency in British public policy to separate purely executive operations from ministerial departments. However, although a Labour minister might not have instinctively turned to an independent trust for assistance, it is unlikely, in view of the need for speed and flexibility, that the decision made at such short notice, was based upon administrative or philosophical considerations. Very probably, the civil servants would have advised him to turn to an independent trust. In their discussions on the evening before the announcement they may have considered and rejected a number of public executive bodies who might do the work. The Supplementary Benefits Commission, for example, was already hard pressed and in any case it had limited legal powers to help families where the head of the household was in full-time work. Although the Commission's staff had experience in making discretionary payments to families, their traditions and procedures were wedded to providing for the essential needs of poor people rather than the generous and imaginative support envisaged as the role of the Fund. The Attendance Allowance Board was similarly pressed, coping with applications for the higher, and newly introduced lower, rate allowance and its staff had no experience of distributing *ad hoc* payments. Officials knew from their experience of supplementary benefits and the attendance allowance how difficult it was for government agencies to exercise discretion flexibly and to justify decisions in marginal cases. The DHSS had had recent experience in the Jimmy Martin case of the public outcry that can result from being forced to make invidious distinctions between different categories of severely handicapped children.

The civil servants may also have considered distributing the money through local authorities, but in one sense it was the inadequacy of existing services that created the need for a Fund. Experience in implementing the Chronically Sick and Disabled Persons Act 1970 had shown how difficult it was to get local authorities to maintain equivalent standards and it would have been impossible to ensure, through the rate support grant, that the money would reach families with handicapped children. To use local authorities to disburse the money would have required special legislation and, even then, the project could have foundered on the rock of the rate support grant and the administrative division between health, housing, and social services. The Fund clearly had to complement existing services, but the decision to establish an independent fund was probably made because speed was imperative – and not to outflank agencies already operating in the field.

The officials might have considered establishing a new trust but it would have taken time to establish and organise, and the Department's first consideration was to provide help quickly. The press and Parliament were demanding help immediately; a solution requiring legislation would have involved unacceptable delay, as well as prolonged and bitter arguments, and the civil servants must have decided that it would take too long to establish an organisation of their own.

So it was natural to turn to an existing trust for help. No doubt, the existing voluntary organisations working for handicapped children, particularly the Lady Hoare Trust, were considered, but their terms of reference were too narrow to enable them to take on the job. Furthermore, to select one of these agencies could possibly introduce jealousy among the organisations. They therefore had to choose a large and respected trust, the terms of which were broad enough to embrace the role envisaged for the Fund.

One reason why a government may choose to operate through an unorthodox agency is that the policy area is experimental; thus, voluntary organisations may be used to 'blaze a trail'. The DHSS was certainly operating in the dark when it established the Family Fund. It has been argued that there was no planning or thinking about this type of operation before the Thalidomide affair and there was little information available to officials at short notice about either the numbers or the needs of handicapped children. The experimental nature of the

Fund was taken up by the press after the announcement and it was perhaps the most important factor influencing the Trust to take on responsibility for its administration. However, it is not likely to have been the reason for turning to the Trust for help. The view in the Department at the time concerning the announcement was that they were making an *ad hoc* response to political circumstances. It was only after the announcement that they became aware of the Family Fund's potential as an experiment in the administration of a social service.

It was not clear from Sir Keith Joseph's statement in the House why the government had settled on £3 million and a further £3 million 'in trust as soon as the cases are no longer *sub judice*'. Clearly, the decision to give the £3 million was made in Cabinet and may have been influenced by the fact that it approximately matched the amount that Distillers were offering then. There appears to have been some confusion at the time of the announcement about the numbers of children that might come within the ambit of the Fund. Speaking about the second £3 million, Sir Keith said:[32]

> It is intended to benefit via the same channel if our experience
> of handling the first £3 million is satisfactory the same limited
> but rather wider than Thalidomide group.

This statement seems to suggest that he intended to restrict the Fund to disabilities broadly comparable with those of Thalidomide children.

> What we have in mind are children suffering from the most severe
> condition analogous to lack of limbs such as those suffering from
> the extremely damaging forms of for instance spina bifida. We have
> some difficulty because we must make a distinction. Because we
> have in mind the sort of children mentioned by the Hon. Member,
> I have had to exclude from this undertaking those who are born
> blind or those who are very shortly after birth discovered to be
> totally deaf. There has to be some limitation.[33]

Judging from these statements it is very probable that at the time of the announcement the Fund was intended to benefit a limited (but unknown) number of *physically* handicapped children. It was only after the announcement and the speculation about eligibility by the voluntary organisations representing different categories of handicapped children that it became clear that a wider range of handicaps, including the mentally handicapped and the blind and deaf, could not be excluded.

The lack of information in the Department about the numbers and nature of handicapped children was probably responsible for the decision to make the money available only to congenitally impaired children. We have since become aware that the non-congenitally handi-capped children in the UK are likely to number less than 10,000. If it had been realised how the Fund would develop, it could have included from the beginning all severely handicapped children. There was no justification for excluding them.

The word 'stress' was not mentioned at the time of the announce-ment. Sir Keith used the words 'burden', 'strain', and 'special needs', but 'stress', which eventually became a key word in the Fund's operation, was not mentioned. Neither did the word 'stress' appear in the minutes of the first meeting between DHSS officials and the Trust's officers. The word first appears, almost in passing, in the document which Lewis Waddilove prepared for the Trust meeting on 11 December. In it he wrote:

> The fund is to be used to relieve family stress directly; there is no question of grant-aiding organisations or institutions.

The point of this sentence was to explain that the help was to be provided directly (rather than indirectly) but the word 'stress' was repeated in subsequent documents and the relief of it was finally incorporated as the purpose of the Family Fund. In such ways are the goals of social policy set.

## The participants in the policy-making process

### The minister

It is not clear what initiative, if any, was taken by Sir Keith Joseph in establishing the Fund and the form which it took. The issue was raised not from within the Department but through pressure from outside, and though he *may* merely have followed official advice, he is unlikely to have done so. He had the reputation within his ministry of being a highly independent figure; he was known as 'The Baron' because of his style of direction, and because during his office he demonstrated his intellectual independence from his advisers by his controversial views on the cycle of deprivation. Not content to rely only on departmental advice, he was an energetic meeter of people and a visitor to agencies and institutions. It is, therefore, difficult to believe that he would have played a passive role during the Thalidomide debate. Yet his depart-ment's policy until quite soon before the debate was to reiterate what services were already being provided and to avoid intervening in the dispute between Distillers and the parents. Even after the debate and despite repeated calls in the press for him to play a part in the settlement, he remained aloof. It is probable that he and his Cabinet colleagues were determined not to embroil the government in the issue, but that they were eventually driven by the crescendo of public outrage and the threatened revolt of their back-benchers to provide some short-term assistance for the families.

## The civil servants

We have shown that the Family Fund was not a policy initiative that had taken years to evolve; nor did it fit easily into the existing pattern of benefits and services or the existing administrative structures within the DHSS. It is, therefore, very unlikely to have resulted from a demand emanating from within the Department. The Thalidomide affair acted as a powerful catalyst in bringing together the various interests within the Department - cash benefits, social services, health, and law. The role of officials in developing the Fund was critical; they were responsible for devising how £6 million could be raised and how it was to be distributed and, after the announcement, for recruiting the Trust and setting out the terms under which it was to operate. (It will probably never be possible to find out who exactly was responsible for extending the Fund outside the various categories of Thalidomide children, but the decision most likely emerged in the course of the urgent discussions between officials and ministers that preceded the debate.) However, the Fund did not spring from the action of officials; their role, like the minister's, was probably reactive.

In view of the limited time between the decision to provide £6 million and the announcement in the Commons, and the fact that the idea of a Fund for handicapped children was completely novel, there could have been no contingency plans and only limited information available to officials. Yet the civil service responded with extraordinary speed and imagination. They were operating in a most favourable context - urgent and general public demands for action, the threat that their minister faced a defeat in the House, and a Cabinet decision that £6 million should be made available. It was because of this climate of opinion and the need for speed that they were able to obtain the resources from the Treasury, cut across their own departmental divisions, override any doubts they themselves might have had about the implication of establishing such a Fund, and waive the consultations that would normally take place with the local authorities' associations and voluntary bodies.

*The private citizen*

Among the individuals who played a decisive part in the establishment of the Family Fund perhaps the outstanding one was David Mason.[34] It is certain that without his determination to stand out against the proposed settlement with Distillers, the issue would certainly not have been raised by the *Daily Mail* and the *Sunday Times*.

The Thalidomide affair was also an unusual example of the 'pressure of public opinion'. The general public was involved as consumers of Distillers' products, as shareholders, as electors of MPs, as correspondents to newspapers, and even in some cases as demonstrators. This public opinion was naturally articulated and shaped by Parliament, the media, and through *ad hoc* pressure groups, but the concern of individual citizens was without doubt an important factor in setting up the Fund.

*The pressure groups*

There was no existing group with the resources, experience, and enthusiasm to harness the issue and press the case. The Lady Hoare Trust, which had been established to provide support for families with Thalidomide-damaged children, was a service-giving agency, and Sir Keith Joseph himself said that his department had never received representations from them on behalf of the families.[35] Lady Hoare herself was ill when the affair broke and though the Trust did provide the Department with information about the children (and show Sir Keith Joseph a film in the House of Commons before the debate), it never actively called for changes in policy. The parents of the Thalidomide children were divided between those who had settled, those who wanted to settle, and those who refused to settle; and the extent to which they were able to participate was also influenced by their legal advisers, Messrs Kimber Bull, who throughout the affair maintained that the best interests of the parents would be served by pursuing their case through the legal channels.

During the campaign, *ad hoc* pressure groups did spring up – notably the shareholders – and the final settlement was a result of the pressure of large City institutions; but the Family Fund did not originate in the information, advice, ideas, or influence of promotional or interest groups.

*The mass media*

A question often asked in discussing the role of the media in policy formation is: Do they reflect public opinion or do they formulate it? The Thalidomide affair is a clear example of the media initiating and carrying through a campaign with the explicit purpose of achieving policy changes. Bruce Page, Phillip Knightley, and Elaine Potter of the *Sunday Times* Insight team had engaged in inquiries into Thalidomide for a number of years. Harold Evans, the editor, finally made the decision to launch the campaign despite the risk of prosecution. He may have been confident that public opinion would be moved by his coverage but in no real sense was the newspaper *reflecting* public opinion; indeed, the public were largely unaware of it. Of course, once the issue had been raised, the *Sunday Times* and the rest of the media reflected public opinion in the sense that they provided a forum for actors in the policy process. But the *Sunday Times* continued to lead opinion and open new fields of action. For example, Tony Lynes was given the names and addresses of other Distillers' shareholders to help him form an action group; a group of those concerned met regularly throughout the campaign in the paper's offices; and Evans kept in close touch with Jack Ashley and certain other MPs. Through the paper's determination to contest the injunctions as far as the House of Lords, it kept the issue alive and involved the rest of Fleet Street; and by publishing lists of the Distillers' shareholders, it ensured the involvement of the institutions. This policy issue is an unusual example of the press formulating public opinion and the action of the *Sunday Times* demonstrates that a newspaper can be the principal cause of policy change.

*Political parties*

The Thalidomide affair was not a party political issue. It is true that Parliament debated an Opposition motion, that the parties followed their whips through the lobbies, and that Barbara Castle, at the Labour Party Conference, committed the parliamentary Labour Party to fighting for a just settlement, but this was no more than the formalism of political debate and the natural stance of an Opposition. The issue arose too suddenly, and with too general a consensus, to develop into a party political issue. The Conservative Party, with its business links, might have been in danger of being associated with Distillers, particularly after the intervention of the Attorney-General to stop the publication of the second *Sunday Times* article. Sir Keith Joseph himself admitted an interest during the Thalidomide debate; he was 'a name at Lloyds', and in so far as insurance money was involved in meeting the settlement for the children, he would, albeit at a great distance, have borne part of the cost. Clearly, this would not have influenced his views one way or the other and is only mentioned here to illustrate the links that existed.[36] But it soon became clear that the business world was as disturbed as anyone by Distillers' actions, and with the Chancellor refusing to 'let Distillers off the hook' with tax concessions and Conservative ministers refusing to be drawn into a defence of Distillers, and with the Labour Party, for the most part, leaving the running to the all-party disablement group in the Commons, the parties managed to avoid an ideological dispute.

*Parliament*

Modern political scientists consider that government, not parliament, is decisive in the making of policy. Parliament has a measure of formal control over policy and may influence the details of it but, in general, priorities for action are determined by government and not Parliament.

This view is qualified by the events leading to the establishment of the Family Fund. Individual MPs, the all-party group on disablement, and the Opposition all evidently played key roles in determining the outcome and, behind the scenes, it is probable that pressure by back-bench Conservative MPs was influential in obtaining government action.

Parliamentary activity during the Thalidomide affair was particularly important because comment in the press was to some extent stifled by the *sub judice* rules. Through parliamentary questions, the tabling of motions and speeches in the adjournment, supply and Queen's Speech debates and, finally, in the full debate, MPs were able to maintain pressure on the government and Distillers. The lead in this was initially taken by the all-party committee on disablement chaired by the deaf MP, Jack Ashley, but as the issue gathered momentum the demands within Parliament became more general. This activity, the specific demand for the establishment of a fund in the Opposition motion, and the fear that they might be defeated in the debate, must have decided the government to announce the establishment of the Family Fund. A defeat in the House would not have brought them down but it would have been a serious embarrassment for them.

It seems clear that in this instance, the policy-making role of ministers and civil servants was negligible. It was action by parties outside government that was decisive in framing the policy adopted.

## Conclusion

This description and analysis of the origins of the Family Fund leaves much to be desired. Any attempt to do justice to the complexity and diversity of the influences, events, and personalities that go to make up the policy-making process is bound to oversimplify, to be selective, and to be in danger of over-emphasising in one place or under-emphasising in another. Even with unfettered access to the necessary information this would be the case; but students of social policy development do not have open access to vital data, particularly the part played by civil servants and government ministers in the policy-making process. As a result any case study must in part be speculative and incomplete.

With this limitation in mind, let us now, however, try to set the Family Fund against Hall *et al.*'s three criteria – legitimacy, feasibility, and support – by which they claim the priority accorded any issue may be assessed.[37]

## Legitimacy

There was certainly some doubt about whether the provision of new help for these children was a legitimate concern for the government. It felt that the Thalidomide-damaged children were no more a state responsibility than any other group of children. The state was not at fault and therefore it had no special responsibility to compensate the parents; this was a private matter between the parents and Distillers. Uncertainty about the proper role of the government went further than this and was evidenced by the establishment of the Royal Commission on Civil Liability and Compensation for Personal Injury. Compensation for injury, except for war and industrial injuries, had not become a legitimate activity of the state. Yet here were new demands for a state fund for Thalidomide children. The government decided that the proper response was to legitimise help for Thalidomide children by including all handicapped children, by denying that it was compensation and presenting it merely as a complement to existing services and, meanwhile, through a Royal Commission addressing itself to the whole question of compensation. While a compensatory payment to one group of handicapped children who had been damaged by a privately manufactured drug was not a legitimate field for government, the extension and improvement of existing services raised no such problems.

## Feasibility

Whether a policy development is feasible not only determines its chances of gaining attention but also helps to explain why one course of action is introduced rather than another. The most important questions regarding feasibility are whether the resources of money, manpower, parliamentary time, or equipment are available. The Family Fund was possible because it was a relatively cheap initiative in money and man-power and called for no parliamentary time. In fact, if there had been time for reflection the government might have decided on other grounds that it was not feasible. There was no existing government machinery for distributing the money; the Fund would create anomalous and overlapping functions between existing administrative units; the size of the population to be served was large; and it would inevitably prove difficult to find an alternative to the provision made by the Fund. If these objections had been formulated, they would have been overridden by the demand to take action of some sort.

## Support

The Family Fund was a measure that attracted extensive approval and certainly improved the government's stock of general support. Indeed, so successful was the initiative that it enabled them to continue to maintain an independent attitude to the Thalidomide settlement.

Hall *et al*. mention other factors affecting the over-all 'image' of an issue which may influence its fortunes. Some of these are:

### Crises

Writing of the welfare state, Myrdal has claimed that:[38]

> all the time new measures were introduced *ad hoc* to serve
> limited and temporary purposes, to safeguard special interests,
> and often to meet an emergency of one sort or another . . . new
> intervention was usually not only motivated by special circum-
> stances – a particular need, an emergency or a pending crisis –
> but also designed accordingly, as limited and often temporary
> measures.

Sir Keith Joseph himself, speaking at a National Association for Mental Health Conference, said, 'I must tell you that one day somebody will write a book . . . about the part that scandal has to play in procuring reform,' and added, 'The sudden revelation of conditions well known to the experts, of which the public is unaware, gives ministers a chance to galvanize their colleagues and get the resources to improve things.'[39]

Sir Keith Joseph faced a mild political crisis over Thalidomide. He was being pressed to give help quickly to the damaged children so that they would not be forced to settle on unfavourable terms with Distillers. The crisis was engineered, but it was real enough at the time and was certainly a vital factor in setting up the Family Fund.

*Origin*

Hall *et al*. suggest that:[40]

> Where an issue constitutes a challenge to a government's competence and is advanced from outside, its recognition is likely to be resisted or ignored. In these circumstances other factors (irrefutable evidence or crises) would have to be particularly favourable if the issue is to make progress.

The demand for a Fund arose from outside government and was expressed first in an all-party motion and then in an Opposition motion. Without the danger that the motion might be supported from the Conservative back-benches, it might have had little chance of success. The government annexed the Opposition demand, extended it to include all children, and presented it as a fresh new idea.

*Information*

It is suggested that the extent to which the existence of a problem can be supported with facts has an impact on progress. This was not true of the Family Fund. At the time when the scheme was devised, the government had little information about the number and nature of the needs of handicapped children and was unclear about what groups of handicapped children should be included in the scheme. We have shown how little research evidence was available before 1973, and though civil servants had access to their professional advisers and Sir Keith Joseph had received information from the Lady Hoare Trust, they had little time in which to clarify what burdens they were seeking to support and why these were not being carried by existing services.

The other participants in the process were convinced of 'the facts' by the case studies presented by the *Sunday Times*.

*Ideology*

There was no conflict between the ideology of the government and the essence of the Family Fund. The Fund was a selective response, calling for no significant increase in public expenditure or civil service manpower and it was to be administered by a private organisation. To the extent to which these factors were considered they must have made it easier for the government to accept the idea of a Fund.

## Some general considerations

In analysing the nature of the Fund, there is a danger of confusing *post hoc* with *propter hoc* considerations. The form that it took is not necessarily a valid guide to the motives underlying its establishment. Indeed we have suggested that it was set up as an unpremeditated response to external demands, announced without clear definition of its purpose or of those whom it was intended to benefit, and unclear as to its mode of operation and its long-term implications. It was subsequently hailed in the press and elsewhere as a new experiment in social policy; but this was a *post hoc* rationalisation designed to raise the status of an institution that had a more expedient purpose.

This, perhaps, explains the disappointment that has been felt at the subsequent response of government to the Family Fund. The DHSS has, for the most part, left the Fund, once established, to its own devices. This has certainly been partly because of the independent status of the Trust and partly because of the Department's confidence that the Trust has managed the Fund successfully, but it is also because there has never been in the government – either among politicians or civil servants – a commitment to broaden the scope of the Fund. There is a natural tendency in social policy for government to concentrate more on the initiation of new policies than to monitor existing ones, and there is also a tendency for the civil service to take a reactive rather than an initiating role. But particularly in the case of the Family Fund, it seems as if the civil service, knowing that the Fund at its inception was an expedient, has continued to view it in that light. Thus, there is as yet no clear picture of what the future of the Fund will be.

This is not to say that the Fund has been viewed with any disdain by ministers and civil servants; indeed, it has become a small weapon in the armoury of successive ministers. Demands for help for vaccine-damaged children, for compensation for children damaged *in utero*, for the attendance allowance to be paid for foster children, and general demands for improvements in policies for the handicapped, have been met with assurances that in addition to its other responsibilities, the Family Fund exists to provide help in such cases. The Fund has, in fact, continued to play the role for which it was devised - to take the heat out of new demands. But as it was never devised as part of a coherent plan to help the families of handicapped children, it has not yet become part of such a plan.

# 3    Organising the Family Fund

When it began to administer the Family Fund, the Joseph Rowntree Memorial Trust had little to go on. Not much was known about the numbers of families that might ask for help, or about the nature of their needs. The Trust had very limited office accommodation and no spare staff, with only three months between the end of December 1972 (when it agreed to take on the Fund) to the beginning of April 1973 when it began to deal with applications. There was no organisation that exactly paralleled it in British public administration. In form, the Family Fund is a Quango - a quasi-non-government organisation - an organisation that is formally or legally independent of government but which is used by government as part of the machinery of public administration. It is a non-government organisation operating at central government level; it is, in effect, wholly dependent on public money; it dispenses this money to individuals; and there is no power of appointment or dismissal of its officials by a government agency. None of these characteristics is unique or even unusual on its own, but the combination of them makes the Family Fund unique.[1]

In seeking to allocate the money, the organisation can be said to have passed through three phases. The behaviour of the organisation and the timing of these phases was certainly the result of the evolution of thinking within the Fund but it was also determined to a considerable extent by three externally determined pressures: the number of applications received by the Fund; the number of cases processed by it; and the rate of expenditure on grants.

These statistics are summarised in Figure 3.1. Broadly speaking, the Fund developed in the first phase in response to the rate of applications and the need to increase the number of grants made. As the rate of grants increased, so did the rate of expenditure, and when the rate of expenditure threatened to exhaust the resources available, the Fund entered the phase of retrenchment. Having found a level of expenditure that fell within the limits of the available resources and having also established an organisation that could cope with the steadied rate of applications, the Fund settled into the third phase of stability.

Of course, this is an over-simplified picture of the working of the

33

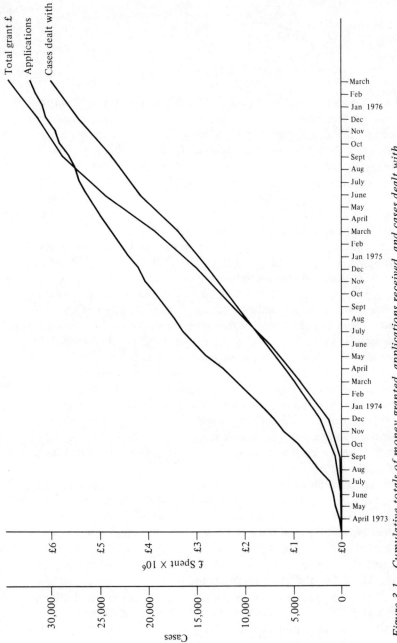

*Figure 3.1    Cumulative totals of money granted, applications received, and cases dealt with*

Fund and the reasons for the changes in its organisation. However, it does provide a background against which to analyse the way in which the Fund operated. Before examining how the Fund developed, we must describe some aspects of its formal structure.

## The Management Committee

The Trust appointed a committee to take responsibility for managing the Fund. This Management Committee comprised four members of the Trust, one of whom was chairman, a consultant paediatrician, a director of social services, the director, and the deputy director of the Trust. Four observers from the DHSS and the Welsh, Scottish, and Northern Ireland offices attended meetings. The Management Committee met ten times during the three-year experimental period, in either York or London. While the Committee took a detailed interest in the work of the Fund, and from time to time reached decisions that were innovative (in the sense that they were independent of advice proffered by the staff), the Fund was in effect managed, and its policy determined, by the staffs of the Trust and of the Fund.

The Management Committee created three other bodies with specific tasks:

1   A Consultative Committee was appointed consisting of members from voluntary organisations, statutory bodies, local authorities, research interests, medical practitioners, and parents to advise on the work of the Fund. The Committee was chaired by a member of the Management Committee and the secretariat was provided by the Fund. The Consultative Committee had no executive functions – it was established to assist the Fund in becoming better known, to help its relations with statutory and voluntary bodies, and to advise on the types of help that it should give and on questions of definition. Although the Consultative Committee gave the Fund some 'feel' of the views of its members and their parent bodies, it was not very active either in making suggestions or in commenting on Fund policy (see chapter 11).

2   A Panel, consisting of two members of the Management Committee, the Trust director, and a consultant paediatrician, was appointed to guide the staff on new issues of principle presented by the applications received by the Fund. The Panel met weekly in the first year of the Fund's operation. To each meeting the senior staff of the Fund brought case papers raising questions about eligibility or the type and scale of the grants that should be made. The Panel was also responsible for reviewing decisions made by the staff where these were questioned

by a parent or outside organisation. Principles that emerged from Panel discussions were ratified by the Management Committee and became internal guide-lines.

3   The consultant paediatrician on the Management Committee was the principal source of reference on difficult questions of definition about the criterion 'very severely congenitally handicapped'. He worked closely with the paediatrician on the Panel at York but eventually found that he needed to consult other colleagues, and so three consultants were appointed to form a Medical Advisory Committee. Most of the work done by this Committee was done via circulating papers, and the Committee made recommendations to the Management Committee on such subjects as the eligibility of mongol children and the criterion of eligibility of children with cystic fibrosis and leukaemia. They also considered a few 'appeals' by applicants who had been refused help on medical grounds.

## Exploratory development

### Staffing

Having established an advisory structure, the Trust set about appointing staff to run the Family Fund. They did not know the size of the administrative operation that faced them, and they believed that their involvement would be a temporary one:[2]

> An administrative structure was needed . . . that could be rapidly expanded as and if demands on the Fund increased in number or complexity and which could also be dispersed at short notice if at the end of three years, other arrangements were made to meet the needs which the government had in mind.

In addition to the existing staff of the Trust, who managed the Fund's investments and grant-making transactions and also took particular responsibility for the Panel, Management Committee, and Consultative Committee, the Trust decided to appoint a secretary to take charge of the Fund. For this post they sought a senior social worker who would be seconded by his or her local authority for the duration of the Fund. In the end, they chose Mr D. Hitch, who had been director of welfare services for Cambridge and who, after reorganisation of the social services, became an assistant director of the Cambridgeshire social services department.

The Fund aimed to respond flexibly to the individual needs of each family without recourse to a body of detailed rules. It therefore employed social workers who were felt to have the professional qualifications for making decisions. The decision to employ social work staff to exercise discretion was crucial in the development of the Fund. A social work ethos dominated the approach to applicants and the Fund's managers found it difficult to direct this professional group. The Trust's director later regretted the decision to employ them to process applications at York. While he valued the caring approach they brought to the work, he felt that the pressures on the Fund were too great for it to operate on social work precepts – 'case work cannot be done at a distance'. He felt that administrative skills were all that were really needed for decisions to be made. Later, as we shall see, the Fund reduced the proportion of social work staff at York. The decision to employ them was a result of the influence of the Trust's assistant director and the involvement of the DHSS Social Work Service in establishment of the Fund. They believed that qualified social workers would be needed to probe behind the initial request for help for other unmet needs, to negotiate with social work and other agencies in the field, and to form an appreciation of the nature of the problems of families with disabled children. The social workers who were recruited were attracted because they would be expected to use their professional judgment flexibly for the benefit of the families affected. In the early days, before the number of applications built up, the professional staff was encouraged to urge families and visiting social workers to think of new and interesting ways of relieving stress; to inquire into needs beyond those covered by the initial request; they were encouraged to advise families of other benefits and services to which they might be entitled; to advocate on behalf of families and, in borderline cases, to give the family the benefit of the doubt. As we shall see, this degree of discretion began to be limited.

*Accommodation*

One of the constraints on the organisation throughout the first two years of its operation was the accommodation available. The Trust had a similar attitude to accommodation as it had to staffing. Until midsummer of 1973, the secretary of the Fund and his staff were accommodated in two offices in the Trust premises. The intention was to run the Fund from these offices and from one large room in a nearby house called The Homestead, owned by the Trust; but by the autumn of 1973, The Homestead was already overcrowded by desks, piles of files, and clerical and social work staff. Additional accommodation was found on the upper floor of a cricket pavilion, also owned by the Trust and in the vicinity of the Trust's offices. Now the Fund was operating from three separate offices and problems of communication arose, with files in various states of processing being passed from one office to another. The upper floor of the cricket pavilion was also soon overcrowded, housing over 10,000 files as well as typists, clerical workers, and social workers in the same space. Following the recommendations of an O and M report, the Fund took over the ground floor of the pavilion and The Homestead was eventually closed.

## *Administrative procedures*

In order to understand the complex nature of the operation, it is worth describing the methods adopted by the Fund in handling applications. Initial applications were received at the Trust office either on a Family Fund application form or as a letter. The assistant secretary would indicate on the letter or application form the action to be taken. If the application was rejected at this stage (usually because of the age criteria), a personal letter was dictated and sent to the parent and the application was filed. If the child was prima facie eligible, a standard letter was sent to the family informing them that their application had been received and they would receive a visit; a social work report form was sent to an agent of the Fund or, if one did not exist in the applicants' area, to the local social services department, asking for a visit to be made; and a notification was always sent to the social services department, asking for comments. At the same time, the application would be registered in both an alphabetical index and a numerically sequenced index, and a file would be prepared and kept in an alphabetical sequence to await the social work report.

When the social work report was received, it was examined to see whether the case was straightforward. If it was, it was linked with the file and passed to staff who examined the reports, completed check sheets, and made a decision. After the decision had been made, letters had to be sent to the family, the social services department, or the agent making the visit and, in the case of grants for cars and washing-machines, to the suppliers.

If the social work report was not a good enough basis for a decision, the file was passed to the social work staff, who had to decide whether to ask for further information from the visiting social worker, a doctor, or the family themselves; or whether to approach the local social services department or other agency to find out why they could not help with the items requested. If it was a simple matter, it would be dealt with by telephone, but usually it involved the issue of standard letters or dictating and typing special letters. The file then went back to the filing system to await a reply. When the reply was received, it was linked to the file and passed back to the social workers for a decision.

The Fund started with the determination that it would avoid the kind of official standard letter commonly issued by the Inland Revenue or the DHSS on social security matters. However, to save secretarial resources, more and more standard letters were printed. The Fund endeavoured to retain personally typed letters for families rejected by the Fund but even they eventually had to be standardised for some types of rejection.

These procedures were evolved by trial and error over a period of two years after the Fund started. While they were being evolved, the Fund's offices moved twice, reorganised and expanded, temporary staff were leaving and new staff were being recruited and trained, and new policies were formulated. Dominating the whole scene was a constant stream of applications to the Fund and thousands of cases waiting to be dealt with. Delay increased the work, for social workers were constantly interrupted by telephone calls from families or their representatives asking about their applications. Often these inquiries could not be answered because the file could not be located.

A huge correspondence streamed into the Fund's offices – social work reports, doctors' letters, letters of thanks from parents, receipts from parents, letters asking about delays, new applications, and re-applications. All these letters had to be linked to files, and because the filing system was too large to be maintained accurately and because the flow of correspondence was too great, not only were mistakes being made but also letters piled up while waiting to be filed. In those cases that required urgent attention (for instance, applications for a holiday grant) efforts had to be made to trace the file which could either be in the filing system, waiting on a social worker's desk for attention or on the coder's desk for coding, awaiting micro-filming, or being micro-filmed. If an important letter was not on the file, it had to be traced by sorting through stacks of unfiled letters.

Gradually, however, the administrative task was brought under control, partly as a result of increases in the staffing of the Fund. The Trust's officers eventually accepted that more full-time permanent staff had to be appointed and that they could not rely only on voluntary, part-time, temporary, or seconded staff. The UK was notionally divided into two parts, each of which was dealt with by a team headed by a senior social worker and consisting of four to five full-time social workers or social work assistants. In addition, the clerical and secretarial staff was increased and was put under the direction of an office manager. The rate of applications, too, declined – in the first quarter of 1975, there was a steady fall from 900–1,000 per month to about 700 per month, while the cases not dealt with fell from over 8,500 in October 1974 to 4,557 by October 1975. Better office accommodation and working conditions increased efficiency, as did improvements in office routines following some of the recommendations of O and M reports in February and June 1974. Even fairly small changes, such as the adoption of perspex envelope files to replace card files requiring punched holes in correspondence, eased the work of the clerical section. One quite substantial innovation was the introduction of micro-filming to clear completed cases from the filing system.

Perhaps the most dramatic increase in the output of the Fund resulted from the improved quality of reports being sent in from the field. This was the result of a number of factors. The social work report form was redesigned more than once and social workers in the field became more familiar with the Fund's procedures. In addition, frustrated by delays in getting social work reports back from social services departments and finding that many that were returned were slipshod, the Fund began to build up a nation-wide network of trained social workers, able to make visits and prepare reports on families within reach of their homes. The Fund made increasing use of these agents. By means, at first, of day training courses which began early in 1974, and then full notes of guidance, issued first in July 1974 in a loose-leaf form and updated from time to time after that, it tried to keep field-workers in touch with developments in the Fund's policies. However, where the quality of the reports improved, the burden of making any necessary follow-up inquiries or negotiating with local agencies was still being carried at York. After experiments in the summer of 1974, the Fund began to get its agents to carry out nego-tiations themselves. Applications to the Fund would be forwarded to the local agents, who would write to the parents, acknowledging the application and making an appointment to visit, and to the social services department; the agents would visit the family and complete the report; seek an opinion if there was doubt about eligibility; nego-tiate with the social services department or other agency, if the help should be provided from social services; and then complete and return the report form. The agents were supplied with standard letter forms, and a regular newsletter informing them of developments in Fund policy. These procedures began to be adopted late in 1974, and soon made an impact on the work at York.

Despite these developments, the discretion of the social worker in the Fund's offices in York began to be constrained by pressure of work and the Panel's decisions. The rising number of applications and cases pending soon made it very difficult for social workers to spend the time needed to carry out the detailed inquiries upon which their discretion had to be based. Alarmed by the backlog, the Fund's managers began to introduce routine procedures and to urge social workers to reduce the time spent on each case. Routine cases were given to un-qualified staff and all were urged to confine themselves to the item requested and not 'try to do casework at a distance'. The social workers, feeling that the problem arose as a result of delays in recruiting staff, were unwilling to accept limits imposed on their professional judgment, and they were not happy in seeing needs that they had recognised go unmet because they did not have the time to intervene. The tensions arising from these restraints on the exercise of professional discretion and the need to speed up the making of grants continued throughout the phase of exploratory development; they were heightened further by the body of rules that began to emerge from the Panel about what kind of help could be given, and from the Medical Advisory Panel about which children were eligible.

Before guide-lines began to emerge from the Panel, the social workers had begun to develop their own unwritten principles. These developed from discussions about each other's cases in the room where they worked and were based on what in their judgment would relieve stress. When the guide-lines ultimately developed by the Panel coincided with or did not differ markedly from those informal procedures which the social workers were already operating, they were accepted without difficulty. However, on a number of issues the Panel laid down principles that conflicted with what the social work staff had been doing, and thought should be done. The differences arose from different interpret-ations of the needs of families and the role of the Fund. The Panel was made up of older and generally more conservative individuals, with less recent direct experience of social work than the professional staff.

Two examples illustrate the conflicts that occurred:

1 *Mongols.* At the start of the Fund all severely mentally handicapped children (IQ less than 50) were considered very severely disabled and eligible for help from the Fund. The staff began to refer cases to the

Panel containing children with IQs over 50 but whose parents had great difficulty in caring for them, including mongol children. The Medical Advisory Committee was asked to consider whether they could be included. They concluded:[3]

> The sub committee is not very happy about the arbitrary use of IQ as a criterion . . . the majority of mongol children fall within a fairly narrow band between 35 and 50 without creating great caring problems. It is considered that the presence or absence of associated disabilities should be the main criterion for making a decision.

This decision was not welcomed by the social work staff. Seeking to extend the eligibility criteria by getting permission to help the mentally handicapped with IQs over 50 with management problems, they were instead being instructed not to assist mongol children with IQs over 35 unless there were other disabilities. They did not accept the view that mongol children did not present great caring problems, and they found themselves faced with making invidious distinctions between different categories of mental handicap. The matter was taken back to the Management Committee at their next meeting in February 1974 with a strong note:

> Recently a larger number of referrals to doctors have been made as a result of the changed policy with regard to the acceptance of mongol children . . . now almost every mongol has to be referred for medical advice . . . . Apart from the additional work involved we are causing disappointment not only in the families concerned but in the agents who prepare the reports for us. There is also disagreement from the Fund's own staff with the decisions now being reached. It is difficult to explain why a mentally retarded child with an IQ of less than 50 is accepted but a mongol child with the same or even lower scale of intelligence is not.
>
> In view of the situation which has developed would the Committee wish to return to the former position.

Despite this recommendation the Medical Advisory Committee[4]

> was still unanimous in the view that medically they would stand by their decision on the grounds that mongol children were different and on the whole easier to manage than similar lower intelligence children of other groups.

However, it was decided that

in order to help the administration of the Fund it was necessary
to have criteria for eligibility which could be interpreted by lay
staff

and the Secretary of the Fund was left to work out such criteria.

The criteria that were eventually adopted were still not identical to
those for other mentally handicapped children but they enabled social
work staff to accept most of those cases that would have been rejected.
The conflict here was between discretion operated by staff who felt
their judgments were as valid as those who had been appointed to
determine policy. In this example the disagreement was also a conflict
between medical opinion and social work opinion. In the next illus-
tration the conflict was between the staff who wanted to exercise their
own discretion and the Panel who wished to impose some restraint on
that discretion.

2 *Telephones.*   As soon as the Fund began to receive requests for
telephones the Panel was set the task of deciding in what circumstances
it was appropriate to give them. Cases were dealt with individually. A
Panel report to the Management Committee on 30 August 1973 recorded:

> Several requests have dealt with telephones. There has been a need
> to call a doctor in connection with severe epileptic fits and, for
> example, a local phone box was often out of order through
> vandalism or parents had to take small children with them. The
> Panel have agreed to provide telephones in these sorts of
> circumstances, but a request was refused when the need was
> merely for the parents to be contacted by the hospital when the
> child happened to be in hospital.

> The policy with regard to the provision of telephones is to be
> discussed further by the Panel.

In November 1973 a report from the York Panel recorded:

> Telephones. The Panel have agreed to provide a telephone for a
> family in which the child suffered from a condition requiring
> immediate contact with the doctor or where for other reasons the
> doctor gave specific advice that the telephone was essential and
> where the local authority was unable to provide them. Broadly
> speaking, telephones were being provided on medical grounds
> rather than social need but not enough of the latter had been
> dealt with to form a principle.

The social work staff became frustrated by these criteria. They meant that they were unable to use their discretion to issue telephones to families where, in their opinion or the visiting social worker's opinion, stress would be relieved by a telephone. It also meant that in order to get a telephone the Fund had to obtain a recommendation from a doctor, which caused more work and delay. The Panel, however, were not as convinced as the staff that a telephone could relieve stress; they were also mindful that the local authorities had responsibility under the Chronically Sick and Disabled Persons Act to give telephones and had adopted very strict criteria. If the Fund gave telephones too easily, might they be overwhelmed with requests and be brought into disrepute? As the chairman of the Panel said, 'we must not do too much, we must not be soft'. The secretary of the Fund continued to press the Panel to accept telephone requests where, in the opinion of the visiting social worker, severe family stress would be relieved, and in February 1974 some guide-lines were accepted by the Management Committee. The social workers were informed:

> We shall still need to refuse applications for a telephone which
> from the terms of the social workers' report seem to be related
> to nothing more than a general desire to be in touch with people
> outside the home or to an understandable appreciation of the
> general convenience which a telephone offers.

Telephones, however, were authorised to be issued if any of eight social circumstances existed, and the secretary of the Fund was authorised to approve the installation and rental of a telephone in other circumstances in which, in his opinion, severe family stress could be relieved. The proportion of families receiving telephones from the Fund rose as a result of this relaxation in criteria from 1.9 per cent in December 1973 to 5.5 per cent in March 1975.

The Panel established criteria on many other items, including holidays abroad; the size of car grants; in what circumstances cars should be issued; speech trainers; toys and play materials; second cars; the purchase of caravans; the treatment of Thalidomide children; housing; central heating; Doman Delecato treatment;[5] visits to Lourdes; and many other matters. The staff remained unhappy about a number of the decisions taken. For example, they could not accept that where it was established that it was essential for the father to have the family car for work, a second car could not be issued to relieve the mother's isolation; they could not understand why colour televisions could only be issued to deaf children when mothers with children with severe behaviour disorders also found that a colour television was the only way of holding the children's attention; or why washing-machines could only be issued to families with incontinent children when many other mothers could by this means be relieved of the burden of washing.

However, despite the resistance of the staff to many of the constraints put upon them, they did become able to operate with more speed and confidence as the body of internal guide-lines built up. Many of the Panel's decisions were welcomed by the staff because they gave staff confidence that their judgments would not be challenged; that they would be upheld in case of dispute; and most important of all, that the Fund was operating with some consistency. One of the lessons learned by the social workers was how difficult it was to operate individual discretion without some guide-lines.

For the time being the organisation at York remained predominantly staffed by social workers operating with a considerable degree of discretion, although the Trust's managers had already decided that an important element in the organisation was[6]

the establishment in the Trust's office of efficient and speedy administrative procedures to deal quickly with a greater number of applications on which decisions can readily be made by persons with some experience of social administration. Social work skills need to be available in this administration in much the same way as are medical skills on which the Trust have regularly called.

## Retrenchment

During the phase of exploratory development, the social workers' discretion had been limited for the most part by the requirement to process grants speedily and the Panel's interpretation of the guide-lines. In the period of retrenchment, to which we now turn, they were to be constrained still further by budgetary pressure until they found themselves left with little discretionary freedom. It was inevitable that financial pressures would begin to affect the work of the Fund, which had developed its procedures without the discipline of a budget. Apart from the costs of administration, the only financial consideration that had any real effect on its early policy-making was the need to *increase* expenditure. Until the end of 1973 the Fund had not succeeded in spending the interest that had accrued on the first £3 million received from the government. By mid-1974, however, the Fund's managers began to consider their rate of expenditure. The Management Committee were told in June 1974, that:[7]

> The Trust's finance officer has calculated that at the present rate of expenditure the Family Fund will be reduced by the end of 1974 to approximately £900,000. Bearing in mind the number of applications . . . in the pipeline . . . the Trust would be unwise to invite further applications after the end of 1974.

In October 1974, this situation was relieved by the announcement that a second £3 million would be made available, and encouraged with these extra resources in December 1974, the DHSS extended the criteria of eligibility to include the non-congenitally very severely disabled.

The first form of retrenchment – the decision to withdraw from the granting of aids and adaptations which could be given by social services departments – resulted not from any immediate financial crisis but from the belief that local authorities, through pressure on their own finances, were transferring their responsibilities to the Fund (this issue is discussed in chapter 13) and that this might exhaust its resources.

The second form was a result partly of an increasing awareness that the Fund might soon face a financial crisis and partly of the announcement in July 1974 that a mobility allowance was to be introduced. It was decided to replace grants for car purchase (worth £750) by grants for car hire (worth £200).

The third form of retrenchment can be attributed explicitly to the need to work within a budgetary framework. In a letter to the trustees on 15 August, the director wrote that the DHSS had agreed that the Fund should continue in operation until the end of 1978.

> It now follows that the administration of the Fund must be related to an annual budget and the Department's first anxiety was whether the Trust would accept such an arrangement as against the 'open ended' discretion and resulting demand on resources that has operated so far. The Department went further and said that if the amount on which the Trust could operate proved to be less than £3 million which is the present approximate annual rate of expenditure then acceptance of the scheme both now and beyond 1978 would be that much easier.
>
> The view that I expressed was that whether or not there was a financial crisis the time had come when some budgetary discipline ought to be introduced to the administration of the Fund, and that this was not inconsistent with the discretionary aspect of the Trust's administration so far. I hoped that in discussion about this change the Department would not put the stress on the need for economy but on a desirable development following a period of two years experiment.[8]

A document, 'Possible areas of Budgetary Control', was presented to the social workers at York and the field-work staff as a 're-emphasis of existing guide-lines'. It identified ways in which the Fund would withdraw from or restrict its help. The types of mobility help available were reduced; grants for low-cost items and repeat grants for families in full employment were to be discontinued; standard letters would be issued to dissuade families from re-applying; help with debts would be restricted; and the Fund's staff at York were asked not to suggest help that the family or visiting social workers had not mentioned.

These policies were successful in reducing expenditure. By the Management Committee meeting in February 1976, when it was reported that the Fund was to have £2.7 million to spend in 1976, the monthly rate of expenditure had already fallen from £378,000 in July 1975 – an annual rate of expenditure of £4.5 million – to £207,000 per month – an annual rate of £2.5 million. Later, as the rate both of applications and of expenditure continued to decline, the Fund was able to relax the budgetary control guide-lines.

The social work staff recruited by the Trust to exercise discretion began to leave and as they left, they were replaced by administrative workers. They left for a variety of reasons but one important one was that they no longer felt that they had sufficient freedom of action.

From early 1976 the Fund has been operating without significant changes, mostly through administrative staff, on the basis of criteria as revised during the period of retrenchment and within a budget of about £2 million per year.

## Conclusion

Two of the themes of this chapter will be familiar to students of organisations:[9]

1   The bureaucratic machinery necessary to implement innovations in social policy led inevitably to increasing rigidity. The task of the Family Fund – the distribution of money to large numbers of families – called for some sort of bureaucratic organisation involving division of labour, hierarchy of offices, and abstract rules and procedures; and the development of these inevitably led to increasing control of front-line units – those exercising professional discretion.

2   The front-line units – in this case the social work staff – experienced many of the conflicts of professionals working in a bureaucratic setting. While the social workers in the Family Fund, in the end, accepted in principle that there should be limits on their discretion to

enable cases to be dealt with more rapidly, they were very reluctant to accept the procedures that were entailed. The managers of the Fund had to take decisions with administrative considerations in mind – which often conflicted with the individual discretionary considerations of the social workers.

While these aspects of organisational behaviour are familiar, of more interest has been the experience of watching the administration of discretion developing within an organisation; there is relatively little literature on discretionary behaviour.[10] No organisation can be entirely rule-bound, nor can it operate without rules. However, the Family Fund was an example of an organisation operating with the very minimum number of rules. At first, the social workers making decisions on cases were constrained only by the guide-lines agreed with the DHSS and their own self-imposed sense of what was fair and effective. The scope of their discretion became limited, first by the exigencies of administration, then by the developing body of internal guide-lines, and finally by budgetary constraints. Michael Hill has written:[11]

> The exercise of discretion occurs when officials are required
> or permitted to make decisions without being given instructions
> which would in effect predetermine those decisions.

As the Family Fund has developed, more and more of the decisions that the staff can make have become predetermined by instructions. Although the Fund never became rule-bound, it was not able to maintain the flexibility that was hoped for.

Much of the debate about discretion in public administration in the last decade has centred on the supplementary benefits scheme. Titmuss, when vice-chairman of the Supplementary Benefits Commission, mounted a biting attack on the 'pathology of legalism' and stoutly defended discretion as an area of flexible, individualised justice.[12] But the administrative problems presented to the Commission in their efforts to exercise their discretionary powers have become overwhelming:[13]

> Our attempts to guide staff in using these powers have created a
> set of rules which have grown increasingly complicated,
> incomprehensible and unpublishable. The constant 'flack'
> provoked by discretion distracts public attention.

Donnison has intimated that the Commission should[14]

> abandon the aspiration to match the benefits we pay to the
> infinite variety of human needs we encounter – the aspiration
> for creative justice.

He has made two distinctions in an attempt to clarify the debate about discretion in supplementary benefits; these distinctions can usefully be applied to the development of discretion in the Family Fund. He distinguished, first, between judgment and discretion. No bureaucracy can avoid making hundreds of judgments every day about, for example, what the legislation means by 'full-time work' or, in the case of the Family Fund, what the guide-lines mean by 'very severe disability'. Judgments can be simplified by establishing rules. In contrast, whether or not to give an 'exceptional needs payment' for a pair of shoes or, in the case of the Family Fund, a clothing grant, is a discretionary decision.

The second distinction is between the levels at which the discretion operates. Discretion can be the responsibility of the Commission which, for instance, lays down rules specifying standard rates of additions for heating; or it can be the responsibility of an individual official deciding to award a pair of shoes. This is an 'individual private and personal decision'. Initially, the Family Fund relied on the officer-level discretion of their social work staff but increasingly this became constrained by the Commission-level discretion of the Panel and Medical Advisory Committee.

In supplementary benefit, rules to control officer-level discretion are introduced for three main reasons:

1 To ensure some degree of consistency or equity in the decisions made at officer level.
2 Because the kind of staff employed by the Commission to make individual discretionary decisions are felt to lack the training or expertise to do so without considerable guidance.
3 Because those who manage the scheme need to be assured that expenditure on discretionary grants is reasonable and can be predicted.

By appointing social workers, the Fund sought to avoid detailed rules; but the need to process grants rapidly, to maintain a degree of equity, and to control expenditure led to increasing rigidity in the administration.

There is no doubt that the Family Fund is still largely a discretionary rather than a legalistic instrument. Social workers in the field and administrative staff in York make discretionary judgments, but they (particularly the staff at York) are not practising individual private and personal discretion but instead, the type of administrative judgments inevitable in any organisation. The range and level of the help available from the Fund has been reduced. The Fund is no longer able to be as flexible and generous as it used to be, and through routinised administrative procedures it may be operating with less individualised responsiveness than it did. However, there is now less variation in the help given to families, greater fairness and consistency, less delay, and more clarity about what can be obtained on behalf of the visiting social workers and families.

# 4     The work of the Family Fund

In later chapters we deal in turn with different aspects of the work of the Family Fund. Now, in order to provide a background, this chapter presents some general information on the size of the grants distributed and the items given by the Fund; discusses the eligibility criteria adopted; and analyses the reasons why families were rejected by the Fund, and the characteristics of re-applicants.

## Size of grants distributed

The amount of money (or the value of help in kind) received by families helped by the Fund was not fixed. The managers believed that the best method of identifying what help families needed to relieve stress was to rely on their expressed needs. These expressed needs were probably only partly determined by felt needs – families would not ask for every item they needed. What they did ask for was determined by what they thought the Family Fund would be prepared to give; what had been obtained by other families they knew; and what a social worker or other member of the helping profession had suggested. Having made their request in a letter or on an application form, the items might be changed during the visit from the social worker, and finally the grant might be varied when the case papers were dealt with by the staff at York.

The average cumulative grant given to the 25,550 families who applied during the first three years of the Fund's operation, and who had received grants up to 30 September 1977 was £348. Families who had applied early on, and possibly re-applied, had of course accumulated larger grants than this, while newer applicants, whose case was only partly dealt with, had acquired much smaller amounts. The over-all distribution of grants was skewed (see Figure 4.1). The average was pushed up by a small number of very large grants and for this reason the median (£250) constitutes a more representative picture of the size of grants.

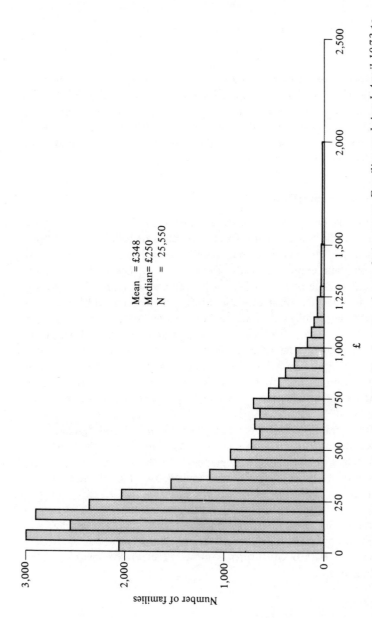

*Figure 4.1   Distribution of number of families by size of cumulative grant. Families applying 1 April 1973 to 31 March 1976. Total £ distributed up to 30 September 1977*

**Items given by the Fund**

The type of help was determined by what the family asked for, by how that was adapted during the process of applying, and by what items the Fund was prepared to give. Table 4.1 summarises the pattern of items requested and given during the first three years of the Fund's operation.

*Table 4.1* *Type of items requested and type of items given to families helped by the Family Fund*

| Item | Requested | | Given | |
|---|---|---|---|---|
| | No. | % of families | No. | % of families |
| Vehicle | 3,955 | 17.2 | 4,789 | 20.4 |
| Fares | 626 | 2.7 | 1,621 | 6.0 |
| Driving lessons | 702 | 3.0 | 2,643 | 9.7 |
| Car hire | 59 | 0.3 | 766 | 3.1 |
| Vehicle repairs | 100 | 0.4 | 346 | 1.4 |
| Petrol/maintenance | 637 | 2.8 | 3,544 | 13.5 |
| Transport general | 378 | 1.6 | 1,138 | 4.8 |
| Clothing | 2,532 | 11.0 | 5,043 | 19.0 |
| Bedding/beds | 2,137 | 9.3 | 4,260 | 17.5 |
| Holidays for child | 200 | 0.9 | 256 | 1.0 |
| Holidays for parents/ others | 71 | 0.3 | 338 | 1.4 |
| Holidays for both | 1,672 | 7.3 | 3,572 | 13.6 |
| Washing-machines | 4,470 | 19.4 | 8,491 | 36.6 |
| Spin-/tumble-dryers | 2,156 | 9.4 | 4,661 | 20.1 |
| Furniture/carpets | 711 | 3.1 | 1,443 | 6.0 |
| Wheelchairs/pushchairs | 551 | 2.4 | 428 | 1.8 |
| Other aids | 800 | 3.5 | 579 | 2.4 |
| Alterations to house | 1,254 | 5.4 | 733 | 3.1 |
| Plumbing | 162 | 0.7 | 324 | 1.4 |
| Home help | 80 | 0.3 | 60 | 0.2 |
| Child minder | 74 | 0.3 | 90 | 0.4 |
| Debts | 239 | 1.0 | 554 | 2.3 |
| Telephones | 1,585 | 6.9 | 1,951 | 7.7 |
| Recreation for child | 1,169 | 5.1 | 1,869 | 7.3 |
| Other | 3,140 | 13.6 | 3,781 | 14.7 |
| Not specified | 2,898 | – | – | – |
| Total items requested | 32,358 | Total items specified | | 29,460 |
| Total families | 23,032 | Total families specifying item | | 20,134 |

The help given with respect to transport and clothing is discussed in detail in chapter 9 and will not be dealt with here. The most common request for help was for a washing-machine. The washing of numerous changes of clothes, of sheets and bedding, nappies and pants was recognised by the Fund as an expensive, time-consuming, and exhausting job – especially if a family had an incontinent child and inadequate laundry facilities. The Fund distributed automatic washing-machines to 36.6 per cent of the families helped and spin- or tumble-driers to 20.1 per cent. The problems of families with incontinent children and the impact the Fund made on these has already been described in a study published by the Disabled Living Foundation.[1]

Requests for help with beds and bedding came from families with incontinent or overactive children who caused heavy wear and tear on beds and bedding; from families who did not have adequate beds and bedding and could not afford to obtain or replace them; and from those who wanted special types of beds or cots in order to, for instance, secure an active mentally handicapped child, or prevent a helpless muscular dystrophy child from falling out of bed. There were no special criteria adopted for this item. As long as the family asked for the item and it was felt that the help given would relieve stress, they obtained it. After spring 1975 there was some tightening up when it was stressed that families should not be given help with needs that might be expected to arise with a normal child. Of the applicants, 9.3 per cent asked for help and 17.5 per cent obtained it. Assistance with beds and bedding was less problematic than with some other items because there was no clear overlap with the responsibilities of other agencies. Social services departments could have helped with these items but the Fund felt that as they did not normally provide such help it was a proper responsibility of the Fund. Recipients of supplementary benefit were after spring 1975 expected to attempt to obtain an exceptional needs payment for these items and only helped if they were refused. The size of grants for beds and bedding depended on the items and/or amounts requested, and there was no standard grant. Families were asked to return receipts for the items they obtained.

Requests for help with holidays came from families wanting help with holidays for the child; for the parents without the child; and, most commonly, for the whole family. The Fund adopted no special criteria. Normally assistance was given for holidays within Britain, though where continental holidays were no more expensive the Fund was initially prepared to help with these. Help with various kinds of holiday was given – a particularly popular choice was holiday camps, but families were also helped to stay in caravans, chalets, rented accommodation, or hotels. Some families asked for and obtained the full cost of their holidays; others asked for a partial contribution only. The level of holiday grants thus depended on how much the holidays cost and what the parents asked for; it also varied according to the contribution made by the local authority. Under the Chronically Sick and Disabled Persons Act 1970, local authority social services departments are enabled to meet the needs of a handicapped person by

> facilitating the taking of holidays whether at holiday homes or otherwise and whether provided under arrangements made by the authority or otherwise (Section 2 (i) f).

Some authorities provide help with holidays under Section 29 of the National Assistance Act 1948, the Mental Health Act 1959, and Section 1 of the Children and Young Persons Act 1963. In addition, local education authorities and the health service were found to be making provision for holidays.

As well as variations in the legislative powers used by local authorities, there were variations in the range of help provided – some authorities limiting their help to group holidays or to holidays run by voluntary bodies. There were also variations in the assessment of eligibility for financial assistance and the amount of help given. In some cases there was still more than one policy operating within the local authority as a result of local government reorganisation. The Family Fund was also operating at a time of very considerable pressure on local authority resources – many authorities made no provision or had reduced the help available to save money.

Following its terms of reference to complement but not substitute for existing provision, the Fund could have given help only in those cases where the local authority had made a contribution to the cost of the child. In practice, because the Fund felt that this would discriminate against families living in the least generous local authority areas, they gave help despite the local authorities' responsibilities. In 1974 and 1975 a circular was sent by the Fund to each local authority to obtain details of the authorities' policy, and families applying for holidays were given help over and above what the authority would give. Later this method was abandoned and only in exceptional cases was the local authority involved. Of the families, 8.5 per cent asked for holidays – 16 per cent of families obtained them.

Families asked for furniture because of the heavy wear and tear caused by the behaviour of the child – for example, a sofa soiled through incontinence. Families with children who lay on the floor a good deal or who crawled or who were at risk of injury if they fell, asked for carpets. The Fund's view was that as wheelchairs and pushchairs could be supplied by artificial limb and appliances centres (ALACs) the Fund should not help. In a limited number of cases, the Fund did help with powered wheelchairs for outdoor use because they were not provided through the health service.

Families asked for items such as special educational toys, speech trainers, colour television, and Possum machines. The Fund developed a policy for each of these items; for example, the extra cost of colour TV rental and licence was given only where a doctor or teacher confirmed that a defect of sight or hearing meant that it was required. Although educational toys should be available from statutory or voluntary sources, the Fund would help with expensive items not obtainable from elsewhere if the child could not go outside. Although the Fund assisted with speech trainers for a time, they came to the view that speech trainers did not relieve stress, so that form of help was discontinued. Outside toys could be provided if either the child's school or an occupational therapist thought they were safe and helped to keep a hyperactive child occupied. Cassette machines or tape-recorders were given if they might calm or soothe a child. The Fund took the view that Possum machines, if they were essential to functioning, should be provided by statutory services.

Apart from recreational aids and telephones, families asked for a variety of different aids to help them look after their child or make him more independent; these included bath aids, shower or lavatory aids, ramps, handrails, and stair lifts. They also asked for adaptations to their houses or gardens – including extra bedrooms, downstairs bathrooms and WCs, playrooms, the widening of doors and passages, central heating, garden fencing, and paving.

The Fund's policy on aids and adaptations passed through a variety of stages. In the first eighteen months to two years, each application was dealt with 'on its merits', subject to guide-lines laid down by the Panel, such as: there was rarely a medical justification for providing full central heating but the Fund could help up to Parker Morris standards with background heating in the living and circulating spaces on the ground floor. Subject also to making inquiries about the willingness of other authorities with responsibilities to contribute towards the cost, the Fund would help by providing grants of, in some cases as much as £3,000.

With the rising rate of expenditure and the belief that local authorities were avoiding their responsibilities by getting the Fund to make the provision, the Fund changed its policies. Grants for aids and adaptations were made only in private housing and only if a local authority in making a grant itself required a parental contribution. Following this policy change, most applicants for help with aids and adaptations were referred to their social services departments and, together with wheelchairs, aid and adaptation remained the only items given by the Fund where the number of applications exceeded the number of grants.

Somewhat to its surprise, the Fund received very few applications for help in the house, though it was prepared to make grants for home helps or child minding. The Fund did, however, receive a number of applications from families in debt. In principle no help was given with expenditure that had already been incurred but the Fund was prepared to help[2]

> when a family clearly had to incur debt beyond normal commitments to solve an urgent problem related to the care of their handicapped child and severe financial stress resulted from this.

The criteria adopted for telephones were more specific than for any other item requested from the Fund. The Panel believed that the local authority model criteria were too stringent, and yet sought to avoid giving telephones on the basis of[3]

> a general desire to be in touch with people outside the house or an understandable appreciation of the general convenience which a telephone offers.

In the end the cost of telephone installation and the first year's rental could be given where a doctor confirmed it was essential on medical grounds; where there was a one-parent family; where there were two or more severely handicapped people in the family; where the family was exceptionally isolated; and in one or two other special situations.

### Eligibility criteria

Guided only by the minister's statement in the House and the letter of agreement sent to the Trust, the Fund faced the task of developing its own eligibility criteria, which it did with the help of the Panel and the Management and Medical Advisory Committees. These criteria were:

### 1   *Age*

Each applicant to the Fund had to be under sixteen. It was quite clear from the minister's statement that the Fund was for children, although no age limit was mentioned. Following discussions between the Trust and the DHSS, the letter of agreement and circular contained the following sentence:[4]

> It will be open to the Trust where circumstances make this
> desirable to continue to give help to the families of children aged
> sixteen and over where these families have previously received help
> from the trustees.

As it turned out, this facility was not used to any great extent and the age of sixteen, when children are eligible for supplementary benefit, became a clear cut-off point.

The age criterion did not present many problems to administer. It is impossible to say how many applications were made by over-age children because they were not all registered. People of all ages asked for help – not only children just over sixteen, but also families caring for mentally handicapped adults in their thirties and forties, as well as people caring for elderly relatives.

## 2   *Location*

The child applying to the Fund had to be living at home. In fact, during the time that the child was in hospital or residential home the family was eligible for help for 'the purpose of visiting or making specific provision for him'.[5] That the Fund should be for children at home was implied in Sir Keith Joseph's announcement, and there is no record of it being discussed further at the meetings that took place later. Following the establishment of the Fund, the Panel helped to work out in what circumstances families with children in hospitals or at residential schools should receive help. Provision could be made to visit children in hospital if other sources of help were not available and the Fund would also provide help to bring children home from schools during the holidays or at week-ends.

## 3   *Very severe disability*

This was the principal criterion applied by the Fund. Sir Keith Joseph had not defined 'very severe disabilities', but it has been suggested in chapter 2 that in his announcement he had in mind a much narrower group than eventually became eligible. He did specifically exclude the blind and deaf, who subsequently qualified for help. In the first meeting with the DHSS, it was mentioned that severely mentally handicapped children should be included, but 'There must be flexibility of interpretation' and 'The DHSS guide-lines must be couched in as general terms as possible in order to defuse criticism'.[6] In the guide-lines agreed with the DHSS, it was left to the Trust and to professional advisers to work out the criteria of severity.

For this purpose the Trust turned for advice to Ross Mitchell, Professor of Child Health at the University of Dundee, who, with a panel of medical colleagues, set about establishing the criteria of very severe disability (and, initially, what conditions were and were not congenital). The first thing that Professor Mitchell did was to distinguish 'disability' (the disorder from which the child suffers) from 'handicap' (the extent to which the child is disadvantaged). He proposed, and the Management Committee accepted, that where the original documents mentioned a Fund for very severely handicapped children, they really meant 'disabled', and that the severity of disability and not handicap should be the test of eligibility. Although the Fund continued to be described as a Fund for *families* with *handicapped* children, it has in fact never been that. It is a fund for families with handicapped children if, and only if, the *children* have a very severe *disability*. The degree of handicap as well as the stress experienced might affect the scale and type of help given but it was not to be taken into account in determining eligibility. This distinction did cause some confusion in the early months, partly because of ambiguous wording in instructions to staff, and partly because of the inherent difficulty in rejecting families facing great burdens but where the child did not meet the disability criterion. However, an exchange of letters in November 1973 between Lewis Waddilove and Ross Mitchell clarified the situation and confirmed that disability should be the criterion.

There were very good reasons for adopting disability and not handicap as the fundamental criterion. Disability could be more objectively assessed – most disabilities were evident to the eye and the medical profession was experienced in distinguishing levels of functional impairment. Handicap, on the other hand, would have been much more difficult to rate and would have had to be judged, in many cases, on the assessment of parents. However, although the decision to take disability as the key criterion was a wise one, it did introduce a disjunction between the qualifying criteria and the need that the Fund was set up to meet. Many children who did not suffer from 'very severe disability' nevertheless needed help so far as the relief of stress was concerned. There was no perfect correlation between the severity of the disability and the problem of management presented by the child.

'Very severe disability' was interpreted by Ross Mitchell in the form of a list of requirements (see Appendix 1) that must be fulfilled in order to qualify for help. This list of requirements was amended as time went on; amendments to the criteria tended to have the effect of narrowing them and reducing the numbers of children eligible. For example, cystic fibrosis – which was initially considered by the social workers as a very severe disability because of the problems of management to which it gave rise – was later accepted for eligibility only if the child was seriously restricted physically by the associated chest condition. Mongols, who like other mentally handicapped children were originally eligible if their IQ was less than 50, were later redefined as eligible only if they had IQs of less than 35. This criterion was subsequently broadened after representation by the staff, and mongols with IQs between 35 and 50 were accepted if they had serious heart defects or other severe disability, or their problems of care were such that an attendance allowance was awarded.

Other criteria were broadened. Thus, the Medical Advisory Committee came to accept that total lack of control of bowel and bladder as a result of organic defects in a child over five was itself a very severe disability. In other cases, too, the staff were enabled to use their discretion and, for example, accept some asthmatic and eczematous children who might previously have been excluded.

Much was left to the discretion and judgment of the individual social workers in York. Doubtful cases were referred to the Panel, but in the early days at least, the benefit of the doubt was given to the family and the child was accepted. But as time went on, there appeared to be a shift in emphasis in the operation of this discretion, and the burden of proof fell more heavily on the family.

## 4   Social and economic circumstances

Social and economic circumstances were not mentioned as criteria in the Minister's statement nor was there any record that they were discussed in the early meetings between the Trust's staff and the DHSS, but in the DHSS letter setting out the agreed criteria, the following sentence appeared:[7]

Those eligible are families . . . who because of their economic
and social circumstances are in need of money, goods or
services which the trustees consider should be provided in

order to relieve stress on the family while the handicapped
child is at home.

In Notes of Guidance for the Panel, when it was first established in
April 1973, the following appeared:[8]

> With regard to the economic circumstances of a family it is not
> intended to introduce a form of means test. The panel will
> however have to be satisfied from the social reports provided
> that the financial circumstances of a family in relation to their
> commitments are such that recourse to the Fund is justified.

In May 1973 the Panel enunciated the following principles regarding
economic circumstances:[9]

1 No form of means test should be employed.
2 When considering the level of income of a family it was
  necessary to take into account what the child's handicap
  did to the way of life of the family by comparison with their
  peers.

Applying these principles did not prove easy. Visiting social workers
were told to ask not for details of income and expenditure but a general
statement about the nature of employment and 'a general indication of
the family's social and economic circumstances is generally all that is
needed'.[10] The Secretary wrote a note for the Management Committee
in October 1974 and this was subsequently incorporated into the Notes
of Guidance to Social Workers, but it was deliberately vague. The figure
of £4,500 per annum was suggested as the kind of salary level where a
grant might not be necessary and the figure was subsequently increased
to £6,000. Social workers were also asked to check whether the social
and economic circumstances were such that the family could reasonably
be expected to provide the items requested from its own resources.

Some of the small number of families whose applications were
rejected on grounds of social and economic circumstance wrote to the
Fund, distressed that they had been turned down on grounds of income
when they had thought that there would be no income test. One letter
of this type said:

> It is humiliating to apply for financial help and one does not do
> that lightly . . . it is an ordeal to have to go through the case with
> your social worker . . . and then be referred to hopelessly over-
> worked, apathetic and inefficient agencies such as social services
> departments.

5    *The request must be appropriate*

The item requested must be (in the words of the agreed guide-lines) 'money, goods or services which the trustees consider should be provided in order to relieve stress on the family while the handicapped child is at home'.[11] How 'stress' became such an important word in the administration of the Fund has been discussed in chapter 2. The relevant sentence in the guide-lines became subtly and significantly changed in the guidance given to social workers:[12]

> The help given must be related to the stress caused by having a
> handicapped child. The Fund cannot be used to solve other
> problems merely because by coincidence there happens to be
> a handicapped child in the family.

This change was justified by reference to Sir Keith Joseph's original statement:

> In many cases the parents need more help in shouldering the
> various burdens which caring for these children entails.[13]

> I emphasise again that this is not compensation. Its purpose is to
> ease the burden of living on those households containing very
> severely congenitally disabled children.[14]

The officers of the Fund believed that this statement implied that they must give help with only those needs that arose out of the care of the child.

Family problems that might be exacerbated by the stress of looking after a handicapped child could not be dealt with by the Fund, if they could not be attributed to the care of the child. For instance, a family asking for help with transport to enable the wife to do the shopping more easily would be refused, but requests for help with transport to 'get out and about' were accepted. With the help of the Panel, criteria were developed covering cars, caravans, central heating, clothing, colour TVs, education, housing, debts, speech trainers, telephones, toys, small grants, furniture, carpets, household equipment, and many other items. Where no criterion existed the social workers had to ask themselves whether the item requested would relieve stress arising out of the care of the handicapped children. This principle was particularly strongly affirmed and emphasised during the early summer of 1975 when the policies of the Fund were reappraised in the light of the reduced resources that were to become available. A mother with a second-hand cooker with only one ring effective, who said 'I can hardly prepare meals for the children' was rejected, and was told 'Our help is limited to assisting in ways which are directly related to the child's handicap and we cannot help with household goods which would be needed irrespective of the presence of a handicapped child.'

## 6  Could the items requested be given by another agency?

In his statement Sir Keith Joseph had said:[15]

> It is not intended that this money should be by way of compensation for being disabled but rather that it should serve to complement the services already being provided.

However, following the meeting between the Trust and the DHSS, the following guide-line was agreed:[16]

> It is for the trustees to decide the form of help which shall be given to eligible families to complement the services provided by statutory and voluntary bodies, but this help may include goods or services which it is within the power of the statutory services to provide.

Here, again, this ruling was difficult for the social work staff to interpret. The powers of existing authorities were wide and it could have been argued that almost all the items provided by the Fund could be supplied by other authorities under existing legislation. The Panel developed policies to guide the staff in making decisions about requests for specific items and within these guide-lines the staff used their judgment. This issue is considered again in chapter 13.

## Rejections

Any agency allocating scarce resources has to discriminate between those who are eligible and those who are not. The Family Fund was no exception. In the light of the criteria applied by the Fund to those who requested help, what distinguished those families to whom it was refused and on what grounds was it withheld?

It should be noted that of those who applied 0.75 per cent died while their application was being processed and 1.7 per cent withdrew their applications after having obtained the item requested from another service. A further 2.7 per cent either withdrew their application for no obvious reason or were assumed to have withdrawn them when repeated attempts to contact the family had failed. Another 0.96 per cent were not assisted for 'other' reasons – they consisted of applicants who were too young or too old, who were fostered, or who failed to make any specific request. But apart from these categories, by March 1976 14.5 per cent of applicants had been rejected because they failed to meet the criteria.

Table 4.2 shows their distribution:

*Table 4.2    Reasons for rejecting families who applied to the Family Fund*

|  | Number | % |
| --- | --- | --- |
| Not very severely disabled | 2,652 | 9.1 |
| Not living at home | 76 | 0.3 |
| Social and economic circumstances | 136 | 0.5 |
| Request not appropriate | 1,346 | 4.6 |
| Total | 4,210 | 14.5 |

*Table 4.3    Rejections by time of application*

| Time of application | Total applications | % rejected |
| --- | --- | --- |
| April–November 1973 | 5,940 | 7.9 |
| December 1973–March 1974 | 4,642 | 8.4 |
| April 1974–July 1974 | 5,085 | 11.4 |
| August 1974–November 1974 | 3,644 | 15.9 |
| December 1974–March 1975 | 3,375 | 18.1 |
| April 1975–July 1975 | 2,765 | 19.4 |
| August 1975–November 1975 | 1,992 | 25.8 |
| Total | 27,443 | 13.4 |

Table 4.3 shows the proportion of applicants rejected according to the date of their first application. Variations in rejection over time are somewhat difficult to interpret because rejections tended to be processed more quickly than acceptances. Table 4.3 restricts the analysis to all applications up to November 1975; only a small proportion of these cases would not have been dealt with by the time of the analysis in April 1976. The Table shows that earlier applicants were more likely to be accepted by the Fund.

A larger proportion of later applicants were rejected as 'not very severely disabled', for 'social and economic circumstances', and because the 'item requested was inappropriate'. Detailed analysis by date of decision reveals that from June 1975 there was a sharp increase in rejection on the third of these grounds. This was the result of the new rules introduced at that time about what constituted an appropriate request.

By April 1976, about 30 per cent of the applications processed each month ended without a grant. Rejecting applications was not easy: it was distressing for families to be told, however sensitively, that the child they were struggling to look after was not considered sufficiently severely handicapped to warrant help. It was also a difficult and demanding job for the social workers to discriminate between cases and to draft letters of rejection. It was particularly hard because some of the families who were rejected because they did not meet the Fund's eligibility criteria were carrying similar, and in some cases greater, burdens than those who were accepted.

Figure 4.2 shows the distribution of handicap scores[17] of 2,832 families with children who have been accepted by the Fund and 328 children who have been rejected because their disability was not considered 'very severe'. These are children who applied after April 1976, when the handicap scale was introduced. Although the mean handicap score of accepted children is significantly higher than that of rejected children, there is a good deal of overlap between the scores. Forty-eight of the 328 rejected children had handicap scores of six or more.

The families who were rejected may not have met the formal criterion of 'very severe disability', but in some instances their *need* was just as great, the *handicap* imposed by the disability was just as severe, and the level of *stress* arising out of the care of the child may have been just as acute.

As in the case of other benefits for the disabled, the Fund criteria do not provide an exact fit between 'families who need help in shouldering the various burdens which caring for these children entails' and the definitions of 'very severe disability'.

Why did the proportion of applicants being rejected apparently increase? Four possible explanations are offered:

1 As time passed the Fund received more applications from families who fell outside the criteria, even when these were interpreted most flexibly.

2 As the Fund progressively developed criteria to define 'very severe disability', the detailed criteria limited the extent to which the staff could use their discretion. When the criteria were very simple, the

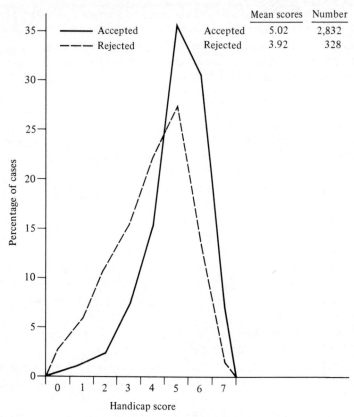

*Figure 4.2    Handicap scores by Family Fund application result*

staff were able to accept a child because there was no rule prohibiting them from doing so. Increasingly complex criteria bound the staff's discretion.

3    The atmosphere in which the staff operated changed. After mid-1975, the need to work within a budget and the replacement of professionally trained social work staff for the most part by administrative staff led to a tighter and more inflexible attitude in decision-making.

4    The increase in the numbers rejected because of 'request inappropriate' took place largely as a result of the Fund's change in policy. After mid-1975, families who asked for wheelchairs, aids and adaptations, and many other items that could be given by another agency were rejected. In addition, the Fund's managers emphasised that the help needed must arise out of the disability.

**Re-applications**

In developing policy in the early days, the Fund's managers did not contemplate that it would become a continuous source of support for families, and the attitude of the Fund to re-applicants has therefore been somewhat ambivalent. On one hand, the Fund accepted that the needs for which families had received help might recur, or that some families might not ask for all they needed in their initial application. On the other hand, with a short-term involvement, with limited resources to distribute, with new families applying, and the belief that there might be many more eligible, it did not encourage families to re-apply. Yet by December 1976, out of 37,094 applicants, 10,837 (29.2 per cent) had applied more than once. The earlier the family had applied, the more likely they were to have re-applied, and by December 1976, this was true of about two-thirds of families who first applied to the Fund in 1973. Some of these families had originally been rejected but were accepted on second application. These included the families of non-congenitally disabled children who were ineligible until the criterion was changed, and families whose child was considered too young at the time of the first application. But the majority of re-applicants had already been helped by the Fund.

Re-applicants to the Fund differed in a number of respects from first applicants. They were more likely to be single parents or to have larger families; less likely to have deaf or mentally handicapped children, and more likely to have spastic, spina bifida or mentally ill children; and more likely to be working-class families, to have an unemployed or sick head of household, and to be receiving the higher rate attendance allowance – that is, to have a more severely disabled child; and less likely to have a wife in work. Overall, then, re-applicants tended to be families who were more hard pressed. However, although all the differences mentioned above were statistically significant, none of them was very dramatic.

Re-applicants ended up by receiving more items and larger average grants from the Family Fund. In their first application, they had asked for the same number of items as all first applicants. However, fewer had asked for the big items – like cars, washing-machines, and aids and adaptations – and more had asked for the smaller items that were likely to recur. To some extent, re-applicants were catching up with the items which they had missed on the first round.

They tended to fall into two groups:

1   As many as half of them re-applied for and obtained another payment from the Fund for needs that were by their nature recurring.

Thus, families asked for holidays each year, a family who had received help with driving lessons might ask for more, or if that family had received a clothing grant it needed more clothes and turned again to the Fund.

2    Some families re-applied to obtain items that they had missed on their first application. Those items that were regarded as non-essential were rejected at the second application, but many had been needed all along, and the family might not have known that they could be obtained from the Fund. Either the visiting social worker had also missed it, or the item was required because of some new development in the child's condition of the family circumstances – an old car or washing-machine that broke down, or a growing child who needed new equipment or clothing.

In mid-1975, as part of the general attempt at budgetary control, the Fund introduced the following guide-lines:[18]

### Repeated grants for the same items

It has been necessary to repeat grants for such items as clothing and bedding . . . to families who seem unable to afford these because of the heavy expenses caused by their handicapped children. Repeated grants for families in full employment who are in receipt of the attendance allowance at the higher rate should no longer be made unless there are exceptional circumstances. . . .

### Subsequent applications

When making a grant in response to an initial application it should be stated both in standard and individual letters that the trustees have assumed that the major areas of stress have been relieved and that no further grants can be made unless there has been a substantial change in the family's circumstances. . . . Grants for continuing expenditure on rentals, maintenance, servicing and repairs should not be made.

For a time these guide-lines were applied very strictly and it became very difficult to obtain second and subsequent grants from the Fund. Later, as the pressure on resources eased and further money was promised, the guide-lines were operated more liberally.

Nevertheless, policy towards re-applicants remained an uneasy compromise between welcoming them as a natural part of a continuous process of help and seeing the Fund as a single contribution service. In some respects, the Fund was saved from having to make a decision about its role because the demands from the families were limited.

# 5    Take-up of the Family Fund

The under-utilisation of benefits and services is one of the most in-triguing problems in social policy, and any study of it presents the research worker with methodological and conceptual difficulties. These have meant that in practice research has not been very success-ful in providing the policy-maker with either reliable estimates of take-up or the reasons for non take-up.

Much of the research on the take-up of cash benefits has been concerned with the means tested benefit system.[1] It appears from this work that benefits that are distributed selectively on the basis of means will not be claimed in some cases by as many as half of those who are eligible. The reasons adduced for this are various – ignorance about the availability of the benefit; difficulties in obtaining, under-standing and completing application forms; lack of incentive in claiming small amounts of benefit; and finally, stigma or an unwillingness to disclose income or identify oneself as a claimant.

There is little evidence about the take-up of contributory and non-means-tested non-contributory benefits and, specifically in this context, about the take-up of these benefits by the disabled. It has generally been assumed that benefits that are selective according to type of disability are more readily claimed than those that are selective by income.[2] The government originally estimated that 10,000 children would qualify for the higher rate attendance allowance and 50,000 for the lower rate. By December 1976, 21,168 were receiving the higher rate and 20,422 the lower.[3] On the other hand, the government esti-mated that 30,000 children would be eligible for the mobility allowance but by 10 October 1977 only 13,687 had claimed. These comparisons probably say as much about the estimates of the eligible population as they do about take-up.

Evidence on the utilisation of services in contrast to benefits is even more difficult to interpret because of the difficulty of establishing need. Demand for health and personal social services is generally considerably less than estimates of need. In the case of the health services, although the evidence is mixed and difficult to interpret because of differences in morbidity, it is generally thought that middle- and upper-income

69

groups are more likely to use services. The same is true in education –
the children of manual workers tend to have worse primary schools
and are less likely to stay on at secondary school or go on to higher
education.[4]

How did the Family Fund fare in comparison with the take-up of
other benefits and services? What proportion of those families eligible
for help from the Fund applied, and how many of them did not do so?
What have we been able to learn about their reasons for not claiming?

There is no single method of answering these questions. It was
beyond the resources of this study to mount a large household survey
to obtain a sample of eligible families and it has been necessary to
build up evidence on take-up piecemeal from a variety of sources as
the three-year 'experimental' period progressed. Evidence was obtained:

1   by a comparison of estimates of the eligible population with
numbers applying to the Family Fund;

2   by an examination of the characteristics of families applying to
the Family Fund to see whether some families are more likely to apply
than others;

3   by experimental attempts to increase take-up in two areas;

4   by an assessment of take-up in three eligible samples.

Each of these will be discussed in turn, and in chapter 7 will be supplemented by an examination of the consumer's view of the Fund.

## Comparison of estimates of the eligible population with the numbers applying to the Family Fund

In this context, the eligible population will be defined as the number of
families in the UK meeting the criteria which were developed by the
Fund of 'very severe disability'. Strictly speaking, only those families
with very severely disabled children in need of items which the Family
Fund can give and which will relieve stress arising out of the handicap
are actually eligible for help from the Family Fund. To establish the
number of families in the UK eligible for help from the Family Fund,
estimates of the prevalence of very severe disabilities were derived from
four sources.[5]

1   Published data on the incidence and prevalence of certain
conditions, including government and local authority registers.

2   A special analysis of the National Child Development study of
every child born in one week in 1958 (see Appendix 2).

3   An analysis of linked local authority and hospital registers in
York (see Appendix 2).

4  An analysis of linked local authority and Family Fund records for Bristol (see Appendix 2).

The best estimate of the prevalence of such children derived from these sources was 6.7 per 1,000, and we can be 95 per cent confident that the prevalence for the UK lies between 83,000 and 106,000. If we take the mid-point of this range – 94,500 – as the best estimate, further adjustments need to be made to reach the eligible population.

First, it is necessary to add the families who became eligible during the first three years of the Fund's operation. It is estimated that about 6,000 very severely disabled children are born and survive each year, and so a further 18,000 children became eligible for the Fund's help during the first three years' operation.

Second, a number of families have more than one severely disabled child. Therefore, to obtain an estimate of the number of families who were eligible for help it is necessary to take account of these. Unfortunately it is not known exactly what proportion of families do have more than one eligible child. Of families with more than one child applying to the Fund, 9.3 per cent stated that they had another disabled child in the family (1.6 per cent had two or more) but not all of these would meet the eligibility criteria. In the absence of any reliable figure, it is reasonable to estimate that 6 per cent of families had more than one very severely disabled child.

These calculations may be summarised thus:

| | |
|---|---|
| Best estimate of prevalence | 94,500 |
| Plus three years' births | 18,000 |
| Less children in the same family | 6,700 |
| Total eligible families | 105,800 |
| Total families who applied to the Family Fund | 28,911* |
| Proportion eligible applying to the Fund | 27.3 per cent |

*Excluding 2,808 who did not meet the severity criteria of the Fund.

## Characteristics of families applying to the Family Fund

Some types of families are more likely to have applied than others. The following variables will be examined: age; class; working wives; family composition; disease; geographical location; time.

*Table 5.1    Age at application*

|        | <1   | 1     | 2     | 3     | 4     | 5     | 6     | 7     |
|--------|------|-------|-------|-------|-------|-------|-------|-------|
| Number | 749  | 1,604 | 2,424 | 2,544 | 2,457 | 2,266 | 2,236 | 2,260 |
| % total | 2.4 | 5.2   | 7.8   | 8.2   | 7.9   | 7.3   | 7.2   | 7.3   |

|        | 8     | 9     | 10    | 11    | 12    | 13    | 14    | 15    |
|--------|-------|-------|-------|-------|-------|-------|-------|-------|
|        | 2,176 | 2,067 | 2,121 | 1,952 | 1,834 | 1,568 | 1,422 | 1,316 |
|        | 7.0   | 6.7   | 6.8   | 6.3   | 5.9   | 5.1   | 4.6   | 4.2   |

## Age at time of application

The prevalence of severe handicap varies according to age. Some conditions, such as muscular dystrophy or cystic fibrosis, do not begin to be disabling until late in childhood; disabilities caused by burns and head injuries may occur at any time after birth; other conditions, such as heart defects, may be improved or cured by surgery. There are many conditions that are not recognised at birth or, if they are diagnosed, the degree of severity of the disability is not easy to assess at a very young age. Moreover, very young disabled children, although they may cause their parents considerable emotional distress, do not necessarily present any more of a burden of the kind which the Family Fund could relieve than would a normal baby of the same age. For instance, all babies, and not just disabled ones, call for extra laundry. This is not to say that families with a very young disabled child would not benefit from help with a washing-machine, but it means that they may be less likely to recognise laundry as a problem arising out of the presence of the handicapped child and will therefore be less likely to apply for help. As we have seen in chapter 4, the Fund took the view that, in general, families with very young children could not receive help.

In Table 5.1, it is clear that if the prevalence of child handicap is equal for each age, fewer families with younger and older children have applied to the Fund.

## Class

Two possibilities arise in considering variations in the rate of applications by social class. On the one hand, because the Fund was distributing items such as clothes and bedding, washing-machines, holidays, and help with transport, it might be expected that there would be fewer applicants from the upper social classes, who might either possess these items already or be able to acquire them. On the other hand, these classes might be expected to be more articulate, to have higher aspirations, perhaps to feel relatively more deprived, and to be better informed about the help available, and for any of these reasons to be more likely to apply to the Fund.

Unfortunately, there are no data on the national class distribution of families with disabled children. It is thought that some conditions are not associated with class and that others are.[6] In the absence of any representative data on families with handicapped children, Table 5.2 compares the class distribution of applicants to the Fund with the class distribution of children from the General Household Survey.

*Table 5.2   Comparison of the social class distribution of applicants to the Family Fund with that of children in the General Household Survey 1973*

| Social class | Family Fund (N = 25,037) | GHS 1973 (N = 7,967) |
| --- | --- | --- |
| I | 2.2 | 5.4 |
| II | 10.6 | 15.0 |
| III non-manual | 11.8 | 15.3 |
| III manual | 52.2 | 42.9 |
| IV | 16.8 | 17.5 |
| V | 6.4 | 3.9 |

It appears from this comparison that applicants to the Fund were more likely to be manual workers.

*Working wives*

Table 5.3 shows that fewer of the wives of applicants to the Fund were able to go out to work to supplement the family income, and that such families were likely for this reason to be more hard pressed than those with normal children.

*Table 5.3   Comparison of the work status of Family Fund families and families in the General Household Survey 1972*

| Working wives | Family Fund (N = 28,980) | GHS 1972 (N = 7,391) |
| --- | --- | --- |
| Full time | 3.8 | 12.8 |
| Part time | 20.4 | 27.9 |

*Family composition*

In Table 5.4 the family composition of Fund applicants is compared with that of the population with dependent children covered by the General Household Survey. A larger proportion of Fund applicants consists of single-parent and larger families. There is no reliable evidence on the distribution of the family types and sizes of all families with disabled children. Some conditions (e.g. mental handicap) are more likely to occur in large families, because mothers of mentally handicapped children tend to be older than average. On the other hand, the birth of a handicapped child is very likely to deter parents from risking another child.[7] It is not known whether the strains of caring for a disabled child cause marriages to break up.

*Table 5.4    Comparison of the family composition of Family Fund families and families in the General Household Survey 1973*

| Family composition | Family Fund (N = 29,845) | GHS 1973 (N = 4,567) |
|---|---|---|
| Couple with two children or less | 47.2 | 68.0 |
| Couple with three children or more | 40.6 | 23.0 |
| Single-parent families | 12.2 | 9.0 |

Over all, these findings indicate that the economic circumstances of families applying to the Fund are lower than for the population as a whole, and also probably lower than the population of all families with disabled children.

*Disease*

The distribution of applicants according to their principal handicapping conditions is given in Table 5.5. There are no comparative data on all families with very severely disabled children, but it has been suspected throughout the first three years of the Fund's operation that families with children with physical disabilities - spina bifida and muscular dystrophy - have been more likely to apply than children with mental or sensory handicaps. This is because the proportion of applicants with spina bifida was as high as 24 per cent in the first year of the Fund's operation but fell back at the end of the period to 11 per cent.

*Geographical location*

There is considerable evidence that the distribution of handicap varies

*Table 5.5    Handicapping condition of applicants to the Family Fund*

| Handicapping condition | Number | % total |
|---|---|---|
| Cancers, malignant tumours | 127 | 0.4 |
| Benign, unspecified tumours | 47 | 0.2 |
| Diabetes | 40 | 0.1 |
| Other endocrine, nutritional, metabolic or allergic diseases | 161 | 0.5 |
| Haemophilia | 161 | 0.5 |
| Other blood diseases | 99 | 0.3 |
| Mental illness (autism) | 1,234 | 4.0 |
| Mental subnormality | 9,972 | 32.3 |
| Polio | 14 | – |
| Cerebral haemorrhage | 37 | 0.1 |
| Multiple sclerosis | 5 | – |
| Cerebral palsy (spastic) | 5,215 | 16.9 |
| Paraplegia/hemiplegia | 154 | 0.5 |
| Epilepsy/convulsions | 933 | 3.0 |
| Head injury | 71 | 0.2 |
| Other CNS | 585 | 1.9 |
| Heart diseases | 635 | 2.1 |
| Bronchitis | 7 | – |
| Asthma | 60 | 0.2 |
| Other lung diseases (cystic fibrosis) | 326 | 1.1 |
| Diseases and defects of digestive system | 99 | 0.3 |
| Renal disease | 146 | 0.5 |
| Diseases and defects of bladder | 104 | 0.3 |
| Diseases of the eye/partial blindness | 313 | 1.0 |
| Deafness | 1,445 | 4.7 |
| Other ear disorders | 20 | 0.1 |
| Blindness | 517 | 1.7 |
| Diseases of the skin | 45 | 0.1 |
| Rheumatoid arthritis | 61 | 0.2 |
| Arthrogryphosis | 75 | 0.2 |
| Muscular dystrophy | 865 | 2.8 |
| Sprains, fractures, etc. | 44 | 0.1 |
| Other diseases of the bone | 493 | 1.6 |
| Amputations | 54 | 0.2 |
| Spina bifida, hydrocephalus | 5,566 | 18.1 |
| Other congenital abnormalities | 889 | 2.9 |
| Burns | 3 | – |
| Ill-defined conditions | 206 | 0.7 |
| Total | 30,828 | 100 |

between different areas.[8] Although for children there is no survey evidence of this, there are published statistics on the regional distribution of attendance allowances being paid to children. If, as has been suggested, the attendance allowance is claimed by the majority of those eligible, the regional distribution of allowances paid can be used with some confidence as an index of the prevalence of handicap in different regions, even though the attendance allowance and Family Fund criteria are not identical.

*Table 5.6    Regional distribution of Family Fund applicants and recipients of attendance allowance*

| Region | Attendance allowance in payment per 1,000 children under sixteen | Family Fund applicants per 1,000 children under sixteen |
|---|---|---|
| Northern | 3.36 | 2.23 |
| Yorkshire and Humberside | 3.12 | 1.97 |
| East Midlands and East Anglia | 2.86 | 3.46 |
| South-East | 2.96 | 1.77 |
| South-West | 2.68 | 1.69 |
| West Midlands | 3.32 | 1.84 |
| North-West | 3.86 | 2.23 |
| Wales | 3.60 | 2.60 |
| Scotland | 2.90 | 2.22 |
| Northern Ireland | 4.47 | 3.09 |

*Source*: *Hansard*, Written Answers, 21 March 1977, cols 411–12.
Figures relate to December 1976.

A correlation analysis of the rates in Table 5.6 gave r = 0.87, significant at the 99 per cent level. Such a high correlation coefficient indicates a very close relationship between the regional distribution of applicants to the Family Fund and the regional distribution of recipients of the attendance allowance. However, there are still variations that are greater than could be expected to occur by chance (a chi-square analysis of awards of the attendance allowance and applicants to the Family Fund by region gives $\chi > 70$, significant at the 99 per cent level). Scotland and Wales had relatively more Family Fund applicants than attendance allowances in payment, and the West Midlands and North-West had relatively fewer Family Fund applicants.

While the regional variations in the rate of applications to the Fund coincide fairly closely with the best available indicator of variations in prevalence, there are nevertheless wide variations in the rate of application to the Fund from different local areas. For instance, within the North-West region, with an over-all rate of 2.45 per 1,000 children under sixteen, Lancashire has a rate of 1.88 and St Helens 4.62.

These variations in application rate may be a function of any of the following factors:

1   variations in the prevalence of severely disabled children;
2   variations in the need of families with disabled children;
3   variations in the provision by the services in the areas;
4   variations in the take-up arising from degrees of awareness of the Fund in different areas.

Information on area variations in prevalence, apart from the regional data discussed above, is not available. Variations in take-up that may have arisen from variations in the awareness of the Fund in different areas is discussed later in this chapter and in chapter 6. An analysis was carried out to examine whether there is any relationship between variations in need and service provision and applications to the Fund in different areas.

In order to attempt to explain the variations in application rates according to area, about 130 variables, covering population structure, vital statistics, employment, housing, provision of personal social services (including aids to households), education and politics, were collected. A simple correlation analysis revealed that there was a relationship between the application rate to the Family Fund and indicators of need and indicators of service provision in any area. Indicators of need were derived from the variables used by Imber to classify local authorities responsible for personal social services.[9] Factors used to reflect the extent of 'service' provision in an area were thirty-one variables drawn from CIPFA and DHSS series.[10]

Three need and service provision indicators were shown to have some predictive value with regard to the application rate to the Family Fund (Table 5.7), and between them explained 43 per cent of the variation in the rate of applications between areas. Authorities where the application rates differed significantly from those predicted on the basis of their levels of need or levels of service provision were identified by an analysis of the residuals produced by the regression analysis. The residual measures the part of the variation in the Family Fund application rate that remains unexplained after taking into account the describing variables. The authorities whose application rates deviated

*Table 5.7   Regression of the Family Fund application rate on the need and service variables*

| Variable | Correlation coefficient | Cumulative proportion of variance explained | Unstandardised regression coefficient | Standard error of B | F ratio |
|---|---|---|---|---|---|
| | R | R² | B | | F |
| % unemployed | 0.54 | 0.29 | 0.012 | 0.003 | 14.6 |
| % on handicapped register | 0.49 | 0.38 | 0.029 | 0.009 | 9.7 |
| % lacking one amenity | 0.49 | 0.43 | 0.002 | 0.001 | 8.2 |
| (Constant) | | | 1.108 | | |

*Note*: On 101 areas, with degrees of freedom 1 and 97, the regression coefficients for all three variables were significant at the 1 per cent level.

most from those predicted on the basis of their levels of need and of service provision are listed in Tables 5.8 and 5.9.

*Table 5.8   Areas with lower application rates than predicted on the basis of need and service indicators (ten most deviant areas ranked by size of residuals)*

| Area | Application rate | Rate per 1,000 less than predicted |
|---|---|---|
| Tower Hamlets | 2.10 | −0.86 |
| Tameside | 2.02 | −0.76 |
| Enfield | 1.53 | −0.75 |
| Isle of Wight | 1.77 | −0.69 |
| Cleveland | 2.45 | −0.67 |
| Humberside | 1.95 | −0.64 |
| Kensington and Chelsea | 2.33 | −0.64 |
| Bromley | 1.61 | −0.60 |
| Rochdale | 2.00 | −0.59 |
| Barnet | 1.59 | −0.58 |

The reasons why certain authorities deviate markedly from their predicted application rates cannot be deduced from the study. The deviations may be the result of external factors, such as the level of publicity about the Fund in the area or the enthusiasm of certain individuals in disseminating information about the Fund. Those areas, however, that have lower application rates than those predicted on the

basis of both needs and services are likely to be areas that would
benefit from more publicity.

*Table 5.9 Areas with higher application rates than predicted on the
basis of need and service indicators (ten most deviant areas ranked
by size of residuals)*

| Area | Application rate | Rate per 1,000 more than predicted |
|------|------------------|------------------------------------|
| Croydon | 3.52 | +1.13 |
| Doncaster | 3.59 | +1.10 |
| Sutton | 3.07 | +1.03 |
| Greenwich | 3.52 | +1.03 |
| Notts | 3.28 | +1.00 |
| Newcastle | 4.06 | +0.86 |
| St Helens | 3.21 | +0.86 |
| Liverpool | 4.37 | +0.83 |
| Salop | 2.74 | +0.69 |
| Coventry | 3.02 | +0.63 |

*Note*: When both need and service indicators are used, only 101 areas
can be included in the analysis. Two of the six areas excluded were
among the most deviant authorities in the analysis based on need
indicators alone: Bury, which had a lower application rate (1.61)
than would have been predicted, and Wirral, which had a higher one
(3.29).

*Time*

The final variable we shall examine among those associated with application rates is the date of first applications. The rate of applications
has not been even over the three years. The number of applications
each month rose to a peak in March 1974, then began to decline, and
after late-1975 levelled off at between 500–600 per month. This does
not necessarily indicate that the Fund has now dealt with the demand
and is merely receiving applications from newly disabled children. There
is only a marginal tendency for more recent applicants to have younger
children, and the vast majority of applicants are still children who
could have applied to the Family Fund from the outset.

As well as variations in the number of applications over the study
period there have also been differences in the character of applicants
over time. Families with children aged 0–5 applied more slowly to the

Fund than the other age groups; large families applied more readily than other family sizes; families in social classes I and II tended to apply faster to the Fund than the other social classes, and although families in classes IV and V were lagging behind the other groups (except class II non-manual) they increased their rate of application in the second half of the Fund's first three years. Families with Thalidomide, autistic and spina bifida children were the quickest to apply to the Fund, and families with children who were epileptic, deaf, or mentally handicapped, were the slowest.

In addition to these differences there was considerable variation in the application rates over time from families living in different regions of the UK. These variations are summarised in Table 5.10.

Families living in Northern Ireland were slow to apply to the Fund in the early period but by the third they had overtaken all the other regions, and it was Scotland and the West Midlands that lagged behind the rest. These variations influenced and were affected by the publicity programme of the Fund. For example, when Northern Ireland was identified as lagging behind other regions a special campaign was launched to encourage applications from the province. Not all the changes in the rates of applications from different regions can be explained by reference to specific publicity campaigns, though. For instance, there appears to have been a spate of applications in the Northern region between the fifth and sixth period when there were no special efforts launched by the Family Fund to encourage applications. The publicity operations of the Fund and their impact are discussed in chapter 6.

### Experimental attempts to increase take-up in two areas

During the experimental period of the Fund, two attempts were made to increase the rate of applications from particular areas and measure the results. In October 1974, an agent was employed for one week to visit Tynemouth and talk about the Fund to as many intermediaries as possible including doctors, social workers, health visitors, and relevant voluntary organisations, and encourage them to assist families to apply. Tynemouth was chosen because at that time it had a low rate of application.

In September 1975, this exercise was repeated in Sandwell (formerly West Bromwich). An agent was employed for four weeks to visit every health, social, and education agency that might have contact with families with handicapped children. The agent visited all the agencies

Table 5.10  *Cumulative per cent of applications to the Family Fund over time, by region*

| Four-month period | Northern | Yorkshire and Humberside | West Midlands | East Anglia | South-East | North-West | East Midlands | South-West | Wales | Northern Ireland | Scotland | UK |
|---|---|---|---|---|---|---|---|---|---|---|---|---|
| 1 | 4.8 | 4.2 | 4.5 | 4.0 | 4.0 | 5.8 | 6.9 | 3.3 | 4.6 | 0.9 | 3.3 | 4.3 |
| 2 | 19.8 | 19.7 | 15.3 | 23.6 | 20.6 | 18.5 | 22.4 | 22.1 | 21.4 | 14.3 | 13.2 | 19.0 |
| 3 | 30.5 | 34.6 | 29.5 | 36.9 | 35.9 | 35.1 | 37.7 | 36.7 | 38.5 | 39.1 | 24.0 | 34.1 |
| 4 | 47.0 | 49.1 | 47.8 | 52.8 | 51.7 | 50.3 | 51.8 | 51.3 | 54.9 | 58.3 | 48.0 | 50.8 |
| 5 | 58.3 | 60.7 | 60.4 | 53.1 | 63.5 | 62.1 | 63.5 | 62.7 | 65.5 | 72.1 | 62.0 | 62.8 |
| 6 | 72.4 | 70.7 | 71.5 | 74.3 | 74.8 | 73.7 | 75.4 | 74.5 | 75.4 | 80.7 | 73.4 | 74.1 |
| 7 | 83.8 | 81.9 | 81.9 | 84.3 | 84.4 | 83.7 | 84.2 | 84.2 | 85.5 | 87.9 | 83.3 | 83.9 |
| 8 | 93.4 | 90.4 | 91.3 | 93.1 | 91.9 | 91.5 | 91.8 | 91.2 | 92.2 | 93.9 | 92.5 | 91.9 |
| 9 | 100.0 | 100.0 | 100.0 | 100.0 | 100.0 | 100.0 | 100.0 | 100.0 | 100.0 | 100.0 | 100.0 | 100.0 |

and in addition spoke to voluntary organisations, community groups, and parents of children at a special school.

The results of both these exercises are summarised in Figure 5.1. Both the interventions appear to have made an impact on take-up. The rate of applications in Tynemouth nearly doubled by March 1975, while the national average rose by only a quarter. However, after March 1975, the rate of increase slowed down and Tynemouth remained with a rate of application below the national average. In West Bromwich, the number of applications was also more than doubled six months after the action phase. During the period when the national average rate per 1,000 increased by only 0.27, the Sandwell rate went up by 1.08. Despite the increases, only Sandwell was lifted above the national average application rate. These results tend to suggest that, particularly in areas with low rates of application, there are still families who can be encouraged to apply to the Fund by the activities of local agents.

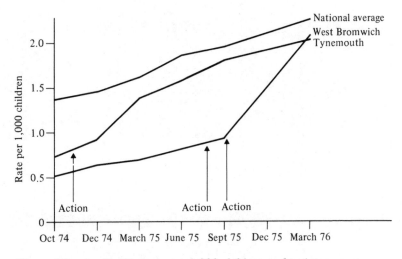

*Figure 5.1    Application rate per 1,000 children under sixteen over time in experimental areas*

### Assessment of take-up in three eligible sub-samples

While the analysis of the characteristics of those applying to the Fund sheds some light on take-up and non take-up, there is really no substitute for a study of claimants and non-claimants in an eligible population. In this study we had no direct access to non-claimants but three attempts were made to obtain information on the proportion of an eligible sample applying to the Fund in York, Bristol, and Leeds.

## 1   *The York study*

A register of all eligible families living in the York district council area was obtained to make estimates of the numbers of families with severely disabled children in the UK. Applicants to the Fund from the York area were then monitored to see what proportion of those on the register applied. By April 1976, 66 or 47.5 per cent of those children classified on the register as 'very severe' had applied to the Family Fund; a further nineteen families had applied who were not classified as 'very severe' on the register; and twenty-eight families had applied who were not on the register at all. All but three of these twenty-eight had a good reason for not being on it. (Seven of them were not 'very severe', one had died before the register was drawn up, eleven had been born after the register was prepared, two had moved to York after the list was prepared, and in four cases, the condition had only manifested itself after the list was prepared.) This suggests that the York register was almost a complete record of eligible families at the time it was drawn up, and that between 45-50 per cent of those children on it classified as 'very severe' have applied to the Fund. The application rate per 1,000 children aged under sixteen was 3.69 in York in March 1976, compared with a national average of 2.24.

## 2   *The Bristol study*

A register of all severely disabled children in Bristol born between 1 April 1959 and 30 April 1969 was developed by Diana Pomeroy at the Department of Child Health, University of Bristol, for a study of their housing problems. The Bristol register provided a prevalence rate of 6.7 per 1,000 children under sixteen. By April 1976, 313 children, or 3.14 per 1,000 under sixteen, had applied from Bristol – about half those eligible for help from the Fund.

The Bristol study also provided some insights into the characteristics of applicants and non-applicants to the Fund. Out of the sample of 255 families in the Bristol study 63.5 per cent said they had heard of the Family Fund and 49.4 per cent had applied. Tables 5.11 to 5.14 summarise the characteristics of the two groups.

The data on impairment tend to confirm that the Fund received fewer applications from families with children with mental handicaps

*Table 5.11   Impairment of applicants and non-applicants to the Family Fund, Bristol sample*

| Impairment | Number | % who had heard of the Fund | % who had applied |
|---|---|---|---|
| Physical | 84 | 61.9 | 53.6 |
| Mental and physical | 23 | 82.6 | 82.6 |
| Mental | 148 | 61.5 | 41.9 |
| Total | 255 | 63.5 | 49.4 |

$\chi^2 = 3.98$ not significant     $\chi^2 = 14.07$ significant at 99%

*Table 5.12   Age of applicants and non-applicants to the Family Fund, Bristol sample*

| Age | Number | % who had heard of the Fund | % who had applied |
|---|---|---|---|
| 7–10 | 140 | 67.9 | 54.3 |
| 11–16 | 114 | 58.8 | 42.1 |

$\chi^2 = 2.25$ not significant     $\chi^2 = 3.73$ not significant

*Table 5.13   Class of applicants and non-applicants to the Family Fund, Bristol sample*

| Class | Number | % who had heard of the Fund | % who had applied |
|---|---|---|---|
| I and II | 39 | 64.1 | 43.6 |
| III non-manual | 21 | 85.7 | 52.3 |
| III manual | 104 | 61.5 | 49.0 |
| IV and V | 41 | 70.7 | 61.0 |
| Single parents | 22 | 59.0 | 42.0 |

$\chi^2 = 54.6$ not significant     $\chi^2 = 3.42$ not significant

*Table 5.14   Functional ability of applicants and non-applicants to the Family Fund, Bristol sample*

| Functional ability rating | Number | % who had heard of the Fund | % who had applied |
|---|---|---|---|
| 1 (High) | 105 | 48.6 | 32.4 |
| 2 | 66 | 65.2 | 51.5 |
| 3 | 38 | 78.9 | 57.9 |
| 4 (Low) | 46 | 82.6 | 76.1 |

$$\chi^2 = 21.4 \qquad \chi^2 = 26.47$$
significant at 99%   significant at 99%

as opposed to physical ones, though as many of the mothers of mentally handicapped children knew about the Fund. The data on age also confirm the suggestion made earlier that fewer older children had applied to the Fund. The data on class were very illuminating: the proportion of the different classes knowing about the Fund showed little variation, but families in social classes I and II were less likely to have applied. There also appeared to be a direct relationship between the functional ability of the child, knowledge of the Family Fund, and whether the family has applied.[11]

## 3   Knowledge of the Family Fund among the parents of children attending special schools in Leeds

While the results presented so far in this chapter provide an indication of the proportion of those eligible who applied to the Fund, as well as telling us something about the characteristics of applicants, we still know very little about why eligible families have not applied. The only way to find out why some families who appear to be eligible have not applied is to find and interview a sample of them. It is, however, difficult to get access to a satisfactory sample. The only readily available one consists of those parents with children at special schools for the severely mentally handicapped. Such a sample is unsatisfactory in a number of respects – it excludes pre-school children, those who have only severe physical disabilities, and mildly mentally handicapped children with physical disabilities. It is, therefore, only representative of school-age children with very severe mental handicaps and, as we have seen, it is possible that of those eligible, a smaller proportion of mentally handicapped than physically handicapped children have applied to the Fund. It is probable that of those eligible, a larger proportion of those over rather than under school age have applied. Nevertheless, a larger proportion of those in schools for the severely mentally handicapped are eligible than those in any other school because, by definition, all such children have IQs of less than 50, which is the Family Fund criterion (except in the case of mongols or children with multiple handicaps).

It was therefore decided to survey a sample of children at schools for the severely mentally handicapped. Following the success of a pilot exercise at Armley Grange School, Leeds, the headmasters of the other six schools for severely mentally handicapped children in Leeds agreed to send a letter and questionnaire to every parent. These were sent via the children. There were 375 families with eligible children at the schools, and 334 of them returned the questionnaire - a response rate of 89.1 per cent.

Before the families were contacted, it was known (from Family Fund records) that 127, or 36.0 per cent of the whole sample, had already applied to the Fund. This was roughly equivalent to an estimate of the proportion of eligible families nationally who had applied at the time, though it was probably a high proportion of eligible mentally handicapped children. The families who had not applied were asked whether they had heard of the Family Fund administered by the Joseph Rowntree Memorial Trust at York. Of the initial sample, 40.5 per cent said they had not heard of the Fund and 23.5 per cent knew about it but had not yet applied (see Table 5.15).

It is remarkable that 40.5 per cent of families with children at these schools said that before they received the letter and questionnaire, they had never heard of the Fund. A number wrote that now they had heard of it, they would like help; others added comments as if to explain why they had not heard about it. There is a link in the responses between ignorance and a misunderstanding of the nature of the Fund. It is as if families had not allowed themselves to be informed about the Fund because they did not think that they were eligible for help. Thus, a mother (with severe financial problems) wrote:

> I think we can't get help because of my income at present but would like to be kept in touch with the Joseph Rowntree Memorial Trust.

Another wrote:

> I didn't think I would get any help because my husband and I both work. I did try to get help (from DHSS presumably) when

*Table 5.15   Results of the exercise mounted in special schools in Leeds*

|                                                              | Total  |
|--------------------------------------------------------------|--------|
| Sample number                                                | 375    |
| Sample response                                              | 334    |
| Response rate                                                | 89.1%  |

BEFORE LETTER

|                                                              |        |
|--------------------------------------------------------------|--------|
| Number who had already applied to Fund (responses)           | 108 ⎫  |
| Number who had already applied to Fund (non-response)        | 19 ⎬   |
| Number who had already applied to Fund (Total)               | 127    |
| Percentage who had already applied to Fund                   | 36.0%  |
| Application results:  Acceptance                             | 121    |
|                    Pending | 0      |
|                    Rejection nvs | 2      |
|                    Rejection other | 4      |
| Number who knew of Fund but hadn't applied                   | 83     |
| Percentage who knew of Fund but hadn't applied               | 23.5%  |
| Reasons: Help not needed at moment                           | 14     |
|        Prefer to manage alone | 0      |
|        Doesn't think child qualifies | 25     |
|        Not enough known about Fund | 52     |
|        Other                | 4*     |
| Number who did not know of Fund                              | 143    |
| Percentage who did not know of Fund                          | 40.5%  |

AFTER LETTER

|                                                              |        |
|--------------------------------------------------------------|--------|
| Numbers applying who knew of Fund                            | 37.3%  |
| Numbers applying who didn't know of Fund                     | 34.2%  |
| Numbers applying Total                                       | 80     |
| Application results:  Acceptance                            | 58     |
|                    Pending | 0      |
|                    Rejection nvs | 3      |
|                    Rejection other | 19     |
| Total now applied                                            | 207    |
| Percentage                                                   | 58.6%  |

*Note*: *Two state child nearly sixteen; one feels material help is not what is needed; one was once turned down (not by Family Fund) and 'won't apply anywhere ever again'.

> I have to take N. to the dentist which is a long way. I have to have a taxi home as he has to be put to sleep. The Social Security say I don't qualify for help as we both work which I think is very unfair.

Again:

> I have not heard about this Fund before this letter but would not think my child would qualify as he gets attendance allowance.

And another:

> I have heard about a Fund that you can get for mentally handicapped children but somebody told me I wouldn't get anything because N. is not physically handicapped.

Following the receipt of the questionnaire, thirty-four of these 143 families applied to the Fund and by May 1977, forty-nine of these families had applied.

The eighty-three families who knew about the Fund but had not applied were asked why they had not done so. They were asked to tick one of four alternative explanations, or give a reason of their own. None of the families said they had not applied 'because they preferred to manage alone'. Twenty-five said they had not applied because they did not think their child was eligible; fourteen said they did not need help at the moment; and fifty-two that they did not know enough about the Fund. All these fifty-two families were sent an explanatory leaflet and application form and by May 1977, thirty-one of them had applied. One parent in this group commented: 'Parents need to know how they qualify for such aid and exactly what they can apply for. It all seems very vague to me.'

At the end of this exercise, when every family in all the special schools in Leeds had been informed about the Fund, the proportion applying was only increased from 35.7 per cent before the survey to 58.6 per cent by May 1977. Only 37.3 per cent of those who already knew about the Fund but had not yet applied were encouraged to do so, and only 34.2 per cent of those who did not know about the Fund before the survey applied after they had been told about it. Of the eighty who applied to the Fund after the survey, nineteen were rejected. (These findings are summarised in Table 5.15.)

So, about a third of the families in this study had already applied to the Fund; nearly two-thirds of the rest had not heard about it; only one in three of those who were informed, applied. It is very difficult to explain why some families – eighty-three in all – did not apply even though they knew about the Fund. Some of them were not in need; others thought their child was ineligible (some rather garbled version of the Family Fund criteria had percolated down to them) but most of the families said they wanted to know more about the Fund before they applied. But again, when they had been given more information, only 58.6 per cent applied.

These confusing and inconclusive results are typical of the findings that have been obtained in other studies which have found that ignorance is the main reason for non take-up and when more information is given, it has resulted in relatively small increases.[12] The Advisory Committee on Rent Rebates and Allowances[13] has recently commented:

> We do not underestimate the difficulties of ascertaining hard statistical facts, of general application, on these elusive problems (take up of rent rebates and allowances and reasons for not claiming), but we feel they are necessary if our assessment of the scheme is to be solidly based .... We think an approach which concentrates on tenants' explanations of their attitudes in their own words, rather than their response to a standard questionnaire, may produce further useful evidence of the reasons why people do not claim.

In chapter 7 applicants' attitudes to the Family Fund are examined in their own words.

## Conclusion

What 'hard statistical facts' about the take-up of the Family Fund emerge from the combination of related studies reviewed in this chapter?

1 The Family Fund is known to about half the families eligible – though only about a third have applied.

2 The numbers applying could be increased by half as much again, if fresh efforts were made to bring the Fund to the notice of families and provide more information to those who know about it.

3 Even with these efforts the total number of families who apply is not likely to rise much beyond half of those who are eligible.

4 Any attempt to increase the number of applications to the Fund will inevitably result in more applications from families who are not eligible, but it is probable that two out of every three will be eligible.

5 It is probable that those families who have applied to the Fund are on average in greater need than those who have not.

6 The main reason why families do not claim is ignorance – ignor-

ance that the Fund exists, that it applies to them, or that they can get help with the particular item that they need. There is no evidence that the stigma of demonstrating need might have prevented families from claiming. The strongest influence in determining the number of claims received must be the low expectations of many of the families and their determination to soldier on without help.

# 6 The publicity programme and source of referrals to the Fund

Let us now examine how applicants found out about the Fund and try to evaluate the efforts that were made to bring its existence to the attention of potential applicants.

## Publicity arrangements

The task of advertising the Fund was put into the hands of a public relations firm - Forman House. Forman House was originally recruited to help with what the Trust expected would be a delicate public relations exercise. Throughout the initial three-year period, the firm provided a general public relations service for the Fund. However, by August 1973, when the Fund was worried by the small number of applications arriving at York, Forman House was asked to prepare a publicity programme. This was worked out in consultation with the Fund's staff and consisted of two main approaches - general editorial publicity, and communication with families through intermediaries.

The firm proposed to build on the initial press conference held to announce the Fund by feeding stories to specialist writers in the quality papers and magazines, and by placing items in local and regional radio and TV programmes. Family advice columnists, social services, and nursing and medical journals were to be briefed; syndicated feature articles were to be circulated to 400 provincial newspapers and individual approaches made to feature editors of national newspapers and magazines; and 'sample' interviews were to be sent to regional and local radio stations. In addition, there was to be a steady flow of news items about the Fund.

When the Fund had been established a circular had been issued by the DHSS to all directors of social services, medical officers of health and chief education officers. Forman House proposed to follow this up by communicating with professional staff at local level through direct mailings of leaflets and posters (with covering letters) to GPs, social workers, health visitors, and special schools. This would be associated with direct approaches to the voluntary organisations representing handicapped children, encouraging their members to apply.

It was recognised at this early stage that the publicity arrangements would need to be phased so as to ensure, as far as possible, an even rate of applications. Administrative statistics were already beginning to show that applications were coming in from different regions at an uneven rate and that publicity should be concentrated on those areas with the lowest take-up. Longer term strategy would depend on the success of efforts made in the first two years, but it was suggested that, if necessary, there could be renewed mailings, exhibitions, production of films, direct advertising, lobbying of MPs, and the production of an annual report.[1]

Before the publicity programme was launched it had to be adapted. The administrative arrangements of the Fund in the autumn of 1973 could not cope with an application rate of more than 1,000 per month and by October 1973 this had already been reached. At a meeting between the secretary and Forman House:[2]

> It was agreed that this rate – of ideally 1,000 per month – was the maximum that currently could be coped with and should be considered the present target level, not to be exceeded for the time being.

But the Fund continued to be unable to process applications at this rate and with a backlog beginning to build up, Forman House had to readjust its programme. The rate of 1,000 per month 'for the time being' became a more permanent aim.

> The prime objective of publicity is to maintain the rate of applications to the Fund at the present level – roughly 1,000 per month, which in general terms will be somewhere close to exhausting the Fund at the end of its three-year period.[3]

It was therefore proposed that media coverage should be used more selectively in those areas with low levels of take-up and while the leaflets that had now been printed should be sent out, the distribution posters should be delayed.

By May, the emphasis of the campaign had shifted further:[4]

> Mr Hitch indicated that from now on the function of press releases on the statistics and activity generally should be to report more on the work of the Fund rather than to stimulate additional enquiries from families except in areas where response had been markedly low. Every occasion should also be seized to encourage statutory social workers investigating applications to report more intelligently.

In a new programme submitted in October 1974, Forman House reported that the task of creating awareness of the Fund among the general public and among intermediaries in contact with potential applicants had been achieved, and that they should now concentrate on improving social workers' understanding of the Fund. They also hoped to achieve some general publicity from the expected announcement of an extension of the Fund's remit to non-congenitally disabled children, but, as it turned out, the minister made this announcement without prior warning in an adjournment debate on vaccine-damaged children in December 1974.[5] A similar occasion when the help of the public relations firm might have been needed was when the Prime Minister announced that he intended to make available the second £3 million to the Fund, but he included it in a package of tax concessions for Thalidomide children without warning the Fund or their public relations firm.

Although the publicity proposals for the second year were agreed at a meeting in January 1975, the Fund's managers asked that direct mailing to intermediaries be delayed while they dealt with the backlog and sorted out the implications of the change of remit. Meanwhile, the newsletter and selective publicity went ahead.

In March 1975, the research team produced a paper on how applicants had heard of the Fund, and this led to a fresh approach by direct mailing to the headmasters of special schools, community physicians (child health), health centres, and consultant paediatricians – but only in the areas of low take-up and in a programme phased over six months.

By the end of three years, efforts to increase the application rate had virtually ended and Forman House was employed exclusively in the production of the newsletter to agents. The Fund's managers felt that it was adequately known about by intermediaries and they feared that fresh efforts to encourage applications would only result in more rejections of families not eligible for help. The Fund was also committed to first, and in some cases second, grants to existing applicants, and feared that a spate of new applicants might lead to overspending.

## The effectiveness of the publicity arrangements

It is not possible to estimate the direct and indirect costs of the Family Fund publicity. During the first three calendar years, Forman House received £29,883 for its services, but it should be noted that a considerable amount of the secretary's time was spent on 'publicity' activities, and that part of the research effort could also be reasonably ascribed to that end. In addition to these hidden costs to the Fund, government departments and local authorities took independent initiatives to bring the Fund's existence to the attention of their staff. Not all those who were successfully informed about the Fund applied to it, and not all those who applied were eligible for help. But if all these uncertain elements are ignored and Forman House's fees alone are divided by the number of applicants applying during the first three years, then each applicant cost 99 pence to attract.

In evaluating any method of information, one would like to know whether it succeeded in raising the rate of applications above what the rate would have been had the method not been adopted. But it is impossible to evaluate the publicity programme in any general or particular way because the process of finding out about the Fund, learning more about it, and then deciding to apply, was often long and involved. A family might have first heard of it from a newspaper or magazine, have learnt more about it at a meeting of a voluntary body, and been encouraged to apply as the result of advice from a social worker.

All the families who applied to the Fund were asked how they learned of the Fund. Table 6.1 summarises the source of information for all families and for those in the ten areas with the highest rate of applications. More families in these areas learned of the Fund through local press coverage, special schools, and fewer through voluntary organisations.

## Newspapers and magazines

Media publicity was one of the two major strategies of the initial publicity programme. Its success cannot be measured only by those families who said they learned of the Fund from this source because media coverage must have led indirectly to informing by friends, relatives, and intermediaries.

By the end of the three-year period, 8.7 per cent of applicants had learned of the Fund directly from media sources. These were most successful in encouraging applicants during the early existence of the Fund, although later there was a decline in the proportion of families hearing about it through local and national newspapers. On different occasions, articles about the Fund in *Woman's Own, Living,* and *Family Circle* caused spates of applications. Until March 1974, there was national coverage in the press and on radio and TV. At this time, Forman House began to concentrate on issuing special releases

*Table 6.1    How all families learned of the Fund and how families in ten areas with highest rate of application per 1,000 children learned of the Fund*

| Source | UK % | Top ten areas % |
|---|---|---|
| National press | 3.3 | 2.9 |
| Local press | 1.8 | 3.4 |
| Magazine | 2.0 | 1.5 |
| Local voluntary organisation | 9.3 | 6.1 |
| National voluntary organisation | 5.4 | 3.2 |
| Health visitor | 10.9 | 11.4 |
| Social services | 18.4 | 18.2 |
| Supplementary benefit | 1.1 | 1.9 |
| Clergy | 0.2 | 0.2 |
| GP | 3.2 | 3.2 |
| Education/school | 15.4 | 21.4 |
| Friend/relative | 14.8 | 16.0 |
| Leaflet/poster | 1.7 | 1.5 |
| Radio | 1.0 | 0.4 |
| TV | 0.6 | 0.6 |
| Hospital/other | 8.0 | 6.1 |
| Attendance allowance | 2.8 | 1.9 |
| Total % | 100 | 100 |
| Number | 28,948 | 3,614 |

in those areas that were shown to have a low rate of application per 1,000 children under sixteen. The effects of these special efforts were monitored but they did not appear to have a significant effect on take-up.

In general, then, it is probably fair to conclude that an area could produce a good rate of application to the Fund without local media coverage playing an important part, and that media coverage alone was not enough to produce a high rate.

## Voluntary organisations

Of the families, 14.7 per cent learned of the Fund through voluntary organisations: 5.4 per cent through national organisations and 9.3 per cent through local branches or parent/teacher associations of special schools. This over-all proportion remained fairly stable, but local branches became a more important source of information than national bodies. It is suspected that some disease categories were more likely to apply than others (see chapter 5) and this may be partly a result of the efforts made by the specialist organisation concerned to encourage applications. Voluntary organisations were not an important factor in determining the application rate in the top ten areas, though in some regions local voluntary organisations made more of an impact than in others. The publicity given by voluntary bodies, and particularly their role in encouraging members to apply, contributed substantially to the take-up of the Fund.

## Local health authorities

Health departments and health visitors were responsible for informing 10.9 per cent of all applicants. In addition, it is estimated that about 6 per cent (most of the 'other' categories in Table 6.1) heard of the Fund from an out-patients' department or hospital clinic. Through time, health visitors became increasingly influential and this may have been the result of leaflets distributed to them through their journal, or circulars and posters sent to health departments. Health authorities or, more precisely, health visitors and community physicians, are in theory in a good position to refer handicapped children, since all children under five years of age should be visited and children of school age will be on school health records.

In practice, except where there are special health visitors for handicapped children, very little of a health visitor's time is taken up with children, and few children over a year old are visited regularly. Nevertheless, health authorities were in a position to refer families and some areas owe much to the efforts made by them to locate families. It was the initiative taken by the medical officers of health in Denbighshire and Derbyshire that resulted in early high rates of application from those areas, and in Northern Ireland the health (and social services) boards were a notably successful source of information.

## Social services departments

Social services departments were responsible for referring 18.4 per cent of all families and this proportion grew as time passed. Some of the best areas had significantly more families referred via this source than in the UK as a whole.

Social services departments tend to know fewer families with handicapped children than either health or education departments, and although they are required to keep a register and provide services for such families, in most areas they will only know families who have been referred for a specific purpose. It is known from the prevalence analysis in York that only 42 per cent of the very severely handicapped were known to the social services departments before they applied. However, considerable efforts were made to inform social workers about the Fund through their professional journals or direct mailings of leaflets and posters. Social workers also got to know about the Fund because, particularly in the early period, their departments were asked to undertake to visit families who had applied in order to assess their applications.

## Supplementary benefits, GPs, and clergy

None of these were important sources of referral. All local supplementary benefit offices had been circulated but although as many as 15 per cent of families applying to the Fund were dependent on supplementary benefit, only 1.1 per cent had been referred by them. The clergy referred only fifty-one families. Considerable effort had gone into encouraging GPs to refer families – posters and leaflets had been sent to their surgeries and notices had appeared in their professional journals, but in all only 3.2 per cent of all families were referred from this source. This indicates not only the well-known difficulty of 'getting through' to GPs but also that although the average general practice will have four children eligible for help from the Fund, they are probably dealt with at local paediatric out-patients' clinics rather than by their GP. The best ten areas over all did not produce any more referrals from GPs than the rest of the country; but some other areas, including Rochdale and Armagh, individually showed higher rates, probably as a result of the initiative of one doctor in each area.

## Education authority/special schools

Although special schools did not produce as many referrals over all as did the social services, they were the most important determinant of the rate of take-up. Of all applicants, 15.4 per cent were informed from this source. Relatively little effort was made initially to encourage referrals by them, though all local education authorities received the first circular, and all the special schools for the severely mentally handicapped in England and Wales received a copy of the Family Fund leaflet. Later, headmasters of schools in areas of low take-up received another letter and leaflet. In the top ten areas over all a much higher proportion of the families learned of the Fund from special schools than in the UK as a whole, and particularly striking rates of referral through the schools came from Manchester, Liverpool, and Southwark. Doncaster owed its position (thirteenth in the take-up 'league') entirely to the efforts of the headmaster of a school for mentally handicapped children.

Headteachers of special schools are not only in a unique position to reach a large number of families with handicapped children but parents may also see these schools as more significant sources of information and help than other agencies. They also meet at the school informally and in PTAs, and thereby encourage each other to apply.

### Friends and relatives

This type of referral is the most imprecise to assess, since information about the Fund may derive from a number of diverse sources. Over all, 14.8 per cent of applications can be attributed to this source and this proportion steadily increased as knowledge of the Fund got around. Regional variations in the top ten areas are not significant but there appears to be a link between those learning of the Fund through the media and those learning from families and relatives.

### Leaflet/poster

Nationally these accounted for only 1.7 per cent of applicants and the proportion fell after December 1973.

### Radio and TV

Coverage on national radio accounted for 0.8 per cent of all applications and local radio produced 0.2. An interview on the Jimmy Young Show probably accounted for most of the radio applications and the percentage declined after that broadcast. Television accounted for 0.6 per cent of all applications nationally and it was not used for any special publicity campaign.

### Attendance allowance

Some months after the start of the Fund the DHSS began to issue leaflets about it to new families with children receiving the attendance allowance. In total, 2.8 per cent of applicants learned of it from this leaflet. If this effort had been sustained and extended to all the 39,000 children receiving the attendance allowance, this might have been a very good method of reaching families, as over 95 per cent of those who applied were already receiving the allowance.

## Conclusion

If every area of the country had applied at the same rate as Doncaster, 89,939 instead of 31,788 children would have applied to the Fund by April 1976; at the same rate as Clwyd, 62,317 families would have applied. Area variation in application rate is a function of prevalence and need, as well as of knowledge about the Fund, but these comparisons nevertheless give a clue to what kinds of application rates might have been achieved if the Fund had had more money to distribute.

Throughout the three-year period, there was a tension between the wish to encourage applications from all those who needed help and the capacity of the organisation and the amount of money available to cope with the resulting demands. The Fund sought to control a sudden rush of applicants at the beginning by phasing-in age groups over the first three months. However, applications were slow to come in and the Fund planned an extensive publicity programme. Within a few months of its starting, this programme had to be altered because applications were in danger of overwhelming the organisation. The organisation was expanded but it took time to recruit and train new staff, develop new procedures for the more rapid throughput of grants, and find and equip adequate office accommodation. In theory, the organisation could have expanded more and more rapidly to cope with a higher rate of applications, but the Trust was wary of establishing too large an organisation for what was still conceived as a temporary involvement, and there was still no certainty that the number of applications was not a passing phase. By the time it became clear that the volume was going to be maintained, the Fund was distributing grants to existing applicants at a rate that came near to exhausting the budget set by the DHSS.

In the case of benefits that have statutory criteria for entitlement, all those who meet the criteria expect to receive the benefit. For example, the amount of money distributed in unemployment benefit depends to some extent on take-up by those eligible, but for the most part it is a function of the number unemployed and the level of the benefit. Expenditure on cash benefits without statutory criteria for entitlement, such as clothing grants administered by local education authorities, depends to a much greater extent on the efforts made by the authority to encourage claims and the amount of help given. The same principle applies to the provision of services – the authority is free to vary expenditure on aids and adaptations, or meals on wheels, by varying the availability of the service to match the budget. If the budget is spent, they are free to seek a supplementary estimate or to suspend the service. In contrast, the Family Fund had finite resources available to it and was set the task of spending this money in a set period of time. What each applicant could obtain from the Fund was not fixed in advance and no one was certain how many families would apply. It therefore had to try and adjust the rate of applications and the help it gave to the limits of its resources. Considerable efforts were made to publicise the existence of the Fund; 31,788 families were encouraged to apply and £6.8 million of the money made available during the Fund's first three years was spent. Without doubt, more families could have been encouraged to apply by a more sustained publicity effort but in that case, the level of help given by the Fund to each family would have had to be reduced. In a publicity programme subject to these constraints, there can be no absolute measure of success. The Fund reached all the families it could afford to reach.

# 7 The consumer's view of the Fund[1]

Any evaluation of a social policy ought to include an assessment of the views of the consumer. In this chapter some findings from the follow-up survey and illustrative quotations from detailed interviews with a sub-sample of it are used to present a consumer's view of the Fund.

First, the views of consumers are of particular relevance to the question of take-up discussed in chapter 5. It may be that one reason why some eligible families fail to claim has something to do with their perceptions or image of the Fund. Second, their views are also essential to an evaluation of the administrative processes of the Fund. Its managers sought to create an agency that could respond flexibly and sensitively to individual needs. How did families experience the process of applying to the Fund? Did they feel they had been treated fairly? How did it compare with their experiences of getting help from other agencies?

The survey that was used to collect these data was carried out in early 1975 and after that date there were changes in the Fund's policies and procedures which may well have altered many families' attitudes. For example, in mid-1975 the Fund began to send out letters trying to discourage re-applications from those families who had had their first requests dealt with. Those who had thought that the Fund was a continuous source of support would have been disappointed to receive these letters. At about this time, decisions were also made by the Fund's managers which effectively reduced the range and size of items that families could receive from the Fund – grants for some aids and adaptations and for the purchase of cars were no longer available. Families who asked for these things and failed to get them felt aggrieved, particularly if they knew about other families who had got such help as a result of an earlier application.

The views quoted in this chapter are those of people who were accepted by the Fund and who received some help. They are therefore the views of those who had reason to be grateful. If the views of families who had been rejected (or who did not apply) had been canvassed, the picture obtained might have been very different.

**Views that might have influenced the family in applying**

A parents' image of the Fund might have affected their readiness to apply. Those who believed that the Fund was a state benefit, paid for out of Exchequer revenue to which they had contributed, might have had a different attitude to it from those who saw it as a private charity financed from private sources. A third of the families interviewed in the follow-up survey did not know how the Fund was established or financed, but more than half believed that it was a private charity financed by the Rowntree/Mackintosh chocolate factory or by private donations.

> 'We thought it might be like a family fund, the Rowntree's family had this fund kind of thing, that's what we thought at first and then it was afterwards that I read about it being a government concern, and then I said, "Well, if it's government why is it coming under Rowntree?" because automatically, Rowntree, you think of the Rowntree chocolate place.'

However, as Table 7.1 shows, no relationship was found between the parents' image of the Fund and their readiness to apply. Families who believed the Fund was a charity took as long to apply as those who knew that it was a state benefit. However, some parents did say that their understanding that the Fund was a private charity inhibited their willingness to apply.

> 'Well, I thought it was cadging, and being very independent you don't like asking for things. I didn't know it was from the government. Since then I've heard about it from television, because they've given them another grant, haven't they? I didn't know a great deal about it. I thought that people just got things if they were very, very poor.
>
> I think people would tend to be a little bit more reticent than if they think it's government money; "If I don't take it, some other so-and-so will." I think it does make a difference. . . . I think more publicity about it being public money would tend to reduce a lot of people's reticence about accepting it.'

There was a general reluctance to apply to the Fund. Even those parents who knew right from the start that it was a government-financed benefit took time to make up their minds to apply and less than half of the sample in the follow-up survey applied immediately on hearing about it.

*Table 7.1    Families' image of the Fund*

| Delay between hearing of the Fund and applying | State benefit | Private charity | Don't know |
|---|---|---|---|
| Applied immediately | 45.5 | 41.1 | 54.0 |
| Applied within three months | 29.5 | 34.2 | 26.4 |
| Applied within three to six months | 13.6 | 13.9 | 11.5 |
| Applied after six months | 11.4 | 10.8 | 8.1 |
| Total | 100% | 100% | 100% |

$\chi^2$ = 6.62 (9 degrees of freedom)
(not significant)

'It depends on your upbringing. If you are used to receiving social benefits I don't suppose you think twice about getting some more but it took me a long time to come to terms, before I applied, with the fact that it was in some way a form of compensation from the government for having a handicapped child. But once I'd accepted that, and the same with the attendance allowance, I obviously applied. I haven't gone on applying.'

As well as the Fund's status and source of revenue, their belief about what they could get from the Fund and what criteria would be applied might also have affected the family in deciding whether and when to apply, as well as what to ask for. They were asked whether they had expected that the Fund would want to have details of their income and that their doctor or social services department would have to be contacted about their application. The replies to these questions analysed in Table 7.2 show that families did not have a very accurate picture of what would be required but that (at least, for those who had applied) it did not really matter.

One reason why some families might have been reluctant to apply was their ignorance about how much money and what items they could ask for. The Fund wanted families to define their own needs and apply for what they thought they needed. Families, on the other hand, wanted to apply for what they thought the Fund would give them. Most thought that there would be a limit on the amount of help they could ask for and only 11 per cent knew that they could ask for whatever they needed. The consequence of this misunderstanding was that 64.7 per cent of families said that there were items that they needed but had not asked for in their initial request, and over 60 per cent of these gave their chief reason as a reluctance to appear greedy.

'I expect I could be considered as a very greedy person but I think in the initial stage Pat was wrong in applying for driving lessons because they were only £30. We could possibly have found that out of our own money. When we applied we couldn't think of anything we wanted without being greedy and it was only after a great deal of badgering from [the peripatetic teacher] that she talked us into having a car.'

*Table 7.2    Expectations of the Fund*

| | Did you think the Fund would – | | |
|---|---|---|---|
| | Want to know details of your income | Want to contact your doctor | Want to contact your social services department |
| Yes, but did not mind | 65.7 | 55.1 | 38.1 |
| Yes, and did mind | 1.7 | 0.3 | 1.3 |
| No, but would not have minded | 30.0 | 44.2 | 56.0 |
| No, and would have minded | 2.6 | 0.3 | 4.6 |
| Total | 100% | 100% | 100% |

*Table 7.3    What prevented you from asking for other things you needed when you first applied to the Fund?*

| | No. | % |
|---|---|---|
| Didn't want to appear greedy | 119 | 60.7 |
| Didn't know you could apply for/get them | 57 | 29.1 |
| Not desperate at the time | 7 | 3.6 |
| Other | 13 | 6.6 |
| Total | 196 | 100% |

As Table 7.3 shows, reluctance to appear greedy was the chief reason given by parents for not asking for things that they needed.

Some parents applied to the Fund without a very clear picture of its scope and purpose. They just knew that it was a source of help from which they might benefit. Although they had no specific urgent needs, they knew that a Fund had been set up to help families like theirs, and they often knew what other families had been given. The families who applied because they felt they had a right to be given help were in a minority.

*Table 7.4    Reason for application*

|  | No. | % |
|---|---|---|
| A crisis | 45 | 14.9 |
| Had been needing items for some time | 127 | 41.9 |
| Heard of/encouraged by families who had<br>    had help | 26 | 8.6 |
| Felt had a right to help | 11 | 3.6 |
| Social worker applied on behalf of family | 55 | 18.2 |
| Referred from/by other agency | 3 | 1.0 |
| Other | 23 | 7.6 |
| More than one | 13 | 4.3 |
| Total | 303 | 100% |

Most of the families made their approach to the Fund with a request for a specific item they felt they needed. In some cases, it was something they had wanted for some time and as soon as they heard about the Fund, they had applied for it.

'I asked straightaway if we could get help with the car. I knew we wanted a car badly, really. I think actually we'd got a car, that was the thing. We'd got the car but the HP was so much each month, you know, we just really couldn't afford it and it was either a question of giving the car up or getting the payments paid off and they helped us pay it off.'

Other families applied only after they had received encouragement from a social worker or a friend.

'I said to her [social worker] I didn't think there was anything he wanted. I didn't really realise what it was. It was the social worker's idea to apply. She said, "You really ought to have something out of it" and she said "Is there anything that Thomas really wants but you feel you can't afford?"'

**Views on process of application**

When the family did apply, how did they experience the process of being visited by a social worker and discussing their application?

Particularly in the early months of the Fund there were considerable delays between the receipt of the application, a visit by a social worker, and the receipt of a grant. These delays arose because the rate of application outstripped the Fund's capacity to deal with them. Only 15.4 per cent of the sample received their first grant within two months of their application and for 17.2 per cent it took longer than six months. For the families, many of whom had plucked up courage to apply for help only after considerable heart-searching, this delay was a source of anxiety. Of the families in the sample, 40 per cent said they had become anxious about the delays and over 18 per cent had actually written or telephoned to find out what was happening. When families were asked whether they had any criticism of the help that they had been given or the process of applying for it, the most common single criticism was aimed at the delay.

After the families had applied, they were visited by a social worker employed by the Fund or by a local authority worker acting on the Fund's behalf. Over 80 per cent of the families found the social worker sympathetic and understanding their problems. The purpose of the social worker's visit was to help families to specify their needs and to identify which of these could most appropriately be met by the Fund. This often involved altering the original request which had been made in ignorance of what could be obtained.

'I put in for the telephone because Stephen has already had one fire and I was terrified in case another time I wouldn't be able to deal with it myself. The girl came out to see me and she asked if we had transport. We had the car but it was well and truly getting past it. Of course I thought no more about it until we got the letter to say we could go and get the car. Believe me, we were over the moon with it and it's been a godsend for getting us out, with having the two of them.'

A number of families were critical of the social worker. Some families felt they had been given insufficient guidance and advice about what they should ask for.

'Well you don't always know what you can ask for. We thought we'd like a bigger place so we asked if they could help with the mortgage . . . but they said they don't help with anything like that. Then I wrote about having patio doors put into Carol's bedroom so that she can have access to the outside but they said that the social services should help with that. . . . I don't think we really knew what you could ask for. We didn't know you could apply for central heating. We had it put in but we didn't know you could ask for help with it . . . all I got was £30 for cupboards.'

In the follow-up survey, 27.5 per cent of those families who had been visited by a social worker had altered their original request as a result of the visit. The great majority of these were happy with the change that had been made and of those who changed, 38 per cent were given more than they had asked for in their initial application.

As well as helping families to clarify what they could obtain from the Fund, a third of the families said that their visiting social worker had helped them in other ways – with claiming benefits, with support and advice, or by putting them in touch with another service or voluntary agency.

The attitudes of families about applying, their ignorance about what they should ask for, and their feelings about the help and advice they obtained from the visiting social worker, all recurred in relation to re-applications. At the time of the follow-up survey, families were asked whether, since their first grant from the Fund, other needs had arisen which the Fund could help with and whether they intended to re-apply. Of the families, 86.5 per cent said that new needs had arisen, though at that time only 27.4 per cent had applied, and a further 12.9 per cent intended to re-apply. Parents were as ambivalent about re-applying as they had been about applying.

> 'I'm not going to apply again . . . I don't think I dare. I'm very grateful to the Family Fund. I've got the car and I'm very grateful to them. But I don't think I would apply again . . . I think I would feel so guilty applying again after having applied twice. But if it wasn't for the Family Fund a car would definitely be out.'

## Parents' views about the Family Fund

When asked whether they were pleased with what they had been given, the vast majority of the families in the follow-up study (97.0 per cent) said that they were. The impact of some items that families received will be discussed in chapters 8 and 9, but families were invited to comment on specific aspects of the Fund's administration in order to probe beneath their widespread feelings of gratitude.

When asked whether they had any criticism of the help they had been given, or the process of applying for it, only 21 per cent of the families said they had. The criticisms they expressed were mainly about delay or of the visiting social worker. There appeared to be little clear relationship between a cause for criticism and the families' willingness to express it. For instance, a family with a spina bifida child had been given a washing-machine, tumble-drier, clothing, and transport help, and yet they were critical of the Fund's delay in dealing with their application. On the other hand, an unsupported West Indian mother with two children was judged by the interviewer to have received less than adequate help. One of her children was cerebral palsied and mentally handicapped. Her initial request was for clothing help and after a visit from a Fund agent, she received a clothing grant of £25.00. However, the child was doubly incontinent and the mother did not possess a washing-machine or drier. He also wore out clothes and bedding and destroyed them, and his mother – who made his clothes by hand – badly needed a sewing-machine. She had no access to private transport and felt greatly restricted in taking the children out and about. This mother was unaware that the Fund might help with any of her other needs. She assumed it was a charity and the agent had not suggested any other form of help. However, she had no criticism of the Fund.

The interviewers in the follow-up survey rated 6 per cent of the sample as having received only barely adequate help, in the sense that though what was given was useful, the families' circumstances justified a larger grant. For example, a family with three children, the youngest of whom was microcephalic, was given £60 for a bed and a gate, but the interviewer felt that the family would also have benefited from help with clothing, transport, heating, a telephone, and fencing. A further 13 per cent were rated as having received poor provision. This meant that the Fund's help had been minimal and the response could have been better. For example, in one family the father was registered as disabled, the mother blind and hard of hearing, the younger child hard of hearing, and the older severely subnormal and with a heart defect. They asked for help with a holiday and received only what they had asked for – £20.00 towards a holiday. But one child was doubly incontinent, his bedding and clothes were heavily worn by incontinence and crawling on the floor, yet the parents possessed neither a washing-machine nor a drier.

In a further 10 per cent of cases, the interviewers merely identified additional items for which there was a clear need and which the Fund would probably have given had they been picked up by the visiting social worker. The most common outstanding needs were for holidays, transport, and clothing. For example, the family of a spastic, blind, and severely retarded child asked for and were given a pushchair costing £19.00, but the child was incontinent and the family would have liked a washing-machine and drier and help with transport. Another family with a mentally handicapped child was given a washing-machine, tumble-drier and heater, but the interviewer commented that they were in desperate need of a holiday.

So in 29 per cent of cases the interviewer felt that there was cause to criticise the Fund but only 21 per cent of the families actually expressed any criticism.

Many of the criticisms were concerned with the amount of publicity and with the amount of information available about what to ask for.

> 'I also think there should be more publicity on what you can apply for. I'm still not sure what I can apply for. OK, household things like the washing-machine and things like this and travel expenses. What else can I apply for?'

A number of families were anxious about having to account for the way they spent the money and other parents raised questions about the fairness of the Fund's procedures.

> 'In London obviously we all talk about what we've got from the Family Fund. Two or three people from the Home Counties applied for and got colour televisions. Three people up here applied for and were refused colour televisions. What's the difference between the Home Counties and here? This is what gets me, it's very much a regional thing. Some regions are getting an awful lot more than others. They would deny this . . . . Whether it is because the social workers here don't put over their case . . . as well as people in the Home Counties or what, I really don't know, but some of the things I've heard of families getting I would never have thought the Family Fund would have dreamt of supplying.'

The great majority approved of the Fund as a method of giving help to families with disabled children (69.9 per cent) and a further 4.6 per cent gave qualified approval.

Some families felt that the ease of application and the minimum of humiliating or discouraging bureaucratic procedures were the particularly attractive aspects of the Fund and other families liked the Fund because they found dealing with it less demanding and stigmatising.

> 'There are so many organisations and things like that that help but they want to know everything and you finish up by being made to feel that you are some sort of – that you are begging for something. I thought it was very good the way they did it. It's only between you and them.'

Others felt an important feature of the Fund was its flexibility and its responsiveness to expressed need. Many families said they had felt a boost to their morale after receiving Family Fund help. They may not have been able to identify and articulate the particular elements of their experience that contributed to this, but they were reassured by the feeling that the Fund was sympathetic to their problems and would be prepared to help when possible. The views expressed by families were developed in the context of their experience in getting assistance from other agencies, such as social services departments, the attendance allowance, and in some cases, supplementary benefits. Certainly, many families who had tried to get help with an aid or adaptation had experienced frustration and delay, and some of those who had claimed the attendance allowance had only succeeded in getting it after a review. Thus, many of the laudatory comments about the Fund were made in comparison with their previous experiences rather than, perhaps, in relation to some ideal standard. In order to see whether families did have a more ideal standard, they were asked whether they could think of a better way for the government to give financial help to families with handicapped children.

*Table 7.5    Can you think of a better way the government could give financial help to families with handicapped children?*

|  | No. | % |
|---|---|---|
| Annual grant to spend as wished | 65 | 21.5 |
| High weekly allowance | 36 | 11.9 |
| More help from local agencies | 19 | 6.3 |
| Annual/weekly money and local help | 25 | 8.3 |
| Other | 58 | 19.1 |
| More than one | 5 | 1.7 |
| Don't know | 95 | 31.4 |
| Total | 303 | 100% |

The results in Table 7.5 show that about a third of the families were unable to think of better ways of giving help. Of those who could, over half favoured cash benefits – most commonly an annual cash grant which they could spend as they wished. The replies of the fifty-eight families in the 'other' category are given in Table 7.6 and again the replies tended to favour cash rather than services.

*Table 7.6   Breakdown of 'other' replies from Table 7.5*

|  | No. |
|---|---|
| Better education/training | 5 |
| Special housing | 5 |
| Holidays/relief care | 6 |
| Social work support/regular visiting | 3 |
| Better services all round | 2 |
| Cars | 1 |
| Tax relief | 1 |
| Large grants as needed from time to time plus money in Trust for later life | 9 |
| Leave Family Fund as it is | 17 |
| Some form of help which doesn't depend on individuals having to ask for things/charity | 9 |
| Total | 58 |

## Conclusion

There is no doubt from this evidence and from the letters of gratitude that have poured into the Fund during its history, that the overwhelming majority of parents who have been helped by the Fund have nothing but praise for it.

These views have been expressed by families who have very low aspirations. Their expectations, based on previous contacts with helping agencies, do not on the whole lead them to expect very much, and internalised values of economic independence and self-sufficiency prevent them from demanding all that they perhaps could from the Fund. The impact of these basic values on their aspirations was reinforced by a considerable confusion about the status and procedures of the Fund and about what they could or should ask for. For many, their initial request was a shot in the dark and what they received was something of a lottery. Far from getting at what families need most, the Fund's policy of leaving it to the family has tended to result in a tentative request for what they think they might get. Of course, as information has spread about what is available, and as visiting social workers have become better informed, the relevance of the initial request and its mediation may have improved.

Perhaps, partly because of the confusion about the Fund's status, partly because of low aspirations, and partly because there was no clear definition of what could be obtained, families did not approach the Fund with any sense of entitlement. Yet, at least for those who applied, it did not seem to matter.

# 8    Relief of stress

In chapter 2 it was shown how, almost by accident, the concept 'relief of stress' became the generally acknowledged substantive aim of the Fund. The circular issued to local authorities by the DHSS when the Fund was established stated: 'The help given is to relieve stress in the family which is due to caring for the handicapped child.'[1]

It is unusual for those evaluating the effectiveness of a social policy to be presented with what at first sight appears to be a clear statement of objectives. However, when it comes to defining the concept of stress as a basis for research, difficulties arise. Stress is a multi-faceted concept and has been used to describe a variety of different phenomena. In the context of families with handicapped children, the word may be used to refer to the physical burdens of care, emotional disturbance created by the child, or even the financial strains resulting from its presence.

'Stress' can also connote stress factors, stress events, felt needs, and stress effects.[2] A *stress factor* is the determining factor in a situation, such as the presence of a disabled child, which leads to stress events. *Stress events* are those happenings that generate stress effects. Harrison identified such stress events in the patient career of children with Perthes disease as diagnosis or hospitalisation. The stress events in caring for a disabled child may be single events such as these, or the cumulative events of the day-to-day grind. Stress events may or may not result in *felt needs* for financial or emotional support, information, or practical help. Whether these felt needs are satisfied may vary the *stress effect* - the physical, emotional, or financial consequences of the event. The stress effects of caring for a handicapped child are likely to vary with the character of the stress factor - the age of the child, degree of disability, and so forth. Stress effects may also vary according to the existence of stress events arising from these disabilities. Does the child require constant attention day or night? Is the condition stable? Is the handicap mental or physical? - and so on. Between the stress event and the stress effect lies a host of variables that may mediate the stress effect. The same stress event may produce different stress effects on the parents, depending on their physical and social environment, their material resources, their attitudes, personalities, and expectations. The stress effect may also vary according to the amount of help they receive to cope with the stress event.

A simple example below illustrates the model:

*Stress model for an incontinent child*

| *Stress factor* | *Stress event* | *Felt need* | *Stress effect* |
|---|---|---|---|
| Incontinent child | Dirty washing | Washing-machine | Exhaustion/ anxiety/ depression |

*Intervening variables*

In this example the stress factor – an incontinent child – causes a stress event: large amounts of dirty washing. The effects of the dirty washing depend on a number of intervening variables, such as the physical capacity of the mother to do the washing, the facilities she has for washing and drying, and the demands of the children. Without a washing-machine, for which she feels a need, she suffers from exhaustion through the labour of constant washing by hand.

How does the Family Fund fit into this model of stress? The Fund took the view that all families caring for a very severely disabled child were under stress and that the best method of relieving that stress was to respond to expressed needs of the families. Sometimes those expressed needs were considered inappropriate by visiting social workers or the Family Fund's staff in the York offices, but to a considerable extent families got what they asked for. The hope behind the strategy was that by meeting the felt needs of families for financial or practical help, they might mediate the effects of the stress event – for example by providing a washing-machine, they would relieve or reduce the anxiety and depression resulting from washing by hand. The Fund could not assist with every kind of felt need – they could provide little in the way of emotional support, advice and counselling, and the amount of practical help they could give was very limited. Nevertheless, the belief behind the Fund was that despite its limitations, helping with basic practical items, like washing-machines, transport, clothing, bedding and so forth, might lead directly or indirectly to the relief of stress effects.

Was this belief justified? As has been suggested, in the context of families with handicapped children, stress effects might be the physical burdens of care. Sir Keith Joseph had said the purpose of the Fund was, 'to ease the burden of living on those households containing very severely congenitally disabled children.'[3]

The simple physical image of stress suggested by this quotation calls for an investigation of how far the families felt that the help provided by the Fund helped them to cope on a day-to-day basis. In the next chapter, the extent to which the Fund's help relieved specific practical burdens is discussed.

Alternatively, stress effects might be taken to mean the financial strain resulting from the presence of a disabled child in the family. The Family Fund distributed grants in cash. The adequacy of this financial help directed to families is discussed in chapter 14 and the financial needs of disabled children have been described elsewhere.[4]

In this chapter we concentrate on the emotional or psychosomatic stress effects. When the effects of stress are discussed it is these conditions - anxiety, depression, and physical illness - which are often described, and we believe that it was hoped that it was this 'malaise' that the Fund's help would relieve.

## The study of malaise

In order to assess the impact of the Fund on this emotional stress, it was necessary to find a reliable and valid scale that would measure stress in families. In the end, it was decided to use the Malaise Inventory for measuring stress in mothers only. The Malaise Inventory is an adaptation of the Cornell Medical Index and was developed in its present form by Rutter and Graham for their study in the Isle of Wight.[5]

### Validity

The scale consists of the following twenty-four questions about emotional and physical/psychosomatic states commonly associated with stress.

#### Malaise scale

| | | |
|---|---|---|
| Do you often have backache? | Yes | No |
| Do you feel tired most of the time? | Yes | No |
| Do you often feel miserable or depressed? | Yes | No |
| Do you often have bad headaches? | Yes | No |
| Do you often get worried about things? | Yes | No |
| Do you usually have great difficulty in falling asleep or staying asleep? | Yes | No |
| Do you usually wake unnecessarily early in the morning? | Yes | No |
| Do you wear yourself out worrying about your health? | Yes | No |

| | | |
|---|---|---|
| Do you often get into a violent rage? | Yes | No |
| Do people often annoy and irritate you? | Yes | No |
| Have you at times had a twitching of the face, head or shoulders? | Yes | No |
| Do you often suddenly become scared for no good reason? | Yes | No |
| Are you scared to be alone when there are no friends near you? | Yes | No |
| Are you easily upset or irritated? | Yes | No |
| Are you frightened of going out alone or of meeting people? | Yes | No |
| Are you constantly keyed up and jittery? | Yes | No |
| Do you suffer from indigestion? | Yes | No |
| Do you often suffer from an upset stomach? | Yes | No |
| Is your appetite poor? | Yes | No |
| Does every little thing get on your nerves and wear you out? | Yes | No |
| Does your heart often race like mad? | Yes | No |
| Do you often have bad pains in your eyes? | Yes | No |
| Are you troubled with rheumatism or fibrositis? | Yes | No |
| Have you ever had a nervous breakdown? | Yes | No |

Rutter and Graham employed the scale to detect emotional disturbance or mental well-being and it has since been used in a number of other studies, notably by Tew and Lawrence,[6] and Dorner,[7] measuring stress among the mothers of spina bifida children. It has also been used as an inventory of maternal health in the Child Health and Education in the Seventies study of every child born in one week in April 1970. Validity is concerned with whether the scale actually measures what it sets out to measure, and it is impossible to establish finally that the malaise inventory is a valid measure of stress because of the lack of clarity in the concept itself. All one can say is that it has been widely used as a measure of stress and appears to be the best scale available.

## Reliability

Reliability is concerned with the reproducibility of the scale. The inventory is completed by the mothers themselves, which should minimise interviewer bias. In an exercise to assess reliability, seventeen families from the follow-up study were asked to complete the inventory again and there was a correlation of 0.96 between their scores. Rutter has also checked the reliability of the scale by asking thirty-five mothers to complete the inventory on two occasions.

> Mothers tended to acknowledge slightly fewer symptoms on the second occasion but there was a high correlation (0.91) between the scores indicating that the pattern of results was very reliable.[8]

To evaluate the impact of the Family Fund, the malaise inventory was used in two studies. In the first, the 303 mothers interviewed in the follow-up study were asked to complete the inventory in order to find out whether the degree of stress could be related to the social characteristics of the families, the nature of the child's handicap and the problems this presented, the help that had been received from statutory and other agencies, and the help that had been received from the Family Fund.

In the second study, in order to provide a validation of the earlier results and the conclusions drawn from them, a sample of mothers who had applied to the Family Fund were asked to complete the malaise inventory before their application had been processed, and again after they had received assistance from the Fund. The purposes of this exercise were to find out whether scores had changed after the mothers had received help from the Fund and whether the scores varied according to any external factor or the help that the families had received.

**First study results**

The mean malaise score obtained in this study of 303 mothers of very severely disabled children was 9.02 (SD = 5.29). This is a higher average score than any other sample to which the scale has been applied. Rutter obtained a mean score of 3.22 in the Isle of Wight[9] and 4.15 in London[10] for general samples of mothers. The CHES study obtained a mean of 4.14 for a sample of over 1,000 mothers living in the South-West,[11] and Dorner obtained a mean score of 5.13 for his sample of the mothers of spina bifida teenagers.[12] Rutter believed that scores over 5 or 6 are outside the normal range and show evidence of disturbance. Nevertheless, 9.02 is similar to the mean score found by Tew and Lawrence in mothers of severely handicapped spina bifida children[13] and it is probably the mean score that one can expect to get in a sample of mothers of very severely disabled children.

Although the over-all score is high, there are nevertheless considerable variations around the mean; some mothers have very low scores, others have scores in the normal range, and others have very high scores. How can these variations be explained?

## Disease

First, the hypothesis that the level of stress revealed by the malaise score would vary according to the disease suffered by the child was tested. It was thought, for instance, that mothers of children dying from cystic fibrosis or muscular dystrophy might have higher scores than children with stable conditions like deafness or blindness; or conditions like spina bifida that present substantial physical burdens might result in higher scores than mongolism which, it is sometimes argued, presents relatively few demands. The mean malaise scores of mothers with children with different diseases were compared. In no case was the difference in scores observed larger than could be expected to occur by chance. This finding suggests that there is nothing specific to a particular disease that causes a mother to experience more or less stress or that personal variables outweigh the effects of any disease constants.

## Type of impairment

The stress scores were then examined to see whether there were any differences between mentally, physically, or multi-impaired children. Physically impaired children present greater physical strain; on the other hand, it might be argued that mentally handicapped children demand more care and attention. No significant differences were found in the malaise scores of mothers of children with different types of impairment.

## Degree of handicap

A scale devised by Jaehnig[14] was used to rank children according to their degree of handicap. The Jaehnig scale divides handicap into three parts - mobility, communication, and capacity for self-care or independence. Mobility is assessed by checking off whether a child can perform eight functions of increasing difficulty. Communication is measured by asking twelve questions covering speech, comprehension, money, and time. Personal independence is assessed by asking twenty questions that cover the capacity of the child to feed, wash, toilet, and dress himself. A total score can be obtained by adding up the three parts of the scale.

These correlation coefficients show that there is no significant tendency for the mothers of the less mobile children, the children with less communication, and the children with less ability to look after themselves, to have a high malaise score. The absence of an association is a remarkable finding. Common sense would suggest that an immobile child, presenting severe management problems and incapable of communication, would produce more stress in a mother than a child with a less severe handicap; these findings, however, suggest that the severity of the handicap is 'neither here nor there'.

*Table 8.1    Relationship between stress and degree of handicap*

| Jaehnig scale | Correlation with malaise scores (N = 303) | |
|---|---|---|
| Mobility | r = −0.00 | Not significant |
| Communication | r = −0.07 | Not significant |
| Personal independence | r = −0.04 | Not significant |
| Total | r = −0.05 | Not significant |

This finding agrees with Dorner's[15] study of the families of seventy teenagers with spina bifida, but conflicts with Tew and Lawrence[16] who found no significant difference between the mothers' malaise scores of mild and moderately handicapped spina bifida children, but found severely handicapped children produced a higher malaise score and in particular mothers with non-mobile and incontinent children scored higher. The Tew and Lawrence study was based on a very small sample and the measures of the severity of handicap they employed were probably less sensitive than the ones employed here.

So far neither the disease, impairment, nor handicap of the child have been found to account for any variation in the mother's stress.

*Age*

Next, the relationship between the age of the child and the age of the mother and the malaise scores was examined. There were no significant linear relationships (r = 0.03 for child's age and r = 0.07 for mother's age) and no significant non-linear differences. Neither the age of the child nor the age of the mother appeared to influence stress.

*Family composition*

If there is no relationship between the stress of mothers and their age, or the age and condition of the child, does the stress vary according to the family composition? The composition of the family of a handicapped child might influence the level of the mother's stress in a variety of ways. Coping with a handicapped child on top of the burdens of other children could lead to greater stress. Alternatively, the rewards or supports provided by other children might compensate for the presence of a handicapped child. There was no significant variation in the mother's malaise score and family size, or between one- and two-parent families. However, the malaise scores of mothers with an only child who was handicapped was 7.11, significantly lower than the score of 9.02 for all the mothers.

### Living standards

The malaise scores of the mothers were next examined to see whether the living standards of the families in the study might mediate the level of stress. There was no relationship between the Registrar General's Classification of Social Class and the level of stress. Mothers in social class V (unskilled manual) had slightly higher levels of stress but the difference was not significant. To examine the relationship between income and stress, the level of net disposable resources was transposed as a fraction of the supplementary benefit scale rates for each family. There was again a slight tendency for the better-off families to have a lower malaise score ($r = 0.24$ not significant) and the group of mothers whose net disposable resources were over 180 per cent of the supplementary benefit scale rates had scores significantly lower than the groups of mothers dependent on supplementary benefits.

The level of stress experienced by mothers did vary according to her satisfaction or dissatisfaction with her role as a housewife or worker. Mothers who were able to do paid work unrestricted had lower malaise scores (6.26) than all other mothers, and those mothers who were not able to work but wanted to, had higher scores (10.32) than mothers who stayed at home and did not want to do paid work (8.64). The variations between these groups of mothers were the largest observed in the analysis and it is interesting to note that only 27.5 per cent of mothers in this sample had paid work compared with 40.7 per cent of the population of all mothers with dependent children.

### Housing

There were no variations in the mother's malaise score according to the pressure on bedroom space or according to whether the house had a garden or yard, bath/shower and hot water, flush toilet, or central heating. A measure of over-all housing standard was obtained by giving one point for every amenity the family possessed. Thus, a family where the child was not forced to share a bedroom, where there was a garden or yard, where there was an inside WC, a usable bathroom and central heating, scored five points. There was no tendency for families with houses of a better standard to have lower malaise scores ($r = 0.02$, not significant). There were nine families in the sample who scored one point or less – indicating very poor housing conditions – but their mean malaise score was not significantly different from the sample as a whole. Finally, the malaise scores were examined according to what the mothers themselves thought about their housing. Mothers who thought their house was unsuitable because of the child, scored significantly higher than those who thought their house was suitable.

## Restriction

One common aspect of life with a handicapped child is the restriction in the lives of one or both parents by the need to provide continuous care of the child and the difficulty of getting out. Mothers were asked whether they thought their leisure activities were restricted at all by their handicapped child. Mothers who described themselves as severely restricted had higher scores than other mothers, but the trouble with this subjective assessment of restriction is that it may well not be independent of the malaise score – mothers with high malaise scores may feel more restricted without actually being more restricted. So mothers were asked how often they went out with or without their husbands for pleasure. The malaise scores did not vary according to the number of times they were able to get out but mothers who said they wanted to get out more scored significantly higher than those who did not.

So while there are clear associations between stress and those mothers who feel restricted, mothers who actually are restricted appear to suffer no more stress than mothers who are able to get out easily.

Whether the family had had a holiday recently did appear to be associated with the level of stress: mothers who had had a holiday during the last year had lower scores than those who had not had a holiday for over three years.

## Help and support

It was thought that the level of stress might vary according to the amount of help received from families, friends, and social workers. In this case, mothers' malaise scores varied according to both an objective and subjective assessment of the help they received. Each mother was scored according to the amount of help (they reported) they received from their husband, children, other relatives or friends, or from paid help. Mothers with most help had lower malaise scores (r = −0.20). Assuming that mothers are reliable in reporting the amount of help they receive, then it appears that those receiving least help do experience most stress. Mothers who reported that they felt that they wanted more help in looking after their child at home scored significantly higher than mothers who did not want additional help. Mothers who said that their families helped a lot had much lower scores than those who said their families could help but did not.

Malaise scores were compared according to the families' contact with a social worker. Over half this sample of families with very severely disabled children had no contact with a social worker but mothers without social work contact had lower malaise scores. It is possible to conclude from this that either social workers are concentrating their efforts where they are most needed, or that social workers enable parents to articulate stress.

## Burdens of care

Earlier it was concluded (with some surprise) that the stress experienced by mothers did not appear to vary according to the capacity of the child to care for itself. However, when mothers were asked whether they felt their child presented a greater management problem than a normal child, those mothers who replied 'much more' scored higher than others. Therefore the malaise scores of mothers were examined to see whether they varied according to particular discrete management problems that the child presented. There were no significant variations according to whether the child had to be fed; neither was there any variation in the scores of mothers with children who were or were not incontinent. However, there was some variation according to three other aspects of management. Mothers of children who needed frequent night attention had higher scores than others; mothers of children who played normally had lower malaise scores; and mothers who reported that their child's health was normal had lower scores than mothers who reported it was only fair or poor. There was also some variation in the malaise score according to the number of times the child had had to be a hospital in-patient: mothers of children with fewer than two in-patient experiences had lower malaise scores than children with three or more. Finally there was some variation in malaise scores according to the degree of activity of the children reported by the mother. Mothers of normally active children scored less than mothers of both underactive and hyperactive children.

## Parents' health

Finally, the malaise scores of mothers were compared according to whether they thought that their, and their husbands', health had been affected by the stress of caring for their handicapped child. Mothers who felt that neither their mental nor physical health had been affected had significantly lower scores than others and mothers who thought that their husbands' health had not been affected scored less than others.

This study set out to trace the independent factors that were associated with variations in the level of stress experienced by mothers of a sample of families with very severely disabled children.[17] It appears that stress did not vary according to the disease, type of impairment, scale of handicap, age of mother and child, family composition and size, social class, housing conditions, and degree of restriction imposed.

Stress scores appeared to increase with the birth order of the child, the amount of night attendance required, if the house was considered unsuitable, if parents felt restricted, if they had not had a holiday recently, or if their health was affected. Scores appeared to decrease as net disposable resources rose, if the mother worked outside the home, if she felt she received enough help and support from relatives and friends, if the child's general health was normal, if it played normally, and was normally active.

These results are unexpected. It is particularly surprising that stress scores do not seem to vary by handicap – according to the degree of mobility of the child, his capacity to communicate, or his personal independence. These first conclusions are largely negative. When it comes to interpreting the factors that do appear to influence the stress experienced by the mother, we have to distinguish between those that are more or less independent. Facts such as whether the mother works or not can be objectively ascertained and it is reasonable in such cases to rely on her own assertion. But her own assessment of a number of other factors relevant to stress may be influenced by her mood and her mood is almost certainly not independent of the stress under which she may labour. Thus, her assessment of her own and her husband's health must, almost by definition, vary according to her subjective feelings; and her assessment of the amount of help she receives, whether the house is suitable and so forth, may also relate more to her mood than to objective reality.

Up to this point, variables have been examined singly but the technique of regression analysis makes it possible to examine variables interacting with one another and to determine whether more of the variation in stress scores is explained if they are taken together. In order to carry out a regression analysis on these data, it is necessary to transpose some of the variables from qualitative to quantitative ones. It is also necessary to distinguish variables that are more or less independent of stress scores.

The variables in Table 8.2 are prima facie the most independent of stress and in combination they explain 20 per cent of the variation in malaise scores:

*Table 8.2    Factors influencing stress scores*

| | Correlation coefficient | Cumulative proportion of variance explained | Unstandardised regression coefficient | Standard error of | F ratio |
|---|---|---|---|---|---|
| | R | R² | B | B | |
| Whether the mother works | 0.25 | 0.06 | 0.998 | 0.316 | 10.0 |
| Time since last holiday | 0.24 | 0.11 | 0.119 | 0.400 | 8.8 |
| Support in the home | −0.20 | 0.15 | −0.998 | 0.471 | 4.5 |
| Order of birth of handicapped child | 0.15 | 0.16 | 0.161 | 1.300 | 1.5 |
| Net disposable resources | −0.24 | 0.18 | −0.241 | 0.209 | 1.3 |
| Standard of housing | −0.00 | 0.18 | 0.551 | 0.354 | 2.4 |
| Level of communication | −0.13 | 0.19 | −0.145 | 0.129 | 1.3 |
| Social class | 0.17 | 0.19 | 0.394 | 0.304 | 1.7 |
| Mother's age | 0.07 | 0.19 | 0.679 | 0.051 | 1.8 |
| Child's age | 0.04 | 0.20 | 0.910 | 0.106 | 0.7 |
| Family size | 0.10 | 0.20 | 0.400 | 0.659 | 0.4 |
| Level of mobility | 0.01 | 0.20 | −0.104 | 0.203 | 0.3 |
| Capacity for self-care | 0.08 | 0.20 | 0.533 | 0.118 | 0.2 |
| (constant) | | | −0.770 | | |

If, in addition to these factors, other variables are added which are partially independent of stress – such as the mother's report of the extent of night attendance required by the child - the amount of variation explained increases to 34.6 per cent. If, in addition to this, the mother's own opinion of her health is added to the regression, the amount of variation explained rises to 45.8 per cent.

However, none of the really independent variables examined either in combination or separately is making a great impact on the level of stress experienced by mothers as measured by the malaise score. Although the findings of this analysis are largely negative, nevertheless they are of importance. There may be other independent factors that have not been uncovered in this study which are important determinants of stress, but we are confident that no external factors that could account for much variation in the malaise score have been overlooked. The alternative hypothesis is that the level of stress is determined by internal factors - the physiology and personality of the mother - and that these internal factors are not affected in any specific way by the external social and physical conditions of the family and the child.

When the factors that appeared to influence variations in malaise scores had been examined, a study was mounted to assess whether any change in malaise occurred as a result of the help given to families by the Family Fund.

## Study of the change in malaise

Three hundred applicants to the Family Fund during February and March 1976 received by post a 'malaise inventory', to be completed before they were visited by a social worker to assess their applications. A covering letter explained that the request had nothing to do with their chances of getting help from the Fund and they were asked to return their forms in confidence to the research team; 259 (86.3 per cent) did so. By December 1976, 201 of these had received a grant from the Fund and thirty-one were found not to be eligible for help. As soon as possible after they received their grants, the mothers were asked, again by post, to complete another malaise inventory. This time 190 (or 94.5 per cent) of those surveyed returned the forms.

The mean score for this sample was similar to the sample of 303 mothers interviewed in their own homes. There was hardly discernible improvement of 0.19 in the scores after Fund help had been received. The correlation between scores was 0.79. In eighty-one cases the mother's level of stress had fallen, but in seventy-eight cases it had increased. No factor could be found that accounted for any amount of the change or its direction. There was no relation between the differences in score and the mother's age, the child's sex or age, the birth order, the number of handicapped children, family composition, family size, working status, class, tenure, whether the mother worked, or whether the family was known to the social services. There was no relation between the difference in the scores and the type, number, or value of the items given by the Family Fund. The amount of money given varied between £30 and £750, with a mean of £173, but the correlation between the amount given and the difference in malaise scores was hardly discernible ($r = -0.08$).

*Table 8.3    Summary of the results of the study of change in malaise scores*

|  | Number | Mean malaise score | S D |
|---|---|---|---|
| Before Family Fund help (all cases) | 259 | 8.67 | 4.41 |
| Before Family Fund help (cases helped) | 190 | 8.66 | 4.45 |
| After Family Fund help (cases helped) | 190 | 8.47 | 4.51 |
| Difference between scores (cases helped) | 190 | 0.19 | 2.88 |

Correlation between scores R = 0.79

There was only one factor that appeared to be associated with changes in stress. Those mothers whose malaise score between tests fluctuated by more than 3 points were significantly less likely to be receiving the attendance allowance. This result might indicate that mothers with children who get the regular income of the attendance allowance are more likely to have more stable, but not necessarily lower, malaise scores.

The variation in the level of the malaise scores confirmed the findings of the earlier study. Of all the variables examined, once again mothers of only children had lower scores and families known to the social services department had higher scores. There was no difference in the level of stress of mothers in families accepted by the Family Fund from that of those who were found not eligible and the correlation between the malaise score and the amount of money given was not significant ($r = 0.12$).

## Conclusion

The first part of this study suggested that the level of stress is not a function of the burdens imposed by the child or the social conditions of the family, but possibly more a function of the personality and even physiology of the mother. If this is true, then it has a bearing on the purpose and operation of the Fund, which attempts to relieve stress by providing goods, services, and cash in order to relieve the burdens of care. Yet if stress does not vary with the ownership of such assets or with the burden of care, then the attempt to relieve stress in this way is bound to fail. The relief of emotional stress may not be a feasible aim of this type of public policy. Public policy may direct itself with some effect to the relief of physical burdens, the monotony of care, the seclusion, the expense and so forth of caring for a handicapped child, but mental or emotional disturbance, as far as it is validly measured by the malaise score, may not be relieved by the provision of goods.

This conclusion was re-examined in the second follow-up study. This confirmed that the level of stress as measured by the malaise inventory is much higher than in any 'normal' sample of mothers, but that little of the variation in the level of stress could be ascribed to the external social and physical conditions of the family and the child. It also indicated that the provision of goods by the Family Fund had not improved the level of mental well-being of mothers. In the absence of a control group it is not possible to conclude that the Fund had no beneficial effect: without its help, the malaise scores might have deteriorated. However, subject to this reservation and the assumptions inherent in the malaise inventory, the conclusion of the studies outlined in this chapter is that the Family Fund was not effective in improving the over-all level of stress in the mothers who applied.

# 9      The relief of burden

Even if no evidence can be found that the Family Fund alleviated stress, as measured by the malaise inventory, there is no doubt that the help it gave was generally much appreciated and, in many cases, made a real and substantial contribution to the practical problems of caring for a disabled child. From the beginning the Fund received a stream of grateful letters from parents, who often described in considerable detail how the money had been spent and what differences it had made to their lives. Very few letters of complaint were received. Some comments by parents are contained in chapter 7.

In this chapter two particular types of burden will be described in an attempt to make an assessment of the Fund's contribution. The two problem areas chosen are mobility and clothing. Together with incontinence,[1] more families received help with these problems than with any others and they are possibly the types of help that the Fund provided most effectively. There were certainly other areas where the Fund was much less successful. In the provision of aids to mobility, education and adaptations, it was circumscribed by limited resources and the problem of overlap with other services. These limitations are discussed in chapters 14 and 15.

## Mobility

The mobility problems of families with a disabled child can be depicted as the normal burdens of infancy extended throughout childhood and into adult life. The presence of a child who cannot walk normally may prevent the whole family from meeting their normal domestic, social, and recreational needs. Even if a handicapped child can walk, it may, because of behaviour disorders, hyperactivity, mental handicap, susceptibility to trauma or infection or a host of other reasons, effectively present a mobility handicap at least as serious as an incapacity to walk. In addition, families with disabled children often have special transport needs in relation to the child's education: thus children at residential schools need to be transported there and back at the beginning and end of each term and parents need to visit the child during the term; special day schools or pre-schools or day-care facilities may be some distance from home and present transport problems not experienced by families with children at local schools. There may be special transport difficulties in relation to the child's medical treatment: most handicapped children visit local hospitals and clinics for treatment more often than normal children; they are also more likely to be in-patients and their families are faced with the difficult problem of visiting. Further, children with specific conditions may be treated at regional or national centres and this presents their parents with special difficulties – delivering and collecting their children, and visiting them if they are in-patients.

The follow-up survey provided some information on the proportion of applicants who had mobility problems. Of the children over two years old, 65.6 per cent were unable to walk independently. In addition, 21.8 per cent were described as hyperactive or overactive and in addition, a few were having fits weekly or more often. Thus, a total of 87.8 per cent of the sample were likely to have serious mobility problems. In addition to these, there were other children not included above: the severely mentally handicapped, possibly also incontinent, without a sense of danger; those with heart, lung or kidney conditions that prevented them from walking, although they were technically able to do so; the deaf and the blind who, especially at an early age, present special problems; and those with severe eczemas or conditions such as haemophilia or brittle bones who are at risk on public transport.

Only 22 per cent of the families in the follow-up survey said that they were not at all restricted in taking their child out. This means that the domestic, social and recreational life of the child and/or the family was inhibited by a mobility handicap in over three-quarters of the applicants to the Fund.

### Transport and medical care

Of the families in the follow-up survey, 70 per cent said that their child attended a hospital or clinic to see a doctor or therapist regularly. Some of these (16 per cent) had to attend more often than monthly and only 12 per cent attended less regularly than every six months. Just over half of the families (51 per cent) said that they had difficulties getting their child to hospital or clinics – these difficulties included the cost of the journey, the awkwardness of the journey, the amount of time it took, and the need to take time off work and the difficulty of using public transport with the child. The other principal problem associated with attending clinics was what to do with the other children

- those mothers with other children who were not at school either had to take them to the hospital/clinic as well or, if it were possible, arrange for friends or relatives to look after them.

In addition to visiting clinics, 82 per cent of the families in the sample had experienced, at least once, their child as a hospital in-patient; in a third of the families the child had been an in-patient at least five times. Parents were asked whether they had had any difficulties in visiting their child while he was in hospital and 59 per cent replied that they had. The more often the child was an in-patient the more likely they were to have difficulties visiting and in a number of cases, such as spina bifida children who typically required repeated bouts of in-patient care in their early years and children sent away to national centres for treatment, visiting became so difficult or costly that parents could not see the child as often as they would have liked.

## Transport and education

As we shall see, there are clear duties on local education authorities to provide transport to enable children to go to school and 80 per cent of those children attending day special schools, ordinary day schools, or day nurseries had no problems transporting their children to school because it was done at the expense of the local education authority by bus or taxi. Not all the pre-school-age children were attending nurseries or playgroups and some of those not attending might have liked to if there had been transport available. The majority of those attending school who mentioned that they had difficulties with transport had complaints about the organisation of the transport - it arrived at unpredictable times, children were collected late and delivered home early, and some children had to be transported to a central collecting point.

The principal transport problems associated with education were borne by those children attending residential schools (10.9 per cent in residential schools and 3.3 per cent in hospital schools). Of the parents, 37 per cent said that they were not able to bring their child home as often as they would like and 48 per cent of the parents said they were not able to visit their children as often as they would like. In all, 70 per cent of the parents with children at residential school had problems visiting or bringing their children home at week-ends or half-term.

## The services that exist to help with mobility problems

Before the Family Fund, and until the advent of the mobility allowance, there was, effectively, no provision to meet the domestic, social, and recreational needs for transport of a family with a handicapped child. There were certainly no clear statutory obligations. The Chronically Sick and Disabled Persons Act empowered social services departments to convey a few children to play-groups, day centres, and clubs, and local voluntary organisations might also provide transport for similar purposes. For the most part, however, families had to use either public transport or run a private car. Of the families in the follow-up survey, 46 per cent had a car available.

From January 1976 the mobility allowance – a cash grant of £7 per week (from November 1977) – began to be phased in for children between the ages of five and fifteen unable, or virtually unable, to walk. By October 1977, 14,213 children were receiving the allowance and it was a badly needed source of help for many families where none had existed before. However, it did not fully meet the need. The age criteria meant that families with immobile children under five – often the age when children have special needs for transport to pre-school play-groups or hospital care – were excluded from benefit. The mobility criteria excluded those families whose children were able to walk but who, nevertheless, because of management problems presented by the children's condition, had equivalently severe difficulties. And those who received the allowance – £5 per week during the period of the study – found that it was not enough to run a car, and so, for many of the families, who have either received a car or a grant towards transport from the Family Fund, the mobility allowance was a net diminution in provision.[2]

The services that exist to help with transport for medical care can be divided into those available for treatment and those available for visiting. It is a principle of the national health service that medical care is free at the point of access and under the Act, area health authorities are required to provide transport when it is medically necessary.[3] However, it became clear from the experience of applicants to the Family Fund that area health authorities differed in their interpretation of what is medically necessary: in some cases, non-ambulant children only were provided with transport and in other cases, it was available only for visits strictly related to medical treatment. Where ambulance transport was provided, it was often extremely inconvenient: if ambulances were organised on routes or circuits, there was often no certainty when the child would be picked up or taken home. Journeys that might have taken ten minutes by car might take over an hour by hospital transport and involve long waits at the hospital or clinic while all the patients in the ambulance were seen. The families who had to transport their children for in- or out-patient treatment at regional or national centres had special problems. In most cases only those families receiving the family income supplement or supplementary benefits could receive a refund of the cost of a journey if the visits were for non-urgent treatment. Even when the area health authority accepted that the journey was medically necessary, it would sometimes refuse help if the journey was a long one.

If the provision of transport for hospital treatment was often inadequate for families with handicapped children, the help available to enable parents to visit their children in hospital was much more problematical. Despite a general recognition that 'Where a child is admitted to hospital his links with his home must be maintained . . . visiting the child without restriction is essential',[4] no single agency has responsibility for providing help. Families on supplementary benefit may get an exceptional needs payment for visiting costs, social services departments can make payments under Section 1 of the Children and Young Persons Act 1963, and a few area health authorities give assistance to parents. However, most of the families who need help with visiting have to seek it, with the help of medical social workers, from voluntary organisations, charities, or hospital endowment funds. The amounts available from these sources to meet the needs of families – especially those travelling long distances to national centres – are never enough.[5]

The transport needs associated with education are better catered for than domestic, social and recreational needs, and those for health care. Section 55 of the Education Act 1944 places a clear duty on local authorities to arrange transport free of charge and most parents are satisfied with the service provided. There are some organisational problems, and children in pre-school play-groups, where the responsibility lies with the social services department, may face special difficulties, but on the whole the service is adequate. However, although LEAs also have a duty to provide transport to residential schools, they tend to restrict their support to the beginning and end of each term and only very rarely help parents with the costs of visiting or bringing the child home at week-ends. A Department of Education and Science administrative memorandum in 1966 reminded education authorities of the importance of these visits and pointed out that:[6]

> When travelling and other expenses are relatively high it may be impossible for parents to visit as often as the interest of the child may require . . . in these circumstances the local education authority may pay part or whole of the parents' travelling and

other expenses incurred in making the visit if they are satisfied
that without a visit the child's special educational treatment
would be impaired and the parents cannot afford the cost.

It was clear from applications to the Family Fund that this directive
was not being interpreted very generously by education authorities.

## The impact of the Family Fund on mobility problems

As soon as the Family Fund became involved with this area of widespread need and limited or non-existent provision, it immediately began
to receive applications for help with transport of all kinds and for many
different purposes. Families sought help with the purchase of cars,
vans, and caravans; the repayment of loans on existing vehicles; train,
bus or taxi fares or the costs of car hire; towards the cost of driving
lessons and the running expenses of cars – repairs, maintenance, fuel,
and lubricants. Families asked for help in order to take the child on
outings or on holiday, to ease the burdens of shopping, to take the
child to hospital, school or clubs and other social activities, and to
enable them to visit residential schools or hospitals.

Faced with these demands the Fund decided that it could not meet
every request for help and, as with other areas of provision, developed
guide-lines within which the Fund's staff and visiting social workers
were expected to use their discretion. The guide-lines were:

1    Transport could be given where the child's condition inhibited
the family's ability to go out of the home, or to go on outings. But
general regard must be had to social and economic circumstances.

2    In general, help with other transport needs was not forthcoming
unless there were exceptional circumstances. Thus, help to enable the
wife to do the shopping or the husband to go to work should not have
been given. The cost of fares to take a child to school or hospital would
only be subsidised if the need was urgent, or the journey expensive. In
principle, the Fund was prepared to help only if the authority responsible
was unable or unwilling to do so. It did help families to visit residential
schools and also was prepared to help with the costs of visiting children
in hospital when all other sources of help had been approached.

The Fund also developed guide-lines about what form the help
should take and, in particular, in what circumstances cars should be
given. The Panel was much exercised over the question of cars – they
were costly, expensive to run, and the Panel worried too about the
propriety of raising the standard of living of families too far above that
of their peers. In the end it was agreed to provide a standard grant of

£500 (rising to £750 as time went on) towards the cost of a second-hand car if no other form of help was more suitable; if a member of the family could drive the car, and meet the maintenance costs and garage it; and if the car would enable the family to go out on outings.

In practice these guide-lines were not strictly adhered to. In particular, the Fund's staff found it difficult to restrict help with cars and other transport solely for the purpose of family outings. Families did, in fact, obtain cars for a whole range of mobility problems and of course, cars which were authorised for 'outings' helped to meet many other needs as well.

In May 1975, the Fund changed its policy with regard to help with transport in order to reduce expenditure and to adjust to the introduction of the mobility allowance. Under the new transport criteria families should no longer receive cars but a self-drive car-hire package of £200 which had been negotiated with a car-hire firm and enabled a family to hire a car for one week-end per month and two weeks' holiday per year. In practice, not all families wanted help in this form and many preferred to accept a cash grant of £200 (eventually £250) in place of the car-hire package. When the mobility allowance began payment, the Fund no longer provided help with transport to those families receiving the allowance, but continued to assist those families which needed help but were not eligible for the mobility allowance.

### Assessment of the Fund's assistance with transport

So, the level of help with transport diminished during the initial three years. The Fund never agreed to meet the general transport problems of families with handicapped children and formally restricted help to the provision of outings – though in practice the help given benefited the family beyond that particular need. The extracts from the following letters from families illustrate the benefits that were obtained from the Family Fund – help that went beyond the purpose of that help.

I have been using it for three weeks now and have found it marvellous for every one of my family to go out together without having to cope with pushchairs and baggage on public transport. This was becoming increasingly difficult due to my daughter's weight. I have also been able to take her shopping with me without having to ask someone to stay with her while I do shopping. I think she seems a happier child not having to be left so often. I have been able to take her to local recreation

areas where she can see other people enjoying themselves which
gives her great pleasure and she can also play ball games from her
chair.

We have also been able to regain contact with our immediate
family which we were not able to see so often.

I can only say thank you again for your help, it is hard to
describe what this has meant to Susan except to say her world
has been opened to a wider place.

With reference to your letter dated 5.6.75 with cheque for £725,
I thank you very much for the help you have given us. I am
pleased to inform you that we have now got the car and are very
happy with it. It is going to make a big difference to us in many
ways. There will be no more worries of how I shall get someone
to look after Kenneth while I attend doctor appointments or go
for the weekly shopping etc. As I can now have Ken with me. We
are also going to be able to get a holiday this year which we found
difficult before. Kenneth enjoys the car very much and we take
him for an outing as often as possible.

The Family Fund enabled us to get a car in January of this year,
we have an Austin 1300 estate. And it has opened up a whole
new world to our son, instead of always being the one who had
to stay home when I went shopping, he can now come and has a
grand time going around the shops which to him, after being so
restricted for so long is an adventure on its own, beside all the
fun outings we have been able to have during the school holidays.

It has also meant that we have all been able to take a more
active part in his school activities, instead of a 2½ hour selection
of bus journeys, we are able to go direct in just over half an hour.
This of course is good for Gary, and all our other children.

The Family Fund has arranged many things all for the better
for all of us and especially Gary, for which we are all very thankful.

The car also means that Gary no longer has to go to hospital
by ambulance but by car (he hated his ambulance trips).

The administrative statistics provide some information on the help
with transport given by the Family Fund (see Table 4.1 on p. 53).

The distribution of items requested and given remained fairly stable
throughout the first three years of the Fund except that after the
policy changes in May 1975, the proportion of families given car hire
or the alternative general cash grant increased and the proportion

receiving vehicles fell. In the case of every item, more families received help with transport than those who asked for it in their initial request and the visiting social workers played a part in suggesting this type of help to applicants. Yet there were also many families who could have benefited from help with transport but who failed to get it. Of the 46.2 per cent of families in the follow-up survey who had no access to private transport a third felt that they had had outstanding transport needs at the time when the Family Fund social worker visited them, but they had not asked for transport. Some families got help with more than one transport item. Of the families in the follow-up survey, 38 per cent obtained at least one form of help with transport. Generally, help with transport, particularly car grants, tended to account for the largest payments made by the Fund and by June 1975, it was estimated that 51 per cent of the Fund's expenditure had been items under this heading.

There is no over-all measure of the effectiveness of the help that the Fund gave with transport. Letters to the Fund, some of which are quoted above, illustrate what some parents felt about it. The follow-up survey results revealed a rather mixed picture. Those families with access to private transport were as likely to feel restricted as those without it, and although cars enabled families to visit children in schools and hospitals more frequently and easily, as many of those with cars as without still complained of the difficulties of doing so. It appeared that families with the more severe mobility problems were more likely to own a car. Thus, those owning vehicles did not have a lesser burden than those who did not possess cars. There can be no doubt that in many cases the Fund transformed the problems of transport that families experienced. In others the second-hand car burdened the family with continual bills for tax insurance and repairs, and became a liability.

One of the limitations of the Fund's help with transport was its one-for-all nature: by March 1976, only 1.7 per cent of families had received a second vehicle, 12.3 per cent had received help with fares more than once, 4.2 per cent had received car hire more than once, and 10.8 per cent had received petrol and maintenance grants more than once. Although for many families the burdens of transport were continuous, families did not treat the Fund as a continuing source of support. The Fund itself left it to families to re-apply, and although it formulated a policy to give an annual grant of £250 for transport to any eligible child, it did not encourage re-application.

The mobility allowance was the only way in which the government reduced the Family Fund's responsibility for the relief of a need during the period under review. The allowance was not introduced for this purpose, and in fixing its criteria, the government did not draw on the experience of the Fund. The mobility allowance criteria were more restrictive than the Fund's in terms of qualifying age and severity, and the level of support provided was considerably lower than that previously given by the Fund. The mobility allowance was really only able to take over some of the responsibilities of the Fund because in order to match it, the Fund lowered the level of part of its provision. With the resources at its disposal, the Fund was not able to sustain the level of grants made for transport in the early period, nor could it provide a continuous service. Although it had previously provided, and still does so, a valuable source of help with *ad hoc* payments for travel to hospital or other exceptional needs, it has not been and cannot be viewed as a permanent service to meet the general transport problems of families with handicapped children.

## Clothing

There are two principal reasons why families with a handicapped child may need help with clothing: the disability itself may result in heavy wear and tear of clothing, or the family may be poor and find it difficult to provide for even the normal clothing requirement of a child. Of course, in many instances, the child's disability results in exceptional wear and tear *and* the family is poor.

Not all disabilities result in exceptional wear and tear of clothing; indeed, some disabilities probably cause less than that expected of a normal child. For instance, a child permanently confined to a wheelchair will not require new shoes as often as an ambulant child (though wheelchair-bound children do tend to wear out trousers rapidly). However, many disabilities do result in exceptionally heavy wear and tear. Incontinence, for example, involves constant changing and washing; dragging feet quickly wear out shoes (one widow who applied to the Fund bought a new pair of sandals costing £5.25 every three weeks for her cerebral palsied daughter); constant rocking or rubbing tends to destroy even the hardest-wearing clothes; some mentally handicapped or mentally ill children systematically destroy clothing; those who crawl or move around on their bottoms cause heavy wear; children with feeding difficulties and who dribble, children with calipers or hearing aids and those with physical abnormalities calling for unusual shapes or sizes, all may have extra clothing needs.

In the follow-up study, mothers were asked whether they thought that their children needed extra clothes, shoes or bedding because of their handicap; 85.5 per cent said that they did. They were asked to try and estimate the extra cost of providing the items needed. The average estimated extra annual cost was £45.29 (SD 26.73).

It is difficult to separate the burden of extra costs of this clothing from the financial circumstances of the families applying to the Fund. For poor families, even the provision and replacement of normal clothing is a source of anxiety. No systematic information on the financial circumstances of families applying to the Family Fund was collected. However, we have already seen that these families were more likely than the general population of families to be hard pressed, and would have had difficulty meeting the normal expenses of child-rearing, quite apart from any extra expense in bringing up a handicapped child.

## The provision of clothing

The Family Fund was operating in a society in which family poverty remains widespread. In 1975, it was estimated that 7.4 million persons were living in families with incomes up to only 40 per cent higher than the supplementary benefits levels.[7] In addition to this substantial problem of poverty, the general living standards of families with children have been declining in relation to other groups.[8] After expenditure on food, housing, and fuel, expenditure on clothing is perhaps the most essential call on family resources. It is not possible to estimate how much families actually spend on clothing children because the major source of data – the Family Expenditure Survey – does not distinguish between expenditure on children's shoes and shoes for the rest of the family. In 1975, the average annual expenditure in one-child families was £11.44 for the child's clothes and £53.56 for the whole family's shoes. Margaret Wynn[9] has shown how clothing costs vary with age, children aged fourteen and fifteen costing more to clothe than adults. The Weaver Committee estimated that the annual clothing costs of the fifteen-year-old at 1955 prices was £30.[10]

If families with disabled children are too poor to meet their clothing needs or cannot afford the extra clothing attributable to the disablement, what other sources of help are there? Apart from the Family Fund, there are four.

    1  *Social services departments*. Social work departments in

Scotland have power, under the Social Work (Scotland) Act, Section 12, to provide material help.

> It shall be the duty of every local authority to promote social
> welfare by making available advice, guidance and assistance on
> such a scale as may be appropriate.

In England and Wales the legislative powers are not so clear. Section 1 of the Children and Young Persons Act 1963 enables departments to make cash payments to families if such payments would reduce the chances of the children coming into care. Section 2a of the National Assistance Act 1948 gives powers to local authorities 'to make arrangements for promoting the welfare of persons . . . permanently handicapped'.

Despite (or perhaps because of) this legislation, few social services departments give assistance with clothing, other than *ad hoc* gifts from dispensary-type funds. Only ten out of 303 families in the follow-up survey had ever received help with clothes, shoes, or bedding from their social services department.

    2  *Supplementary Benefits Commission.*  The normal clothing requirements of recipients of supplementary benefits are expected to be met out of the scale rates of benefit. Families with an exceptional need may apply for either an exceptional needs payment – a lump-sum grant which is given for the purchase of a particular item or items – or an exceptional circumstance addition, by which scale rates are increased to meet special expenses.

Exceptional needs payments are entirely discretionary, although the Commission's officers are guided by a list of normal clothing requirements (BO 40). In 1976, 1.1 million such payments were made to supplementary benefits recipients and 58.3 per cent of these were for help with children's clothes and shoes.[11] In 1968, the average clothing grant to children was £5.55 and the Commission spent nearly £800,000 on these grants.[12]

The Supplementary Benefits Act 1976 enables the Commission to help families with urgent needs who do not receive supplementary benefits, but it is very rare for such families to be helped with items like clothing.

Only two families in the follow-up sample said they had ever received help to buy extra shoes, clothes, or bedding from the Supplementary Benefits Commission.

3 *Education authorities.* Under Section 5 of the 1948 Education Act, local education authorities (LEAs) were given permissive powers in this field 'where it appears to a local authority that a pupil . . . is unable by reason of the inadequacy or suitability of his clothing to take full advantage of the education provided at school, the authority may provide him with such clothing as in the opinion of the authority is necessary for the purpose of ensuring that he is sufficiently and suitably clad while he remains a pupil at the school'.

In practice, most LEAs provide (i) grants for distinctive clothing required to be worn by secondary school children, and (ii) grants to all children to buy essential clothing. Both grants are normally means-tested and so are only available to the children of poorer families.

There has been considerable criticism over the years of the low level of grants and the narrow limits of the means tests employed by most LEAs.[13] Only eleven families in the follow-up study said that they had ever received extra shoes, clothes, or bedding from their local authority.

4 *Voluntary organisations.* A number of voluntary organisations make *ad hoc* payments to families for shoes and clothing but aid from this quarter is not extensive: only six families in the follow-up survey said that they had ever received help with clothing or bedding from a voluntary organisation.

To sum up, before the Family Fund was established, there was really no other source of help with clothing. Social services departments do not have wide enough powers to help with clothes and shoes; education authorities have powers if the clothing is required for school and if the family meets a test of means. The Supplementary Benefits Commission has discretionary powers to help those dependent on supplementary benefit but even those families with quite exceptional needs rarely get extra help from that source. There was no agency with the single responsibility to meet the clothing needs of handicapped children, and few of the families concerned had any help at all in this respect.

## How the Family Fund helped with clothing

By April 1976, 5,043 families, or 19 per cent of all families helped, had been given grants for this purpose. Only 11 per cent of families actually asked for assistance but the visiting social worker, or the social worker processing the applications at York, decided that other families too needed help of this kind and so more families were given clothing grants than asked for them.

At the start, the Fund responded to every individual request from a family. However, before long, the Fund's officers decided that it was more sensible to make a standard grant of £30 in response to all applications for clothing. This grant was increased from time to time and had reached £50 by April 1976. It was varied from family to family and those who asked for help with shoes tended to continue to get the grant needed for this item.

By December 1973, 49 per cent of the families applying had received grants totalling less than £60 and the Fund's managers began to be concerned about the amount of time spent in processing these small grants, which tended to be for clothing and bedding. There was a backlog of 5,000 cases not yet dealt with and it was costing about £20 to process each grant. At the Management Committee on 29 November 1973, it was insisted that:[14]

> A case could probably have to be put to the DHSS about this
> (small grants) as the provision of these small items should be a
> local operation carried out by people who are ordinarily visiting
> the families and should not be something that is processed
> through a national organisation such as the Trust.

In a note for the Management Committee on 28 February 1974, the secretary of the Fund discussed whether small grants, if they were to be made at all, could be made without a social worker visit and the matter became one of the issues raised with the DHSS in a paper on the administration of the Fund that was presented to it in August 1974.

> The trustees believe that the procedures they have devised
> for the administration of the Family Fund are not well adapted
> for the nation-wide distribution of grants for clothing and
> bedding nor is a central Fund the right source for such help
> . . . . Clearly discretion in such cases would be better exercised
> by a local organisation otherwise in touch with the family.[15]

The DHSS reply to this was given to the Management Committee on 3 December 1974. It said that the point was taken but that it was hoped that the Fund would carry on making these grants because there was no certainty about who else had the power to do it. The Secretary of State thought that it was within the competence of local authorities under Section 29 of the National Assistance Act 1948, but he was unwilling to issue a circular on the subject because of the difficulty of asking local authorities to do more at a time when their expenditure was being cut back.

By May 1975, the Fund was trying to reduce its expenditure and a list of ways of doing this was drawn up.[16] Two suggestions were that grants of less than £50 were not justified and should be discontinued, and that families on supplementary benefit should be urged to seek exceptional needs payments before grants from the Family Fund were considered. Although these suggestions were approved at the Management Committee on 26 September 1975, small grants – including grants for clothing – continued to be made, though the social workers had more regard to the 'social and economic circumstances' of the families applying for them. The suggested changes in the treatment of supplementary benefit claimants were more rigorously enforced. All families asking for items that could be obtained through exceptional needs payments were required to obtain a letter from their local supplementary benefits office refusing the help requested before the Fund would step in. The Fund's staff were not unhappy about this procedure and went to considerable lengths to check that families did tell the Fund if help was refused by the Supplementary Benefits Commission. In the end, the majority of supplementary benefit applicants, either because they were refused an exceptional needs payment or because the exceptional needs payment was inadequate to meet their needs, obtained help from the Fund. The Fund presented to the DHSS some cases where an exceptional needs payment had been refused and the result of this initiative was that an instruction was sent to local supplementary benefit offices, urging the staff to have greater regard to the exceptional needs for families with disabled children. The Fund's staff believed that the Commission became more generous in the treatment of families with handicapped children as a result of this instruction, but the situation in which families on supplementary benefit could only get help from the Fund after they had been refused by the Supplementary Benefits Commission, while families with incomes from other sources would receive grants directly from the Family Fund, continued to be anomalous.

### Assessment of the Fund's help with clothing

The Fund remains the principal source of help with clothing available to families with handicapped children but it is not the best mechanism for meeting these needs. Families cannot afford to buy clothing because their incomes are too low or are inadequate to meet the exceptionally heavy needs attributable to disablement. In either case, discretionary *ad hoc* payments administered from a central Fund are bound to fail.

The problem of family poverty can only be resolved by adequate family support schemes, such as child benefits. The Family Fund does not meet the extra clothing costs - only a minority of families with these extra costs get help with them, and the majority of those who have received a clothing grant have received it only once. Yet clothing remains a recurring cost to the family, and distributing small grants, as the Fund has recognised, is not cost effective. Yet so long as no more comprehensive provision exists the Family Fund continues to provide a small but useful source of help with the clothing costs of a disabled child.

## Conclusion

This chapter has sought to show that in the provision of second-hand cars and other transport help and in the provision of clothing grants, the Family Fund met needs that were not being covered adequately by existing services and yet were important burdens carried by families with handicapped children. In the case of cars, it was not able to sustain the level of grants required to purchase a car, and its help tended to be of a once-off nature. The provision of clothing grants filled a gap in existing provision but was probably not an appropriate responsibility for a centrally organised fund. Conclusions reached in this chapter will be further discussed in chapters 14 and 15.

# 10    Cost effectiveness

In this chapter we examine the cost of administering the Family Fund and attempt to answer three questions. How much did the Fund cost to run? Was this more or less than other agencies performing similar functions? Could the Fund be run at less cost and maintain the existing level of service?

## How much did the Fund cost to run?

For a number of reasons there is no one answer to that question. It depends on the date of the calculation and what costs are included in it.

From the beginning, the Trust insisted that the administrative costs of the Fund should be separately earmarked, because they wished to avoid spending on administration any of the £3 million intended for families. They also undertook to finance from their own resources the research project associated with the Fund (although the DHSS later made a substantial contribution to the costs of the research programme). Throughout the period of this review, the costs of the core administration – the director of the Trust, the finance officer, and three secretaries, although they were heavily engaged in Fund business, were not charged to the Fund.

Perhaps the best way of expressing the cost of administration is the ratio of administrative cost to each £ distributed to families. This cost ratio depends on the amount distributed as well as the administrative costs, and both of these have changed with time. In the early days, when the Fund was processing a lot of applications but before many grants had been made, the expenses ratio was relatively high. Later, after mid-1975, with the cessation of grants for cars and for aids and adaptations, the size of the grants began to fall and the expenses ratio rose again. The costs of administration also varied. In the early period, the majority of social work reports on families were provided at no cost to the Fund by workers from social services departments. Because of the delays in the return of reports by social services departments and because the reports were often not completed correctly, the Fund began to recruit and train its own paid corps of agents. At first, the system of payment to agents was on a sessional basis but as the number of agents increased, sessional payments were found to be too expensive and the Fund began to pay a fee for each visit, plus travelling expenses. There were also changes in the staffing costs at York. Over the period, the Fund recruited a professionally trained social work staff to process applications there. As the application rate to the Fund declined and its systems of operation became routinised, the social work staff left and the Fund operated with fewer trained social workers and two teams of administrative staff.

To take account of some of these changes three cost ratios have been calculated below:

1   The actual administrative cost borne by the DHSS for each of the four years 1973-7.

2   The additional cost that was borne by social services departments - that is, how much more it would have cost the Fund if all visits had been carried out by the Fund's own agents.

3   The cost of the Fund after the end of the three-year experimental period when it was operating at a stable level.


## 1   *Administrative costs of the Fund*

Although the picture is not as clear as it might be (because accounting methods have not been consistent throughout) Table 10.1 does show that the total administrative costs rose to a peak in 1975. The increase was the result of the build-up of staff in the headquarters at York and the growing use of agents on a fee per service basis. Although the administrative costs were higher in 1975 than 1974, the actual amount of money distributed to families was less. The increase in costs in 1975 was almost entirely due to the increased use of agents. In 1976, when fewer families were helped, expenditure on administration declined, thanks largely to a drop in the cost of publicity and savings on administrative salaries. But the cost of the agents increased.

The relationship between the actual administrative tasks and administrative costs is shown more clearly in Table 10.2. The cost per £ paid was as high as 16.1 per cent in 1973, but in 1974 and 1975 it fell as the average payment to each family rose. But towards the end of 1975, grants for cars and for aids and adaptations were stopped, and with smaller payments to new families applying to the Fund and only small savings in the cost of processing each case, the average cost of each £ distributed rose. Over the whole period, each £ distributed by the Fund cost 6.6p to distribute. It cost £19.61 to provide a grant to each family helped.

*Table 10.1   Administrative expenditure of the Family Fund (year ending 31 December)*

|                                   | 1973    | 1974     | 1975     | 1976     | Total    |
|-----------------------------------|---------|----------|----------|----------|----------|
| Administrative salaries }         | 23,887  | 79,665   | 78,988   | 65,547   | 369,398  |
| Agents' claims               }    |         |          | 53,529   | 67,782   |          |
| Travelling expenses               | 3,781[1] | 14,852[1] | 1,803    | 2,007    | 22,443   |
| Publicity                         | 4,967   | 17,172   | 7,744    | 7,144    | 37,027   |
| Printing and stationery           | 4,074   | 10,333   | 12,525   | 10,983   | 37,915   |
| Postage and telephone             | 3,161   | 9,450    | 8,214    | 8,460    | 29,285   |
| Office equipment and furniture    | 4,480   | 4,602    | 2,549    | 2,884    | 14,515   |
| Light, heat and overheads         | 1,759   | 3,016    | 3,714    | 4,482    | 12,971   |
| Professional fees                 | 50      | 258      | 832      | 1,106    | 2,246    |
| Contribution to the research programme[2] | –       | 12,500   | 12,500   | –        | 25,000   |
|                                   | £46,159 | £151,848 | £182,398 | £170,395 | £550,800 |

*Notes:* [1] Includes travelling expenses of field workers.
[2] Attributed as a cost to the Fund because the research programme provided statistics and intelligence on its workings.

*Table 10.2   Payments and cost ratios for each year ending 31 December, 1973–6*

|                                      | 1973    | 1974      | 1975      | 1976      | Total     |
|--------------------------------------|---------|-----------|-----------|-----------|-----------|
| Administrative costs £               | 46,159  | 151,848   | 182,398   | 170,395   | 550,800   |
| Money granted £                      | 286,363 | 2,677,344 | 3,268,898 | 2,083,807 | 8,316,412 |
| Number of families receiving first grants | 1,880   | 10,327    | 9,367     | 6,492     | 28,066    |
| Number of payments made              | 2,334   | 16,198    | 19,797    | 16,980    | 55,309    |
| Average payment £                    | 123     | 165       | 165       | 123       | 150       |
| Cost per £ paid %                    | 16.1    | 5.67      | 5.58      | 8.18      | 6.62      |
| Cost per payment £                   | 19.7    | 9.37      | 9.21      | 10.04     | 9.96      |
| Cost per family £                    | 24.55   | 14.70     | 19.47     | 26.25     | 19.61     |

## 2   Savings in administrative costs due to unpaid work of social services social workers

At the start, very few families were visited by the Fund's own agents but by the end of the period, most of them were. Over all, 60.1 per cent of the families who had received a grant by April 1976 had had their original application assessed without charge to the Fund by workers from statutory agencies. If £7 is taken as the average agent's fee over the whole period, then the total extra cost that the Fund would have borne can be estimated as:

Agent's fee (£7) × proportion of families visited without charge to the Fund (60.1%) × total families helped 1973-6 (28,092) = £118,183.

Thus the ratio of costs per £ paid for the whole period of the Fund to 31 December 1976 should be increased from 6.6 per cent to 8.0 per cent.

## 3   Administrative costs of the Fund as it is now operating

To obtain a picture of the administrative costs of the Fund at the level of expenditure that has now been set for it and using the methods that have now been developed to process claims, we can use figures for the twelve months ending 31 December 1977 (see Table 10.3).

*Table 10.3   Payments and cost ratio for the year ending 31 December 1977*

| | |
|---|---:|
| Administrative costs £ | 161,391 |
| Money granted £ | 2,199,677 |
| Number of families receiving first grants | 5,171 |
| Number of payments made | 17,283 |
| Average payment £ | 127 |
| Cost per £ paid % | 7.3 |
| Cost per payment £ | 9.3 |
| Costs per family £ | 31.21 |

The Fund is now operating on a budget of £1.8 million per year and £200,000 per year for administrative expenses – that is, a budgeted level of administrative costs of about 11 per cent. This level has not yet been reached by the Fund. Indeed, there was some reduction in the costs ratio in 1977 as a result of savings under a number of heads, but mainly because an increasing proportion of the money distributed was in second and subsequent grants without a home visit by an agent.

The Fund has benefited from the Trust's investment strategy. The DHSS has paid in advance the money it has made available. Thus, the first £3 million was made available as soon as the Fund began operation in April 1973, and all of it was not distributed until January 1975, by which time the second £3 million had already been received. This was not spent until the end of 1975 and the £2.7 million (including administrative expenses) received in March 1976 until the end of that year. The Fund's financial managers have invested these large balances as Certificates of Deposit maturing at variable dates. It has been a delicate business ensuring that deposits mature in time to be available to pay grants to families but not too soon to lose interest. At one time in early 1975, the Fund had serious cash-flow problems because of a delay in receiving an annual grant from the DHSS, but towards the end of that year after the cut-back in payments for cars and aids and adaptations, it found itself with an unexpected surplus which had to be re-invested.

The net result of the Fund's investment strategy is that over the period to the end of December 1976, it accumulated £717,080 in interest, which is more than the total cost of administration for the same period (see Table 10.4). To put it another way, it had been possible to distribute to families the money that was made available by the DHSS for administrative expenses.

*Table 10.4    Interest earned on balances held by the Family Fund compared with administrative costs. Years ending 31 December 1975–6*

|  | 1973 | 1974 | 1975 | 1976 | Total |
|---|---|---|---|---|---|
| Interest earned | 195,593 | 265,936 | 181,246 | 88,688 | 731,463 |
| Less bank charges | 264 | 2,208 | 5,049 | 6,862 | 14,383 |
| Balance | 195,329 | 263,728 | 176,197 | 81,826 | 717,080 |
| Administrative costs | 46,159 | 151,848 | 182,398 | 170,395 | 550,800 |

## Was the Fund cheaper to run than other agencies?

There are no other agencies identical with the Family Fund but two with some similarities are the Supplementary Benefits Commission and the Attendance Allowance Board.

The supplementary benefits scheme is a vast undertaking, making payments that determined the living standards of 9 per cent of the population in 1976.[1] Most of the expenditure on supplementary benefits is in the form of regular weekly scale-rate payments. However, each claimant for supplementary benefits has to undergo an individual assessment of eligibility which is most commonly carried out in a local office but which may involve a home visit. In addition, many of the applications for benefit result in relatively short-term payments. As well as the scale rate of benefit payable to claimants, those with exceptional needs or in exceptional circumstances may ask for an addition, either in a lump sum or by way of a regular weekly addition to the scale rate. Applications for exceptional needs payments generally involve a visit to the claimant's house. The administrative costs of the supplementary benefits scheme vary according to the type of claimant.[2] The elderly, who tend to be long-term claimants, present lower administrative costs than other claimants. Over all, every £1 costs 10.2p to distribute to supplementary benefit claimants. Each discretionary addition to the basic scale rates of benefit costs considerably more than this. The Supplementary Benefits Commission[3] estimates that discretionary additions take up 6 per cent of staff time to distribute 5 per cent of total benefits but that exceptional needs payments costs twice as much to administer as exceptional circumstances additions. This means that it costs roughly £8 million to distribute £24 million in exceptional needs payments, that is, 30p per £1 distributed or £7.18 per exceptional needs payment. It is perhaps no wonder that the Supplementary Benefits Commission's annual report[4] described these payments as 'an exceedingly inefficient way of getting money into the hands of our claimants'.

The attendance allowance scheme is similar to the Family Fund in that it involves a home visit to assess the degree of disability. The home visits are carried out by doctors who are paid a fee by the Board. Their reports are scrutinised by DHSS medical staff, who decide whether the applicant meets the medical criteria. Any similarity with the Family Fund ceases when a decision is made, because the attendance allowance is not a capital sum like the Family Fund grant but a relatively generous weekly allowance, paid subject to there being no change in the recipients' circumstances for a period fixed according to the nature of the condition. Recipients are re-examined at the end of the period but 60 per cent of the awards are for life.

The fees paid to doctors for visiting applicants are more generous than those paid to social worker agents by the Family Fund: it is estimated that each case costs about £15 to assess. The attendance allowance was introduced in stages from 1971 and during the 'take-on' period, administrative costs were relatively high, but by 1976-7 the scheme was running at a fairly routine level and the cost of distributing £130 million in benefit was £3.9 million or 3 per cent.[5]

Compared with supplementary benefits, the administrative costs of the Family Fund are not excessive. They are higher than those of the attendance allowance but this is because the level of benefit, even at the lower rate, is much higher for the attendance allowance than for the Family Fund. Up to the end of 1976, the Fund distributed just over £8.3 million to 28,092 families at a cost per £ paid of 6.6p. If, instead of receiving lump-sum grants at the Family Fund level, these families had been given the equivalent of the attendance allowance for three years at the lower rate of £8.15 per week, in April 1977 it would have cost only 1.5p per £ paid.

The cost per £1 distributed by the Fund is a good deal less than the cost of distributing exceptional needs payments in the supplementary benefits scheme. This is probably not because this scheme is running less efficiently than the Family Fund but because the level of exceptional needs payments is much lower than Family Fund grants. The cost per exceptional needs payment in 1976 was £7.18 but the cost per *payment* of the Family Fund was £10.04.

## Could the Fund be less costly?

Can any savings be made in the present methods of assessing each case? About 40 per cent of the costs of administration goes in paying fees and expenses to field-work staff and another 40 per cent is absorbed by salaries of staff vetting the field-workers' reports. Substantial savings in administrative costs could only really come from a reduction in one or both of these heads of expenditure.

Given that experience has taught that it is not possible to rely on the staff of social services departments to provide speedy and comprehensive reports on applicants, and given, too, that it is necessary to make home visits to check that an applicant is eligible and to ensure that the requests are appropriate, then the methods devised by the Family Fund have a number of advantages. First, the social workers recruited by the Fund carry out home visits for lower fees than doctors would have charged. The current fee of £7 per visit plus expenses, is about half the fee currently paid to doctors visiting on behalf of the Attendance Allowance Board. It is interesting to note that the assessment of attendance requirements for the attendance allowance which is arguably largely a social question is carried out by doctors, whereas the assessment of very severe disability which is arguably largely a medical question is carried out by social workers. There is a long tradition of using doctors to do assessments for state benefits for the disabled but it might be cheaper and no less efficient if the DHSS were to use social workers. Second, working for the Fund has given many trained social workers who had to give up work to have a family the opportunity of part-time employment. This is difficult to get in many areas and has obvious benefits for the individuals concerned in sustaining their interest in social work and giving them a chance to keep up to date in practice. However, the Fund has also demonstrated that there is a cadre of trained and experienced social workers covering every area of the country, ready and eager to do part-time work. The Fund agents were recruited without advertising but through contacts and by word of mouth, and they remain a resource for the future.

There is little scope for savings in agents' fees in respect of those families who apply again. Such cases are only visited again when the information on the file is so old that it is considered inadequate or where there has been a marked change in family circumstances, such as a marriage breakdown. Where such a visit is necessary, the agent receives a smaller fee. There might be scope for dealing with applications for small amounts without a home visit. The Supplementary Benefits Commission, which in the past carried out home visits even for the most trivial application, have started giving exceptional needs payments for less than £30 without a home visit. However, the circumstances are not strictly comparable, as the Supplementary Benefits Commission already knows a good deal about the circumstances of applicants for exceptional needs payments, whereas the Fund knows nothing about its new applicants.

What about savings in the organisation at York? During the experimental period and since, there have been continual changes taking place in office routines, staffing levels, office layout, and so forth. Banks of shelving containing files have been replaced with micro-filmed records and micro-card readers; individually typed and dictated letters have been replaced by standard printed letters; open-ended questions on social work report forms have given way to 'tick box' layouts; and professionally qualified social work staff have been replaced, for the most part, by administrative staff. The routinisation of procedure has not occurred without some loss in the flexibility and sensitivity of the organisation. Families, who in the past received individually dictated letters which had regard to their own particular circumstances, are now as likely as not to receive a standard letter which, while it is sensitively worded, cannot respond to individual circumstances. The office staff at York still have to make difficult judgments and further dilution of the numbers or calibre of staff may lead to less sensitive decisions.

## Conclusion

While there is no reason to regard the Fund as having been excessively costly to administer, there is cause for concern in the future. Administrative costs are bound to rise with inflation and, unless the resources that are made available to the Fund also rise, the ratio of administrative costs to the money distributed to families will increase. Each payment the Fund makes is already costing over £9, and about 7p is being spent on administration for every £1 distributed. However, it is inevitable that a system involving discretionary judgments about each individual case will be costly to administer, and there must be a point where the costs of distributing each £1 become too high to justify the existing system of administration in relation to the size of grants made.

# 11     Implicit aims

So far, we have been concerned with the extent to which the Family Fund succeeded in achieving explicit aims or publicly acknowledged goals. As well as publicly acknowledged goals every social policy has certain implicit aims or motives. These are the aspirations of the participants which are not publicly acknowledged. In this chapter, an attempt is made to assess the extent to which the Family Fund achieved some implicit aims. The discussion will concentrate entirely on the extent to which the aims of the two principal organisations concerned with the Fund – the government and the Joseph Rowntree Memorial Trust – were achieved.

## Government

In the case of the government, a number of implicit aspirations can be suggested. In the early days, it hoped that the establishment of the Fund would relieve the demands on 'the minister' to intervene in the dispute between Distillers and the families of Thalidomide-damaged children. Subsequently, it was in the interests of the government that the Fund should continue to be a source of political credit, co-operating within the constraints imposed and not making unreasonable demands or raising embarrassing public or private criticism.

The Fund became a small but useful instrument in the sense that the government has been able to claim new developments. For example, in announcing that £5 million was to be made available to the Thalidomide Children Trust in lieu of tax that they would be required to pay on the awards from Distillers, the Prime Minister was at the same time able to say that £3 million would be granted to the Family Fund. The fact that this £3 million had already been promised did nothing to detract from the value of the credit redounding to the government of appearing to be giving *more* help to families with a handicapped child. The extension of the terms of the Fund to non-congenitally disabled children served a similarly useful purpose. The announcement was to be made by the minister in an adjournment debate on vaccine-damaged children[1] but unfortunately time ran out before he reached that point

152

in his speech. The news subsequently appeared in the press but it enabled the minister to counter demands for a compensatory payment for the families of vaccine-damaged children by a concession over the terms of reference of the Family Fund. The terms were not extended *for* that purpose; it had already been realised by the government and the Trust that the restriction to the congenitally disabled was inequitable and that to broaden the area of flexibility would not result in a substantial additional burden on the resources available. The fact that the timing of the announcement coincided with demands for help for vaccine-damaged children was providential. In other ways, too - in speeches to public meetings or in the House and in answer to parliamentary questions - ministers could claim political credit for the families helped by the Fund and the money distributed.

This store of credit might have dried up if the Fund had become the focus of complaint. It was suggested in chapter 2 that one of the government's motives in turning to independent bodies to perform difficult or controversial tasks is to 'pass the poisoned chalice' - that is, to avoid criticism that may arise. On balance, we felt that this was probably not a motivating factor in persuading the government to turn to the Family Fund. Nevertheless, the fact that the work of the Fund resulted in very little complaint is remarkable. The Fund was created at a time when there was already considerable criticism of the provision for the disabled made by government and local authorities and its terms of reference gave it wide discretionary powers to help families who failed to get help from existing sources. Having regard to this critical environment, given also the growing militancy of welfare rights organisations over the operation of administrative discretion, the limits on its resources and the numbers in need, the Family Fund might have been expected to cause more trouble for government despite its independent status.

In order to evaluate the volume of complaint about the Fund, it is necessary to describe the channels for complaint that existed.[2] The most formal channel of complaint of administrative action is through the courts. No legal action has been brought against the Fund, and it is questionable whether the general law relating to charities provides suitable remedies for questioning and altering decisions taken in the course of day-to-day administration.[3] Individuals with a grievance could take up their case with their MPs and there has been a trickle of letters to the DHSS or directly to the Family Fund from this source. Dissatisfied with the results of an informal approach, an MP might possibly try to refer an issue to the Parliamentary Commissioner, but no such referral has in fact been made, and it is difficult to see how the Commissioner could review an individual discretionary decision even under the most liberal interpretation of the Parliamentary Commissioner Act 1967. He would probably have to restrict his consideration to whether the DHSS had properly supervised the guide-lines agreed between the Joseph Rowntree Memorial Trust and the DHSS.

Between the start of the Fund and April 1976, there has been some activity in Parliament concerned with the Fund. Apart from its mention in an adjournment debate, there have been fifteen parliamentary questions, but all of them were of a general nature, asking for details of the number and nature of grants and the eligibility criteria.[4] None could be described as critical. In fact, the only criticism in Parliament was during a debate on a private member's bill which aimed to provide the right of compensation to children damaged *in utero*.[5] Two MPs, Mr Lewis Carter Jones and Dr Vaughan, criticised the Fund for procedures that were 'too cumbersome', for refusing subsequent requests, and for refusing to give Possum equipment. These criticisms were rebutted by the Solicitor-General, who pointed out the limits of the Fund's resources. Otherwise, the Fund has not been discussed in Parliament. No member has asked a question about an individual decision, nor has the Fund's policy been criticised through an adjournment debate or private member's bill or motion. Reports that one MP, Greville Janner, was to call for a ministerial inquiry into the operation of the Fund appeared in some provincial newspapers in August 1973 but his attention was diverted by the Arab–Israel war and his threat was not followed up.

More difficult to assess are the complaints about policy in individual cases brought to the attention of the government by families, voluntary organisations or, in a few cases, statutory bodies such as local authorities. Most grievances of this type have come directly to the Fund and have been dealt with at that level, but complaints have found their way to the DHSS. They have all been dealt with by officials, none has required the active intervention of a minister and none has aroused the kind of public attention that was caused by decisions by the Attendance Allowance Board (over Jimmy Martin) or the interpretation of the Chronic Sick and Disabled Persons Act 1970, by local authorities.

Nor has there been much criticism in the press. A press campaign was partly responsible for the establishment of the Fund but thereafter newpapers restricted their coverage to responding to the Fund's own press release. Apart from this, and articles by members of the research unit and the staff of the Fund, the journals have not evinced much interest.

It is clear from this that the Fund has been operating in a supportive political atmosphere and has not presented the government with burdensome political problems. What about the administrative difficulties it has created? Unusual though its status is within the machinery of public administration, the government is responsible for accounting for its work. Strictly speaking, financial accountability is exercised by the Exchequer and Audit Department and the Public Accounts Committee. They are responsible for ensuring that a grant in aid by the Exchequer is expended for the purpose for which it has been authorised. The Family Fund was subjected to two 'inspection audits'. Inspection audits are the normal method of audit where bodies receive a greater part of their income from public funds. There is no formal responsibility on the Exchequer and Audit Department to visit every year and the fact that they did so in two successive years indicates that they were particularly interested in the operation of the Fund. The responsibilities of the Department go beyond fiscal to process accountability. The Controller and Auditor-General reports to the Public Accounts Committee which decides whether on the basis of the report to make a recommendation to the relevant government department. None of the appropriation accounts covering the years in question has contained comments from the Controller and Auditor-General and one can assume from this and the verbal assurances given to the Trust's officers that he was well satisfied with the work of the Fund.

The government department responsible for the administration of the Fund has been the DHSS and, within it, the division responsible for the physically handicapped. The DHSS established its own mechanisms for the fiscal accountability of the Fund and maintained scrutiny over its finances by receiving quarterly accounts of payments and expenses.

Beyond these routine forms of scrutiny, the DHSS has had a rather limited involvement in the day-to-day work of the Fund. It chose to exercise little formal control over and above the minimum requirements of public accountability. DHSS officials have not intervened on their own initiative on matters relating to the policy of the Fund and, though they are members of the Management Committee, have played a comparatively unobtrusive part in its activities. So, the Fund cannot be said to have created onerous administrative burdens for the DHSS. Indeed, perhaps the only time after its establishment that officials and ministers were heavily engaged in Family Fund business was during the negotiations with the Treasury over the question of financing the Fund beyond the £6 million originally promised.

To sum up, the implicit aims of the government have been achieved by the Family Fund. It has produced remarkably little in the way of political and administrative burdens for the government and has been a continuous source of credit throughout its history.

## Joseph Rowntree Memorial Trust

Chapter 2 described how the Joseph Rowntree Memorial Trust agreed to take on the administration of the Family Fund only after careful consideration and with considerable misgivings. The trustees feared that public concern over the treatment of the Thalidomide children by the Distillers Company might spread over to the Trust. They were not at all certain that their experience equipped them for the task and were worried lest the Family Fund would swamp the routine work of the Trust.

So, the Trust too had a number of implicit aspirations for the Fund – that credit and not discredit to the Trust would result from the new responsibilities and that the work of the Trust would not be overwhelmed. Have these implicit aims been achieved? Perhaps the clearest evidence that they have is that the Trust was prepared to continue to administer the Fund beyond the initial three-year period, at first to the end of 1978 and then subsequently 'for an indefinite period'.[6] The Fund has not been administered without difficulties or anxieties. In the early days, the trustees were alarmed by the slow trickle of applications and the fact that the money was not being spent. Later, there were anxieties about the backlog of cases not dealt with and the slow speed at which they were being processed and, later still, the high rate at which money was being dispersed. There were difficulties in finding suitable accommodation and differences between some of the staff of the Fund and the Trust's managers. Despite the recruitment of new staff to run the Fund, the Trust's staff and some of the trustees were burdened with extra work arising from it.

However, these burdens were more than offset by the advantages that accrued to the Trust through its administration of the Fund. Because of it, the Rowntree Memorial Trust and its officials became better known than ever before. The Fund itself came to be widely known as the 'Rowntree Trust' and its work was appreciated by the families concerned, by voluntary and statutory agencies, and by the government. The Trust's anxiety that it might be overwhelmed with complaints and disputes about its decisions proved to be unfounded. In order to process these complaints, from the beginning the Fund established the Panel on top of the normal process of the review of complaints by senior officials. If 'applicants' were not satisfied by the decision of the Panel they could ask to have their case considered by the trustees on the Management Committee of the Fund. As criteria were developed the Panel met less often, until it eventually stopped meeting altogether. From that point onwards, all disputes were dealt with by the director of the Trust. The Fund never advertised a 'right of appeal' and families or their representatives rarely couched their complaints in this form. 'Appeals' could really only be made to the good nature of the Fund's managers. Those who did complain appeared to be satisfied by a letter explaining the decision in their case or the general policy of the Fund. Some dissatisfied families took their case further by complaining to their MPs or the DHSS but none of these cases produced adverse public reaction. Complaints received by the Fund were greatly outnumbered by expressions of appreciation.

The other 'safety-valve' that was established by the Trust was the Consultative Committee. Its purpose was to provide a forum for interested bodies to discuss the Fund's policies, to acquaint Fund managers with the general climate of opinion within the community, and perhaps to defuse criticism that might otherwise have been directed through external and public channels. As it turned out, the Consultative Committee never became an adversary of the Fund and with the exception of one or two parent representative members was entirely supportive of the Fund's work. The representatives of the voluntary organisations never used the Committee to raise questions about the Fund's policy and as attendances at meetings declined, the Fund's managers began to question its role and usefulness. Fund officials even tried to induce it to play a more critical role by deliberately raising controversial subjects for discussion, but with little success, and it came to meet less and less often.

Its amicable relationship with the DHSS throughout the period certainly helped the Trust to achieve its implicit aims. Although the Trust had insisted on being given considerable discretion in administering the Fund, it did expect that surveillance by the DHSS would be sharper than it was. Indeed, the lightness of DHSS supervision caused the managers some anxiety. Their exchanges with DHSS were dominated not by disputes over decisions taken but by concern to persuade the Department to decide about the Fund's future.

Even the extra administrative burden attributed to the Fund brought some compensations to the Trust. It gave it a new interest and challenge and economies of scale enabled the Trust, as a whole, to run more efficiently.

## Conclusion

The general lack of querulousness surrounding the Fund is quite remarkable. It is explained partly by the way the Fund has been managed,
partly by the nature of the clientele and their perception of the Fund
as discussed in chapter 7, partly by the generally beneficial nature of
its work and partly, perhaps, because the Fund was a new agency. As
it settled down to more routine methods of operating and as beneficiaries
and their representatives found out more about procedures, and as
more families re-apply, the constraints on the budget, the restrictions
on the types of grants given, and the increased rate of rejections, might
have given rise to greater conflict. There is no evidence that it has done
so up to date.

# 12    Equity and the Family Fund

A scheme like the Family Fund, characterised by flexible administration and allowing an unusual degree of individual discretion, inevitably raises questions about equity. The principle of equity demands that like cases should be treated alike and unlike cases should be treated unlike in order that a distributive system should be fair and just.[1] Equity in this context simply means 'fair shares' but it raises difficult problems of degree – 'if people's needs are unequal, how unequal are they and what kind of apportionment will secure equity?'.[2] For most cash benefits in British social policy, equity is maintained by treating each case equally by entitlements defined by statute. In the provision of personal social services and supplementary benefits there is considerably more scope for discrimination between cases on the basis of discretionary judgments.[3]

Most of the literature on discretion and equity has been concerned with supplementary benefits and it is worth discussing briefly the differences between the Fund and supplementary benefits. The discretionary powers of the supplementary benefits scheme for the most part enable additional payments to be made to supplement basic scale-rate allowances for a population which by definition is poor. These cash grants are part of an income maintenance programme. In contrast, the Family Fund was making relatively larger cash grants to a population which was not defined by economic circumstances and where the purpose of the grant was not income maintenance. The importance of these contrasts has to do with the different purposes of the grants and their relative sizes. On the one hand, an inequity in the supplementary benefits scheme between one claimant getting an exceptional needs payment of £10 for a pair of shoes and another receiving nothing may be considered less unjust than an inequity between a grant of £30 and one of over £1,000 from the Family Fund. On the other hand, because the supplementary benefits scheme is concerned with primary income maintenance needs, any inequity may be considered less justifiable than variations in occasional grants which have nothing to do with income maintenance.

The policy-makers who established the Family Fund could have decided that every applicant who met the criteria should receive a uniform cash grant - indeed, it was open to the Trust to decide that that was the best way in which to distribute the money. However, this option was not considered because at a very early stage it was assumed that what was needed was an operation that could respond flexibly to the felt needs of each family. The arguments for flexibility were very powerful. In the attendance allowance there was already a cash benefit that gave uniform assistance to most of those families concerned. What was needed now was a system that could respond to the individual needs of each family. Families' needs varied with the handicap of the child and their own social and economic circumstances. In addition, one of the purposes of the Fund was to equalise provision between local authorities and this called for discrimination between cases. Even if this were not reason enough, there were other arguments for using a flexible discretionary basis for the distribution of the money - for example, relatively little was known about the number of families who would be eligible, how many would apply, what and how much they would ask for. The cash available was limited to £3 million with a promise of another £3 million at some unspecified date. A flexible system allowed for experimentation and adaptation in the light of experience and made it possible, if it became necessary, to adjust the grants made to the resources available. Finally, a discretionary system ensured that the Fund did not become the victim of 'the pathology of legalism'.[4] With discretionary power in the hands of the Fund to make, withhold or vary grants, it was less likely to be subject to dispute at the margin.

These, then, were the arguments in favour of distributing the money to the families on the basis of judgments about the individual circumstances of each applicant. However, the question still remains: was the distribution of the money made available to the Fund equitable? The rest of this chapter is concerned to discover whether the procedures adopted did result in an equitable distribution of the resources.

The test of equity is that cases which are similar in all relevant respects should receive the same benefits and those which are different should receive proportionately different ones. The difficulty faced by those attempting to discover to what extent these tests have been met is to get agreement about what are the *relevant respects* and what is the *benefit*. While the degree of disability of the child might be considered relevant to varying the help given, should the income of the family or its general social circumstances also be taken into account? If agreement is reached about these criteria, which in principle can be objectively ascertained, what about the professional judgments of social workers, which may not be objectively ascertainable but could be considered relevant to a benefit designed to relieve stress? In assessing the benefits derived by the family, one is faced with similar problems. The help given in terms of the amount of money and/or type of item can be established, but it could be argued that these are no more than 'inputs' and that what really ought to be investigated are the 'outputs' – in this case, for instance, the extent to which the help given has relieved stress or burden.

In grappling with these problems it has been necessary to simplify. Variations between families are expressed in monetary terms – in terms of the total cumulative amount of money received from the Fund. The 'relevant respects' examined here are a limited number of broad categories.

The value of the items that each family has received from the Fund has varied considerably. The mean cumulative grant of £291 for the whole period hides very great variations. The size distribution of grants is summarised in Figure 4.1 on p. 52 and they range from a single grant of £2.50 for a mattress cover to grants totalling £3,762 for major house adaptations for a family with two cerebral palsied children. In theory, this variation could be equitable – the cases may be so unlike as to justify being treated as differently as this. What has to be established is whether and to what extent there were unjustifiable variations resulting from the discretionary administration of the Fund. In the analysis below, variations are divided into those which prima facie appear to be unjustifiable, those where there are possible justifications, and those where there are probable justifications.

First, it is necessary to say a little more about the overriding variations that arise as a result of the date of the first application (see Figure 12.1). Some of the factors contributing to this variation could in principle be justified. For instance, grants varying with inflation, or early applicants receiving additional payments as their needs change, or new needs develop, may be justified. However, variations resulting from adaptations in policy may be less easy to justify from the applicants' point of view. Thus, families could ask for and receive a grant of up to £750 for a second-hand car during the first two years of the Fund but as a result of policy changes in mid-1975, families applying after that – even if they were identical with earlier applicants in all relevant respects – could receive only a grant of up to £240 for a year's car hire. This type of inequity, though possibly inevitable from an administrative viewpoint, was nevertheless a source of grievance: some families could not understand why they could receive only car hire while others with similar or lesser needs had received a car.

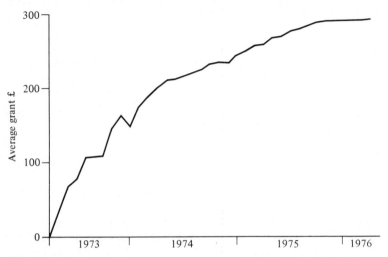

*Figure 12.1    Cumulative average grant – April 1973 to March 1976*

## Variations that may not be justifiable

If what a family received from the Fund depended to some extent on the knowledge, training, values, competence, or prejudice of those handling its case, it is difficult to see how such a variation can be justified. One of the great dilemmas in a discretionary system is that it relies on individual employees using discretionary judgments. If that discretion is limited by set criteria, then flexibility – the advantage of discretion – is diminished, but if discretion is given free rein, then equitable treatment rests on the identical judgments by employees. Initially, the Fund relied for the most part on the discretionary judgments of professionally qualified social workers. Later, some fixed criteria were introduced and a body of agents was appointed and trained to carry out the majority of visits to families' homes. There is some evidence that these measures increased uniformity in making decisions. However, there is also evidence that the grants received by families did vary to some extent according to who carried out the visit. Some social workers' reports were slipshod, others were well informed about the Fund and evidenced remarkable care, imagination and a clear concern to ensure that families were fully informed of the help that was available from the Fund and other agencies. To some extent these variations could be ironed out when the file was scrutinised at the York office. However, there was a limit to the extent to which social workers based at York could negotiate cases, and except in the cases of the most obviously incompetent reports, they relied on the judgment of the visiting social workers.

In Table 12.1 the mean grant given to families in each of the first four years is compared for those where the initial home visit was done by an agent of the Fund and those where the visit was done by another social worker – usually an employee of the social services department.

*Table 12.1   Mean size of grant by type of worker visiting the family*

|  | Family Fund agent | | | | Other social worker | | | |
|---|---|---|---|---|---|---|---|---|
|  | N | % | Mean | SD | N | % | Mean | SD |
| First year | 970 | 22.6 | 445 | 351 | 3,316 | 77.4 | 418 | 352 |
| Second year | 3,585 | 35.2 | 370 | 309 | 6,591 | 64.8 | 370 | 329 |
| Third year | 4,253 | 50.7 | 280 | 220 | 4,129 | 49.3 | 279 | 238 |
| Fourth year | 1,123 | 53.7 | 201 | 148 | 968 | 46.3 | 202 | 177 |
| Over all | 9,931 | 39.8 | 320 | 273 | 15,004 | 60.2 | 344 | 311 |

At first glance it appears that families visited by agents of the Fund received lower grants on average than those visited by other workers, but this difference is merely a function of the fact that later applicants (who received smaller grants) were more likely to be visited by an agent. If this variation is controlled by looking at the mean size of grant within each time period, the size of grant is identical except for the first year of the Fund's operation, when agents were recommending larger grants than other social workers.

There was one further opportunity during the experimental period of the Fund to analyse the impact of different methods of administration on variations in what families received. Up to January 1974, all reports sent to York by visiting social workers were vetted by professionally qualified social workers on the staff. In early 1974, to increase the throughput of grants, applications were divided into two groups: those where the request was of a straightforward nature, the child clearly qualified and no further inquiries were needed before a grant could be given; and those where some further inquiries were needed before a grant could be given. The first type was dealt with by one of two non-professionally qualified workers acting as 'rapid processors' operating a routine vetting and recommending system; the second type by social workers in the normal manner.

To test the hypothesis that families dealt with by the rapid process might do worse, samples were taken of cases completed by the rapid processors and the qualified social workers. No significant differences were found in the mean grants per family or the mean numbers of items given either by the different methods of operation or by individual workers within them.

In conclusion, it was found that what families got from the Fund depended to some extent on who visited them to do the assessment, and particularly in the earliest phase of the work, agents employed by the Fund tended to recommend higher grants on average than workers already employed in another agency. However, while these differences existed (and they are significant at 95 per cent level), they really only account for a small amount of the variation in the level of grants over all and there are wider differences between other factors.

## Variations that are possibly justifiable

There are two variations in the level of grant between families that are possibly justifiable: these are the area where the family lives, and the social class of the head of the family. These will be discussed in turn.

### 1    *Area*

There were considerable variations in the mean size of grants made to families living in different regions of the UK from £278 in Northern Ireland to £351 in Wales. These variations are summarised by region in Table 12.2.

There are a number of possible explanations for these regional differences. One hypothesis is that the variation may have been a result of the influence of the social workers visiting families in each area. For example, a particularly energetic and efficient agent doing most of her visits in one local area may have been responsible for an increase in the mean level of payments to families in that area. It is probable that influences of this type would have been rather diffuse because agents tended to visit families in different local authority areas and where local authority workers did the visits, more than one worker would visit families. However, the Fund staff in York thought that local agents may have been responsible for the high average grants in some areas including Redbridge (Mean - £454), Greenwich (£389), Bexley (£384), and Tower Hamlets (£380). Another possible reason to account for the variation in the size of grants is the variation in the quality of the

*Table 12.2  Mean size of grant by region*

| Region | N | Mean | SD |
|---|---|---|---|
| Northern | 1,598 | 309 | 277 |
| Yorks. and Humberside | 2,108 | 333 | 303 |
| West Midlands | 2,215 | 326 | 290 |
| East Anglia | 583 | 275 | 258 |
| South-East | 6,386 | 341 | 306 |
| North-West | 3,364 | 333 | 282 |
| E. Midlands | 1,701 | 307 | 263 |
| South-West | 1,549 | 290 | 287 |
| Wales | 1,596 | 351 | 308 |
| Northern Ireland | 1,369 | 278 | 282 |
| Scotland | 2,726 | 346 | 309 |
| Total | 25,195 | 326 | 294 |

*Note*: $F = 13.5$ df $10/25184$. Significant at 99 per cent level.

services in the different area. To test this hypothesis an analysis was carried out to examine whether there was any relationship between the mean size of grant and the level of provision in a particular area. An index of provision was produced by taking the number of handicapped children assisted with an aid, adaptation, telephone, radio and TV per 1,000 children under sixteen for each local authority. The correlation of the aids per 1,000 children against the mean £ granted in each area was +0.19 (not significant). Therefore, we concluded that there is no relationship between the level of local authority provision and the size of grant given by the Family Fund.

## 2  Social class

Table 12.3 shows how the amount of money granted by the Fund varied by social class.

Social class is only a crude indicator of living standards, but in general one can certainly expect families and single parents in social classes IV and V to be worse off than the families of non-manual workers. It appears from these results that families who were less well-off received on average smaller grants from the Family Fund. This was certainly true in the first three years of the Fund's operation and while the differences began to narrow following the decision not to make grants for the purchase of second-hand cars and adaptations, the over-all difference remained.

What families received from the Fund depended on how much they

Table 12.3　Mean size of grant by class

| | I, II and III non-manual | | | III manual | | | IV and V | | | Single parents | | |
|---|---|---|---|---|---|---|---|---|---|---|---|---|
| | N | Mean | SD | N | Mean | SD | N | Mean | SD | N | Mean | SD |
| First year | 724 | 469 | 393 | 1,723 | 453 | 361 | 876 | 399 | 338 | 593 | 333 | 286 |
| Second year | 1,834 | 395 | 363 | 4,745 | 391 | 318 | 2,065 | 345 | 285 | 1,142 | 297 | 266 |
| Third year | 1,811 | 296 | 254 | 3,641 | 290 | 234 | 1,697 | 266 | 207 | 1,012 | 240 | 192 |
| (Fourth year) | 429 | 202 | 139 | 1,007 | 202 | 160 | 323 | 186 | 124 | 267 | 199 | 136 |
| Total | 4,798 | 352 | 325 | 11,116 | 350 | 299 | 4,961 | 317 | 271 | 3,014 | 276 | 242 |

asked for. Inevitably, middle- and upper-income families are more articulate and have higher aspirations. They might already possess the cheaper items that the Fund offered and they were more likely to seek help with the more expensive ones – adaptations, equipment, and cars. Lower-income families feel stress because they lack the cheaper and more basic items – clothing, bedding, and furniture. Even if they aspired to a car (the most common expensive item), they may have been refused if the Fund felt that they could not afford to run it.

These variations were the inevitable result of the terms of reference of the Fund and its administrative procedures. Its aim was to relieve stress in families arising out of the care of a handicapped child. The Fund believed that the best way of identifying what might relieve stress was to ask the parents. One of the earliest principles decided was that there should be no means test. Not only would such a test have added enormously to the complexity of administration and conflicted with the discretion and flexibility of the operation, but it was also recognised that even relatively well-off families experienced difficulty in finding the money to acquire some of the more expensive items given by the Fund.

Regard was to be given to 'social and economic circumstances' but only 0.5 per cent of applicants were rejected on these grounds (see chapter 4). One way in which the Fund might have ensured that 'the inarticulate' obtained the items they needed would have been to ask the visiting social worker to check whether each family visited had each of the items that the Fund could and would give and that would relieve stress. Although the Fund did encourage visiting social workers to use their imagination and think of new and original ways of helping, it was always wary of agents going to families with a checklist of items and recommending everything that they needed and that would relieve stress. If they had done this without limiting criteria, the money available would have been quickly exhausted: with them, the discretion and flexibility of the social workers and the Fund would have been circumscribed until every item given had its own eligibility test.

It is thought to be a common phenomenon in social policy that the more articulate derive greater benefit from social services, but where this occurs, it does because they are more likely to ask for a service. In the field of cash benefits – apart from the issue of take-up – benefits are either distributed as an *equal* sum to each person who falls into a certain category of need, or they may vary progressively according to means. In contrast, the Fund has been distributing a *variable* sum to those in certain categories of need and that variable sum has borne a regressive relationship to means. This is a novel result of the exercise of discretion and difficult to justify in terms of the principle of equity outlined above or traditions in the administration of benefits.

Variation by social class in the size of grants might have been justifiable if the grants had been larger for poorer families. The converse was true. However, as can be seen in Table 12.3, the variation by social class has diminished and there are other factors associated with wider variations in the mean size of grants given by the Fund.

**Variations that are probably justifiable**

*Age*

The influence of a child's age on the needs of a family is likely to be complex. For example, as a child grows older, the physical burdens of care are likely to increase (though there are some conditions where capacity for self-care increases with age). On the other hand, parents of young children are less likely to have acquired the items that the Fund gives, and may therefore be more likely to ask for them. Table 12.4 summarises the variations over time in the average grant to families with disabled children of pre-school, primary school, and secondary school ages at the times of their application.

*Table 12.4    Mean size of grant by age*

| | Age at application | | | | | | | | |
|---|---|---|---|---|---|---|---|---|---|
| | 0–5 | | | 6–10 | | | 11–16 | | |
| | N | Mean | SD | N | Mean | SD | N | Mean | SD |
| First year | 1,330 | 460 | 360 | 1,647 | 446 | 356 | 1,383 | 360 | 332 |
| Second year | 3,931 | 382 | 332 | 3,756 | 390 | 322 | 2,517 | 324 | 306 |
| Third year | 3,415 | 283 | 224 | 2,852 | 292 | 241 | 2,048 | 256 | 219 |
| Fourth year | 949 | 208 | 149 | 695 | 203 | 140 | 495 | 181 | 203 |
| Total | 9,625 | 341 | 297 | 8,950 | 355 | 303 | 6,443 | 299 | 284 |

In each period the pre-school and primary school age children received a larger average grant than the 11–16-year-olds.

*Family composition*

As with age, the influences of the family type and size are likely to be complex. Large families can be expected to be more hard pressed; on the other hand, they may be longer established and have acquired the range of assets that the Fund granted. There was, in fact, little difference in the mean size of grants to large and small two-parent families but those to single-parent families tended to be smaller (see Table 12.5). This variation between two-parent and single-parent families diminished over time.

*Table 12.5   Mean size of grant by family composition*

| Family composition | N | Mean | SD |
|---|---|---|---|
| Small two-parent families (less than three children) | 11,725 | 338 | 305 |
| Large two-parent families (three + children) | 10,078 | 333 | 296 |
| Unmarried mothers | 320 | 267 | 199 |
| Divorced/separated mothers | 2,009 | 272 | 239 |
| Widows | 520 | 253 | 255 |
| Single fathers | 154 | 247 | 230 |
| Total | 24,806 | 328 | 295 |

*Disability*

Over recent years, as new benefits for the disabled have been introduced and new principles have begun to govern the criteria adopted for allocating these benefits, the old principles of allocation based on a test of means or on contribution conditions have been displaced by a disability test. For example, the attendance allowance is awarded on a test of capacity for self-care or attendance needs, with a higher rate given to those with a greater handicap, and the mobility allowance is assessed on the basis of walking capacity. The principle that the most severely disabled should have priority in the allocation of benefits was enunciated in a White Paper:[5]

> Better provision for the severely disabled must come before
> further provision for the less severely disabled.

The Family Fund was also restricted to the 'very severely disabled' but in view of the variation in the size of grants made to different families, did the amount of help given vary according to the degree of disability of the children? The question has been examined in a number of different ways.

1   *Handicapping disorder or disease.*   Table 12.6 shows that

there have been substantial differences in the mean size of grants made to families with children with different disorders. In general, it appears that children with disorders such as spina bifida, cerebral palsy, and muscular dystrophy have received larger grants than those with mental handicaps and sensory disorders. The deaf and blind have also received smaller grants. These differences are certainly partly a function of the needs that arise from different conditions but they are also probably a function of what items families with different types of handicapped children sought and what the Fund was prepared to give. Thus, families with children with mobility handicaps would tend to ask for and receive help with cars, car hire, or other aids and adaptations to ease mobility, whereas children with sensory handicaps would tend to ask for educational toys, TV links, and speech trainers, none of which the Fund was generally prepared to provide because they were items that should have been obtainable from existing authorities.

*Table 12.6   Mean size of grant by disease*

| Principal cause of handicap (extract) | N | Mean | SD |
|---|---|---|---|
| Mental illness (autism) | 1,119 | 360 | 365 |
| Mental subnormality | 8,091 | 290 | 249 |
| Cerebral palsy | 4,471 | 359 | 304 |
| Epilepsy | 768 | 305 | 267 |
| Other CNS | 517 | 352 | 278 |
| Heart disease | 453 | 267 | 304 |
| Deafness | 1,099 | 202 | 181 |
| Blindness | 452 | 280 | 276 |
| Muscular dystrophy | 762 | 432 | 378 |
| Bone diseases | 352 | 309 | 282 |
| Spina bifida | 4,938 | 435 | 336 |
| Other congenital diseases | 605 | 300 | 296 |

2   *Disability and handicap.*   In the follow-up survey, children were classified according to the Jaehnig scale.[6] The results in Table 12.7 were obtained in a correlation analysis of the parts of the Jaehnig scale and the mean size of grant.

These results indicated that there was no relationship between the level of grants and the over-all capacity of the child but there was a slight tendency for the most immobile children and the most mentally handicapped children to receive larger grants. These findings were confirmed by an analysis of applicants to the Fund after April 1976. Applicants were rated according to their disability, child handicap, and parental handicap.[7] The correlation in Table 12.8 was obtained.

*Table 12.7   Size of grant by degree of handicap*

| Degree of | N | Correlation with mean size of grant |
|---|---|---|
| Mobility handicap | 303 | −0.25 (significant at 99 per cent level) |
| Comprehension | 303 | −0.15 (significant at 99 per cent level) |
| Capacity for self-care | 303 | −0.03 (not significant) |
| Over all | 303 | −0.01 (not significant) |

*Table 12.8   Size of grant by degree of disability and handicap*

| | N | Correlation with mean grant |
|---|---|---|
| Disability | 2,144 | 0.11 (significant at 99 per cent level) |
| Child handicap | 2,144 | 0.15 (significant at 99 per cent level) |
| Parental handicap | 2,144 | 0.16 (significant at 99 per cent level) |

Although there is a significant positive relationship between disability and handicap and the size of Family Fund grants, the size of the correlation coefficient is not large and the relationship is therefore weak.

Having found that there are variations in the grants given to families by the Family Fund according to the age of the child, family type, disease, disability and handicap, social class, area and agency making the report, which of these factors associated with variations in the size of grant is most important? The problem with the analysis up to this point is that the variables examined are not independent of one another. For instance, the prevalence of certain diseases varies with social class[8] and the variations in the mean size of grant by disease may merely be the result of variations by social class and vice versa.

It is possible to give some indication of the relative importance of the variables using a step-wise variance analysis programme (automatic interaction detection (AID)) developed by Sonquist and Morgan.[9] AID assists in selecting those combinations of variables that are *most* related to variation in the size of grants. The results are best expressed in the form of a 'tree structure'. Thanks to the number of cases in the Family Fund analysis, the AID analysis split the Family Fund cases into thirty-nine groups. The most important results were obtained in the first five splits and a tree structure of these splits is given in Figure 12.2.

The first split divides the cases into those applying in years one and two and those applying in years three and four. The second split divides the former group according to social class - single parents and unskilled manual are split off from the other classes. This latter group is again split by time and then year two is split by region and so on.

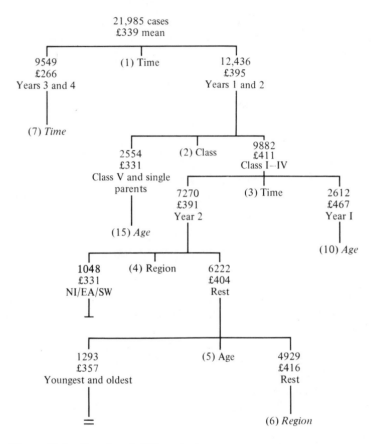

*Figure 12.2    Results of AID analysis*

The meaning of this is that the period when the family first applied is the most important factor in determining the size of the grant. Having controlled for that, class for the earlier applicants is the most important factor in determining the size of grants - then time again, then region, and then age. In combination with these variables, agency of report and family composition do not appear to have an influence on variations in the size of grants.

## Conclusion

What can be concluded from this examination of the distribution of cash grants using a system characterised by discretionary principles? Has it been possible in a discretionary system to ensure that like cases were treated alike? The analysis so far has, of necessity, been of a general summary nature, whereas concern about equity derives from a comparison of individual cases. From such a comparison, it has certainly been possible to isolate cases where, on the basis of the principle of equity, there are prima facie grounds for saying that the distribution of support by the Family Fund has been unfair. For instance, why should Mrs W., a separated mother living in a one-room flat with a totally physically and mentally handicapped child, receive only £30 for clothes, while Mr and Mrs B., with a hydrocephalic child with similar handicaps, get £700 for a car, tax and insurance, plus a washing-machine? It is very difficult to argue that these differences reflect variations in stress felt by the families. It appears much more likely that in one case either the family obtained all that it asked for or the visiting agent explored other needs that were not expressed in its original application. In the other case, the agent merely rubber-stamped what the family asked for. Added together and analysed as a whole, variations in the treatment of cases have not been as dramatic as the example quoted; nevertheless, they have existed. A middle-class family living in south-east England, visited by a Fund's agent, applying early to the Fund, with a child suffering from muscular dystrophy, having two parents, and aged between five and ten, could expect to get a larger grant from the Fund than a working-class single parent living in Northern Ireland, applying recently to the Fund, with a deaf child aged over eleven, and visited by a social services department worker. These cases were unlike and have been treated unlike, but it is doubtful whether the respects in which they were unlike justified the way in which they were treated. Different levels of grant could be justified on the basis of different handicaps, of different ages of the children or even of area if there was evidence that the variation was related to level of provision. However, it is very difficult to justify smaller grants to single-parent families, working-class families, families who apply to the Fund late and who happen to be visited by less competent social workers. Certainly, to families and the 'taxpayer' these differences are hard to understand. However, there are three arguments for discounting these inequities.

First, it could be argued that these variations were to a great extent the result of the inexperience of the Fund in the early period, and that as policy has developed, there has been a marked diminution in them. Grants have become more standardised; new applicants are now more likely to get smaller grants of less varied amounts; variations by family type and dependent on the social worker making the report no longer exist, while those by class, region, child's age, and handicapping condition have diminished. Nevertheless, they still exist and in individual cases there are striking differences in the level of grants awarded.

Second, it could be argued that the aim of the Family Fund was not to treat families equitably but to use the money available to relieve stress. The issue is not the amount of money given to a family but whether the grant achieved a reduction in stress. The conclusion of chapter 8 was that grants, large or small, did not do so.

Finally, any inequity might be offset by the flexibility, speed and ease of administration and general responsiveness of a discretionary system. Any attempt to restrict the freedom of social workers by imposing further criteria would introduce further rigidity into the system. This was certainly a view held by the managers of the Trust:[10]

> There is no entitlement and because we are using discretion
> flexibly we cannot be called upon to show that our grants are
> equitable.

# 13 The boundary problem

There is no single agency responsible for meeting the needs of families with handicapped children and the Family Fund has had to operate in a multi-organisational context. In chapter 2, it was suggested that one of the government's motives for creating a new independent agency was to bypass the rigidities, impecuniosity, and inertia of the existing agencies. As far as the families were concerned, and certainly in the earlier period of its existence, the ability of the Fund to complement existing provision was something of a godsend. As well as meeting needs that no statutory agency had powers to meet, it could enlarge the work of other agencies by increasing the range of choice and the level of provision. For example, families who lived in social service department areas where no provision was made for holidays for handicapped children could obtain help from the Fund. In these situations, it played an equalising role. In other ways the Fund acted to 'top up' the provision made by local agencies – for instance, by making a grant to enable the parents to go on holiday with a child who was being financed by the local authority. Sir Keith Joseph had said:[1]

> It is . . . intended that this money . . . should serve to complement the services already being provided by statutory and voluntary bodies to help the families concerned.

However, the guide-lines agreed with the DHSS stated:[2]

> It is for the trustees to decide the form of help which shall be given to eligible families to complement the services provided by statutory and voluntary bodies but this help may include goods or services which is within the power of the statutory services to provide.

The circular to local authorities announcing the establishment of the Fund had warned that they 'should not however regard this as in any way relieving them of their statutory responsibilities'.[3] Much of the early work of the Panel in laying down internal guide-lines about what items could or could not be given by the Fund was directed to the questions whether the item was obtainable from an existing service or not, and, if it was, was the Fund complementing or substituting for that help? One of the problems faced was in deciding what items could be given by other agencies – cars and washing-machines clearly could not be given by other statutory agencies, while health care and education certainly should be provided. However, other items were more problematical – fares to hospitals, visits to special schools, nursing and mobility aids, house adaptations. All of these could be provided under existing legislation but in some areas they were being provided either not at all or only to a very limited extent.

The Panel divided items into three categories:

1    Those such as education, medical treatment and housing, where there was a clear statutory responsibility and the Fund would not help.

2    Holidays, fares to visit children in hospital, aids and adaptations and the like, where the Fund would complement existing provision.

3    Transport, washing-machines and other aids where there was no statutory responsibility.

The second category created most difficulties. If a family applied for an item that could be given by another agency, a good deal of effort had to be devoted to finding out whether the responsible agency was prepared to help. If it was unable to help or would do so only after undue delay, the Fund reserved the right to provide the help itself. Although these negotiations were time-consuming, they often resulted in an offer being made by the agency which had previously refused to help. For example, one director of social work in Scotland wrote:

> Mrs B., our social worker, was in error in suggesting that your Family Fund make some provision toward the cost of providing a shower unit. This authority, in common with other local authorities, has a statutory obligation to provide necessary aids and adaptations.

The task of negotiation with other agencies was not made easier by the fact that the Fund's operations coincided with local authority reorganisation and the new authorities either did not have policies or had inherited two or more policies (and levels of expenditure) from their predecessors.

## A study of the overlap with other agencies

A small study was made of the files of a sample of 158 families who had applied to the Fund for items that could have been given by other agencies, and the investigation reveals the range of explanations given by authorities for not helping families.

Of the families in the sample, thirteen asked the Fund for telephones. In two of these cases the social services authority eventually agreed to help. Those who refused help gave the following reasons: budget exhausted (2), handicap not severe enough (1), parental income too high (1), family not isolated enough (1). Two authorities simply did not provide telephones for handicapped children.

Of the families in the sample, fifty-five sought help with adaptations. In seventeen of these the social services department was persuaded to meet the whole of the cost and partial contributions were made in a further nine. Among those unable to assist, the following reasons were given for their refusal: budget exhausted (10), request not the direct result of handicap (4), parental income too high (5), handicap not severe enough (1). One authority, Bolton, suggested that instead of a downstairs extension, the handicapped child's bed should be brought downstairs and put in the kitchen. (The child was incontinent and the bathroom was upstairs.) Northamptonshire admitted that their 1974-5 budget for home adaptations was *less* than the £1,700 needed by *one* family to build an extra bedroom.

Of the nineteen applications to the Family Fund for assistance with family holidays that were examined, six had received a local authority contribution towards the child's holiday. The most common reason given by authorities for not contributing, was that they only provided holidays in their own homes.

Of the sixteen Family Fund applications analysed for wheelchairs and other personal aids, seven were eventually met by the appropriate authority, two were refused by the authority on medical grounds, and in one case Croydon stated that the type of chair requested was not available from the social services department.

Of the requests to the Family Fund analysed, six involved the provision of day-time or domiciliary care for the handicapped child. Two requests for nursery places were met by the social services departments, but a request for the taxi fares to take a child to nursery was refused by Plymouth City Council. Of the three requests for home helps, one was met by the social services department.

Of the cases examined, twelve were applications for clothing, shoes, prams and furniture. In three cases the local authority was persuaded to help. Derbyshire stated that their budget for clothing was inadequate to meet the request, while Glasgow said they could only supply a pram if it was donated to them by a voluntary organisation.

In addition, eight cases were analysed where the social services departments had powers to make payments under Section I of the Children and Young Persons Act 1963, three for rent arrears, and five for fuel debts. In only one case was the local authority persuaded to meet the whole debt, and in two more a partial contribution was made. In the other areas budgets were inadequate. The City of Cardiff refused a payment because the children were already in care. The Fund's social workers felt that payment would have prevented the mother's eviction and enabled the children to return home.

Of the applications, two involved help towards school clothing, and six involved transport to school. In only one case was the local education authority persuaded to meet the family's request completely, and in three more a partial contribution was made.

Of the seven applications analysed that related to the powers of area health authorities, four were for nappies and three for fares for hospital visits. Of the applications for nappies, three were referred back to the appropriate athority by the Family Fund, but in only one case was there evidence that the request was eventually met.

Only three of the Family Fund cases analysed related to the powers of the Supplementary Benefits Commission to make exceptional circumstance additions. One of these was for fares, one for a special diet and laundry expenses for an incontinent child, and the third family needed extra heating, a special diet, and money for fares for their child. There was no record of any of these families ever having received payments from the Supplementary Benefits Commission to cover these extra costs.

Of the thirty-five requests to the Family Fund for which exceptional needs payments could have been made, by far the most common single items were for clothing (sixteen cases) and bedding (four cases).

At the time of the study the Family Fund tended to assist families on supplementary benefit regardless of the responsibilities of the Commission and so in twenty-three of the thirty-eight cases examined there was no record of their dealings with the Commission. In nine cases payments had been made that were felt to be inadequate for the child's needs and in six cases applications had been refused.

## The Fund's response to overlap

The administrative burden imposed by the advocacy involved in persuading local health and social services to meet the needs that they had powers to meet was one of the factors that led the Fund to reappraise its policy. Social workers were having to write two or three times to local authorities to get an indication of what they intended to do.

> There is at present a backlog of reports awaiting action involving a delay of four to six weeks before grants can be processed for action . . . a more serious problem is the large volume of letters which have accumulated and which the filing staff cannot cope with . . . . Enquiries by telephone are also delaying work.[4]

A report on the workings of the Fund was prepared for the DHSS. It contained the following paragraph:[5]

> The Trust feels some concern at the extent to which it is being asked to use its powers to give help which is clearly within the competence of statutory bodies, especially the social services departments. Requests of this sort have increased markedly with the present restriction on local authority budgets. Some authorities accept readily that a particular need should be met from local authority funds, but express the hope that the Family Fund will help because local funds are exhausted. Other authorities exercise considerable ingenuity in discovering the kind of grants the Fund will make, and thus concentrate their own resources elsewhere. The Trust feared this development at the outset; for this reason it asked for, and received, authority to respond to a request, notwithstanding that the help sought lay within the powers of a public authority. The trustees accepted the responsibility to relieve stress arising directly from the presence of a congenitally severely handicapped child in ways which complement the functions of local authorities. They have been able to meet categories of need which it would be extremely difficult for any particular local authority to regard as within its competence. . . . The Fund is now being asked increasingly to meet needs which are clearly within the competence of local authorities, but which are declined simply by reason of the limited resources at present available to the authority. . . . A grant in aid to the Trust which may have been justified by evidence of unmet need cannot be depended on if it is to be used simply to add a measure of flexibility to the allocation of limited resources by local authorities.

The DHSS was less worried than the Family Fund by this passing on of responsibility. At the next meeting in December, the DHSS official on the Management Committee felt that it was inevitable that the Family Fund would supplement as well as complement social services provision because social services had such wide powers. Later, in a letter (9 December 1974) commenting on the points raised in the Fund's paper, it did not refer to the issue and only urged the Fund to continue to make grants for the costs of visiting children in hospital (another overlapping function that had been referred to in the Fund's paper).

By April 1975, the belief was growing among the Fund's staff that economic pressures on local authorities meant that the Fund was increasingly being forced to substitute for local authority provision and because by this time it was clear that it might cause the Fund's finances to be drained with embarrassing speed, the DHSS also became concerned.

There was no statistical evidence that requests for aids and adaptations were increasing. The proportion of families asking for adaptations was always small and had declined somewhat from 7.1 per cent in December 1973 to 6.2 per cent in March 1975. Requests for aids had also declined from 4.1 per cent in December 1973 to 3.5 per cent in March 1975. The belief that demands on the Fund were being increasingly transferred from local authorities probably stemmed from requests that came to the attention of the Fund's managers, coupled with the fact that the backlog of cases not dealt with tended to contain a larger proportion of requests for aids and adaptations because they took longer to deal with.

The Trust's resolve was strengthened when the Secretary of State for Social Services announced:[6]

> I am satisfied that local authorities are aware of the mandatory
> nature of Section 2. Once they accept that need exists in respect
> of one of the services listed in the Section it is incumbent on them
> to make arrangements to meet that need.

Before this announcement neither the Family Fund nor social services departments were certain that local authorities had a mandatory duty to meet needs even if they recognised that a need existed. A meeting was arranged between members of the Trust and the Executive Committee of the Association of Directors of Social Services. The Trust presented proposals that the Directors accepted. In future, the Fund would only consider requests where it was[7]

> urgent to prevent a breakdown in family functioning but
> exceptional circumstances place provision of the particular help
> requested outside the duty of the local authority . . . under

Section 2 of the Chronically Sick and Disabled Persons Act
1973 and limited resources make it impossible to provide adequate
help in the exercise of permissive function under Section 29 of the
National Assistance Act.

For its part, the Trust agreed not to tell families who asked the Fund
for help with aids and adaptations that the local authority had a specific
duty to help.

The result of this step was that the Fund effectively stopped making
grants for aids and adaptations. Families who applied for these items
were sent a standard letter informing them that the Fund could not
help and suggesting that their local social services department might
offer 'advice and help'.

Although the Fund moved out of provision of aids and adaptations
it continued to provide help with telephones and holidays – both of
which were social services department responsibilities. The telephone
criteria were only marginally more liberal than those generally adopted
by social services departments and expenditure on telephones was not
excessive.

Holidays presented less difficulty, both in numbers being
referred and the amount of money involved. Grants for
family holidays should continue as before.[8]

If the original motive for stopping aids and adaptations was the administrative burden they imposed and the belief that local authorities were
using the Fund to replace their own provision, it became linked later in
1975 with the attempts to reduce the rate of expenditure of the Fund.
The Fund also altered its approach to applications for other items
which other agencies had powers to provide. As we have already described in chapter 9, families on supplementary benefit who asked for
items that could be given as exceptional needs payments were referred
back to the Supplementary Benefits Commission before they could be
helped by the Fund. The decision to stop car grants and give car-hire
grants equivalent to the mobility allowance to those not eligible for it
was also taken partly to avoid overlap with this.

## Negative competition

Overlapping functions in the private sector lead to competition for
business – for example between one washing powder and another. In
the public sector there *are* examples of agencies competing with each
other to provide a service but when this occurs in the provision of

social services, the result is commonly negative competition. If more than one agency share responsibility, they tend to try and 'pass the buck'. The Supplementary Benefits Commission, because it is a residual service, tends to suffer from boundary disputes. Its powers to help with exceptional needs overlap with social services departments' powers to make cash payments to prevent children coming into care and with education authorities' powers to provide school clothing. Also in its 1976 report[9] the Commission pointed out how its powers to help with housing costs overlapped with rent rebates. Boundary disputes between the health and personal social services also occur most commonly in the fields of after-care or the long-term care of the mentally ill or handicapped. Despite the efforts to settle these types of boundary dispute by joint financing arrangements or agreement about responsibility, there is inevitably a tendency for the consumer to suffer. The overlap problem affected the Family Fund because it was established with limited resources and wide powers to make discretionary grants in an area where other agencies had wide powers to help in similar ways. Yet for four reasons the provision made by those agencies was very limited.

First, the legislation governing the powers of the existing agencies was for the most part permissive and not mandatory, and central government lacked the power through the block grant system to ensure that money made available for the disabled is actually spent on them. As a report on the implementation of the Chronically Sick and Disabled Persons Act pointed out, the £270 million Sir Keith Joseph made available to implement the Act in November 1971 could have been spent on roads or home helps instead.[10]

Second, when, after 1975, the Secretary of State confirmed that Section 2 of the Chronically Sick and Disabled Persons Act was mandatory, central government lacked the ability to oblige local authorities to make provision. The duty imposed by Section 2 was subject to the local authority accepting that there was a need and it was left to the authority to define it: 'Criteria of need are matters for authorities to determine in the light of resources.'[11]

Third, where the restraint in public expenditure forced local authorities to restrict what help they did provide, the DHSS was unwilling to exhort them by means of circulars to improve provision at the same time as other circulars were stating:[12]

No further growth in services is provided for. The government recognise therefore that local authorities will not be able to meet all the demands for these services and that difficult choices will

have to be made in selecting priorities . . . some services may
have to be provided at a reduced scale.

Fourth, the level of provision by social services departments in the
area of overlap was very low. The legislative powers were relatively
new ones and had not been absorbed into the mainstream of social
services' spending before restraint on public expenditure restricted
expansion and then led to cuts in provision. The best source of data
on what was being provided is not very reliable[13] and is only available
for England. Although there is no indication from the statistics in Table
13.1 that provision deteriorated (except for holidays in 1974–5 and
telephones in 1975–6), it does show how low provision was.

The figures in brackets in Table 13.1 are the numbers of families in
the UK helped by the Family Fund in the same period. The classification
of items is not strictly comparable and gives a rough indication only.
In a number of cases, items classified as aids in the DHSS statistics are
not classified as aids in Family Fund statistics. The totals for the Family
Fund are the totals of all families helped with any item, not just items
that could have been given by social services. These data are not available.

Despite the limitations of the figures, comparison between the
provision by social services in England and that by the Family Fund in
the UK provides some indication of their respective contributions.

## 1   Telephones

The Fund carried the main burden in the provision of telephones. The
social services criteria were so restricted that the Fund, even with its
own limited categories that could be helped, was giving many more
telephones than were the social services. The reduction in the number
in 1975–6 may have been the result of the Fund's intervention or of
public expenditure cuts.

## 2   Adaptations

In terms of the numbers, the contribution of the Fund towards adaptations appears only minor, and it declined after 1975, while local
authority adaptations continued to expand. However, the figures in
Table 13.1 cannot be taken at face value. About half the adaptations
made by local authorities were to local authority dwellings, and about
two-thirds of those to private dwellings cost less than £150 each. The
Fund's assistance was restricted to private adaptations and although it
is not possible to say exactly what the average Fund grant for adaptations

*Table 13.1   Numbers of certain items given to families with handicapped children by social services departments in England*

| Year | Social services (England) | | | | Total households helped (excluding holidays) |
|---|---|---|---|---|---|
| | Telephones | Adaptations | Holidays | Other aids | |
| 1972–3 | 139 | 930 | 4,344 | 1,568 | 2,137 |
| 1973–4 | 205 ( 109) | 1,308 (152) | 5,303 ( 363) | 2,322 (135) | 3,563 ( 4,345) |
| 1974–5 | 278 ( 755) | 1,686 (564) | 5,172 (1,608) | 3,052 (816) | 4,623 (10,402) |
| 1975–6 | 198 (1,087) | 1,944 (341) | 5,867 (2,195) | 3,382 ( 56) | 4,643 ( 8,721) |

*Notes*: Sources of social services statistics:

1972–3 Local Authority Social Services Departments Aids to Households, DHSS SR6 1974.

1973–4 Local Authority Social Services Departments Aids to Households, DHSS SR6 1975.

1974–5 Personal Social Services Local Authority Statistics Aids to Households, DHSS A/F 75/4 1976.

1975–6 Personal Social Services Local Authority Statistics Aids to Households, DHSS A/F 76/4 1977.

was, it was generally considerably higher than the average grant of £300. According to CIPFA, local authorities spent less than £3 million on adaptations in England and Wales in the year ending April 1975.[14] In the same year, only 837 households containing handicapped children received help with adaptations to private property (and only 337 of these cost over £100). Some 18,749 households got help with adaptations so that children in private households constituted 4.5 per cent of the total. If only 4.5 per cent of the £3 million spent on adaptations in England and Wales benefited children in private households, then expenditure on these families by social services departments could have been as little as £135,000. The Family Fund almost certainly spent more than this on that proportion of the 564 families who lived in England and were helped with adaptations in the year ending April 1975.

## 3 Holidays

The number of holidays provided by social services departments declined in 1974-5 but rose again in 1975-6, while the number of families helped with holidays by the Family Fund increased. It is not likely that the decline in social services provision was the direct result of Family Fund provision. More probably, the decline was the result of restraints in local authority expenditure. Family Fund help was not a direct substitute for local authority help, as the Fund assisted with family holidays whereas social services provision tended to be restricted to holidays for the child. However, although local authorities continued to help with more holidays than did the Family Fund, there was, whether by design or otherwise, some shift of responsibility towards the Family Fund.

## 4 Aids

The figures are most unreliable with respect to aids, but it does appear that Fund contributions increased to about a quarter of social services provision in 1974-5 but declined very quickly in 1975-6 with the policy changes that were adopted. Over all, the number of eligible households helped with aids and adaptations has increased since the implementation of the Chronically Sick and Disabled Persons Act. The rate of increase was slower between 1973 and 1976 than it had been between 1972 and 1974. How far this was due to the Family Fund relieving local authorities of their responsibilities and how far it was the result of restraint in public expenditure is impossible to say.

It is impossible to assess the 'cost' of the overlap dilemma – that is, how far the help given by the Family Fund was offset by a reduction, absolute or in growth, of provision by other agencies. As has been argued in chapter 9, the changes brought in by the Fund to match the mobility allowance resulted in a reduction in the level of Fund help given for transport. The officials of the Supplementary Benefits Commission were instructed to disregard the Fund's help and the Fund was later instrumental in a letter being issued to local offices, drawing managers' attention to the exceptional needs of their claimants with disabled children. After the Fund's change of policy on aids and adaptations, there was a drop in the proportion of families receiving this kind of help from 4.8 per cent getting adaptations and 4.7 per cent getting aids in March 1975 to 4.1 per cent getting adaptations and 3.8 per cent getting aids in December 1976. However, this drop was not as dramatic as might have been expected and there is no evidence, as we have seen, that social services provision declined. In other areas of provision, the Fund managed to avoid substituting for existing provision by either finding a complementary role – as in the provision of telephones and holidays – or by not offering help at all or only in very exceptional cases – for example medical treatment, transport for hospital treatment, or wheelchairs. It is probable that some established voluntary organisations in the field were relieved of making small grants to some of their poorer members by the grants for clothing and bedding from the Family Fund.

### Conclusion

The limitations of the provisions made by local authorities and the powerlessness of government to do anything about it were two of the factors that had made it necessary to establish a Fund in the first place. The Fund was founded both because there were gaps in provision *and* because of the inadequate level of existing provision. It was able to fill some of the gaps but it found it could not take on the responsibility for the inadequacy in existing provision. The position might have been different either if existing provision had been able to expand more rapidly, or if the Fund had been financed to enable it to continue to pick up those needs that local authorities were unable to meet. The dilemma of the Fund was that, in abandoning the doctrine that the Fund would provide for unmet needs regardless of the responsibility of other agencies, it was renouncing one feature that made it such an effective source of help for families. In attempting to avoid becoming the dustbin of other agencies' unwanted cases, the Fund either refused help altogether or only agreed to help as a last resort. This meant that families who needed help either did not get it or had to negotiate with social services departments or supplementary benefits before they could be helped. Yet it was precisely this feature of fragmented administration which the Family Fund existed to alleviate.

There have been profits as well as losses arising from the boundary problems. The Fund has had a catalytic effect on some existing services. However, because of the boundary problems, it has not been able to sustain its original flexible and creative role, and has ended by performing more restricted and limited functions than it started with.

# 14    Adequacy of the Family Fund

As soon as Sir Keith Joseph announced the establishment of a Fund of
£3 million to help families with handicapped children, MPs questioned
the adequacy of this sum of money. How far would £3 million, even
with a promise of a further £3 million, go in helping such families? The
previous chapters have contributed to an evaluation of what was
achieved. During the first three years of the Fund's work, £6.8 million
was distributed to 23,468 families. The families received on average
£291 each, or the equivalent of £1.87 per week over the three years.
Of course, the benefit of the Fund's help cannot be assessed only in
cash terms - the items given to families or the things that they were
enabled to buy often brought benefits out of proportion to their cost.
Even families who received only a small grant commonly expressed how
much their morale had been raised by it. For them it had a symbolic
value as a recognition that they were caring for a severely disabled child
and that they deserved help.

In order to assess the contribution made by the Fund to the solution
of the problems of child handicap, it is necessary to view the Fund in
the context of other sources of support for families with handicapped
children.

### Services

Recent years have seen the consolidation of a legislative framework for
the provision of services to disabled people: the reorganisation of local
authority, health, and personal social services; and the introduction of
new cash benefits for which handicapped children are eligible. Yet
families with handicapped children are still not receiving coherent and
comprehensive support to help them to shoulder the burdens of care.
The picture that emerges from applicants to the Family Fund is that
these families are often very isolated. For the most part, they are left
alone to come to terms with the birth and diagnosis of their child's
illness; they continue to cope alone; they meet the child's special
needs from their own resources and if they learn about the benefits
and services that exist, they often do so casually or through their own

efforts; and if they receive help, it may often come after considerable frustration and delay.[1]

Despite the reorganisation of the health services and local government and the unification of the personal social services, the coherence of services for families with disabled children has not necessarily been improved.[2] There is no one unified agency that specialises in the problems associated with child handicap. Families will, if they are lucky, encounter the health services (both in hospital and in the community), special education and education assessment sections of the local education authority, local authority housing departments, social workers, income maintenance and other statutory financial benefits, as well as the Family Fund and voluntary welfare and self-help groups, at different times in their child's life. Thus, families may tend to fall in and out of contact with helping agencies and there is no one *locus* (a 'single door') which they can easily identify as being responsible for furnishing them with information and advice about the range of facilities and benefits available; for supporting them in times of crisis; for arranging a system of relief from the burdens of care; or even just being available for support and encouragement when it is needed.

This continued fragmentation of responsibilities among a number of agencies may have reduced the effectiveness of other moves to rationalise services, and particularly the effectiveness of generic social work and health visiting support. The professional workers with whom a family comes into contact may be unsure of information that lies outside their own sphere of expertise. Social workers may be unfamiliar with the health authority's incontinence service; health visitors may neglect to check whether a family is in receipt of the attendance allowance; and both may forget the extra payments available to families on supplementary benefit who have additional financial burdens caused by the handicapped child. Both of these factors can make it more difficult for the parents of a handicapped child to find out what services and benefits they may be entitled to, and how to set about obtaining them.

Neither the child health nor the personal social services have the resources at present to provide a service of support for this group of families. With the exception of a few notable centres, the paediatric and child health services are hard pressed to cope with the treatment of illness, let alone fulfil secondary and tertiary preventative functions. The personal social services have had difficulties in implementing fully the intentions of Sections 1 and 2 of the Chronically Sick and Disabled Persons Act 1970. Social workers who are carrying heavy case-loads may have to concentrate the bulk of their time and effort into dealing with crises rather than in providing regular support to families who appear to have no immediate pressing needs. Newly referred families may have their practical requests dealt with, but because of the pressure of time and resources, fail to become part of a long-term case-load unless their need for personal support is acute or family breakdown is threatened.

Within the personal social services the shift away from specialist organisations may have increased such problems. Some social services departments are now beginning to introduce specialist teams of social workers to deal with areas of work such as mental health, but it is unlikely that the relatively small group of families with severely handi-capped children in any local area, and which on the whole appear to cope without undue crises, would become the focus of such a division of labour.

A recent Central Council for Education and Training in Social Work report highlights the scant attention which is paid in social work training to work with the handicapped, and this lack of priority means that many social workers who are in touch with families with handicapped children can be ill-equipped to recognise and deal with needs as they arise.[3]

It is in this context that the adequacy of the Family Fund should be assessed. For those involved in the work of the Fund, either as employees or as research workers, there is a danger of exaggerating its importance. The Fund has probably made a greater impression on families just because of the lack of support they receive from other agencies, but it is necessary to record its limitations in the context of the hunger that it and other studies have revealed for both emotional and material support. The Fund has not met this need for a service of sustained and systematic support for families with handicapped children. Fund agents repeatedly drew its attention to families who needed *regular* support - whether advice, advocacy, encouragement, or counselling. They did advise families on issues outside the particular purpose of the Family Fund assessment and in chapter 7 we have seen that the atten-tion and concern given by the visiting social workers was valued by parents. However, the Fund was not established as a social work agency and agents were not encouraged to get involved with families. Any family needing social work support and not getting it was referred to their social services department.

## Benefits

The Fund was never conceived as a source of social work support for families with disabled children and its adequacy should more fairly be assessed in terms of a source of material support.

Since the Fund was founded, there has been little public discussion about cash support for families caring for children with physical or mental impairments. Both policy developments and discussion have concentrated on adults.[4] In their social security proposals for the disabled, the government, with the support of the Opposition, presented[5] and then enacted a non-contributory invalidity benefit for those adults who, if they had been able to work, would have received the invalidity pension: an invalid care allowance for *adult* breadwinners who have to stay at home to look after a disabled person. A non-contributory invalidity benefit for disabled married women unable to do their housework was added after some delay in November 1977. The only new benefit for disabled children has been the mobility allowance, which has been payable to children over five who cannot walk. Apart from the mobility allowance, no new provisions for children were envisaged or discussed in the White Paper. One curious paragraph suggested that there was no need for more money for families with handicapped children.[6]

> Perhaps, particularly in the case of children, the extra cost is an aspect as much of belief as to the benefits which might be gained were extra financial resources available, as it is something based on evidence that more money is actually being spent on disabled individuals than would be spent on the same individuals if they were not disabled.

Yet the paragraphs in the report devoted to disabled children admitted that the presence of such a child in a family could present financial needs for a family in four ways:

1    It could prevent or reduce parents' earnings.

2    It could involve extra costs in providing items to care for or stimulate the child.

3    It could involve payments for services that the parents might normally provide themselves.

4    It could involve additional physical and emotional demands on the parents that might be partially compensated for by cash.

The Secretary of State, in her introduction to the report, stated:[7]

> Where disabled children are concerned we lack adequate information about their numbers and the precise character of their needs,

and the report promised that[8]

the government will be sponsoring research to help answer some of the hitherto unanswered questions about disabled children and their needs.

A good deal of research has now been commissioned by the DHSS and this will be of value in planning future provision. However, research on the Family Fund has already indicated that families with handicapped children have to carry heavy extra expenses and that their incomes tend to be lower than other families'.[9] Given the wide variations in the type and severity of handicap among children, it is difficult to generalise about the type or the level of expenses borne by their families. It is also difficult in practice to say that the problems that families with handicapped children have in paying for these items are not also sometimes shared by all families with dependent children. But the experience of the Family Fund has shown that these needs traverse the whole range of disabilities and are not restricted to the very severely physically or mentally disabled.

It has been estimated that disregarding the income lost to parents of a severely disabled child, the extra expenditure necessary on clothing and bedding, washing and incontinence equipment amounted to an average 'extra cost' of £2.10 per week in 1975.[10]

## Attendance allowance

Up to a point, these needs are already recognised in existing social provision for families with a handicapped child. The motivation for the benefits that exist is not clearly expressed. For instance, the purpose of attendance allowance was described in the House of Commons paper as 'to help those among the disabled who require a considerable degree of personal attention'.[11]

But 'degree of personal attention' is not the purpose of the benefit. The purpose of the benefit is the 'help' that is given, but what is that help for? Was it to provide an income supplement because of loss of earnings or extra expenses? Was it to compensate the child or the parent for loss and damage? Was it to support and encourage families to keep their children at home?

For those families receiving it, the attendance allowance has probably helped with all these things. It is providing a relatively generous tax free and non means-tested cash supplement that is not taken into account in assessing other benefits to about 40,000 of the more severely disabled children in Britain. However, this leaves about 40,000 severely disabled children who do not meet the attendance allowance criteria.

The test of helplessness or need for attendance does not incorporate all those families who need the help that the allowance provides.

In the light of this criticism of the attendance allowance:[12]

> The government [has] carefully considered whether . . . there is a case for change in the scope of the allowance . . . there is no solid basis for a further extension of the allowances . . . further extension would produce a benefit for disablement as such rather than for attendance needs.

This argument is difficult to follow. War pensions have five rates of constant attendance. The attendance allowance as it is paid to children is a recognition of the burden carried by parents and is a compensation for the sacrifices they make on behalf of their disabled children and in the absence of any other benefit for this purpose, it is already a benefit for disablement as such.[13]

However, there are problems in extending the allowance downwards to incorporate children with lesser degrees of attendance requirements. It would be difficult for parliamentary draughtsmen to construct a form of words that would include groups at present excluded from eligibility, such as some children with sensory defects, those at risk of sudden or acute conditions, or those suffering from serious disabilities who have tried to manage, and at the same time exclude the kind of care and attention that would be devoted to a normal child. The attendance allowance would also continue to put a premium on dependency. The harder a child and its parents strove to overcome their disability, the less they would get from the state.

## A comprehensive benefit scheme

In the absence of other benefits, the attendance allowance has become a 'catch-all' scheme, expected to provide compensation, support and encouragement, assistance with extra expenses as well as income maintenance. If it were part of a comprehensive package of benefits for disabled children, its limitations would be easier to justify. A comprehensive income scheme for disabled people has been the demand for many years by representative organisations. In the fullest description of such a scheme, the Disability Alliance recommended a system taking the following form.[14]

1   A disablement allowance paid according to the degree of functional incapacity to compensate disabled people for the extent to which they are restricted from following normal activities.

2   An invalid or disablement pension to be paid to all those who cannot earn.

3   Special allowances to meet the expenses of certain disabilities, including an accommodation allowance.

The need for an invalidity or disablement pension does not arise in the case of disabled children, who, like all children, are expected to be dependent on their parents. But this structure can be adapted to meet the needs that arise in the case of disabled children in the following form:

i   A compensatory payment for the degree of the severity of the disability.

ii   An income to compensate relatives for the sacrifices they make in caring for the disabled child.

iii   A child benefit scheme that bears some relation to the normal costs of child-rearing.

iv   An income to help the disabled person or the family pay for the extra things needed because of the disability.

The first need for a compensatory payment is presently met in those exceptional circumstances where a child's damage can be attributed to the fault of a third party. The government has already accepted responsibility for making such payments to vaccine-damaged children and the Royal Commission on Civil Liability and Compensation for Personal Injury has considered such a scheme for a wider group.

The attendance allowance caters for some relatives in respect of the second need. Although the money received is spent on the extra expenses of disablement, it is given to those families who are most likely to have an income loss because of the need to attend to their child. The third need is met in part by child benefits and child tax allowances. The fourth need for an expenses allowance is met at present by the Family Fund, the mobility allowance, and the service- as opposed to cash-providing agencies.

The mobility allowance has already been discussed in chapter 9. Now that it is to be paid at the rate of £10 per week, it is of greater benefit than it was, but it is still taxable, still payable only to those children who cannot walk and still restricted to children over five. To become a benefit for the expenses of mobility, the allowance needs to escape from the constraints of its conception and design as a benefit primarily concerned to replace the invalid trike for working-age, physically handicapped adults.[15] The criteria need to include all those children who present mobility problems, including uncontrolled epileptics, severe asthmatics, those suffering from cystic fibrosis, the blind, the deaf and the mentally ill or handicapped who are difficult to control on public transport. The allowance also needs to be extended to children between two and five if it is really to provide for the extra expenses of all handicapped children with mobility problems.

If the mobility allowance were extended to cover mobility expenses, the remaining routine expenses of disablement – incontinence, extra clothing and bedding, recreation, feeding and so forth – would be left to the Family Fund. How adequate is the Fund to fill this role? Although in many instances it has been a valuable and valued contribution to the relief of the burdens of care, its impact should not be exaggerated. It has made an average contribution of £291 over three years and £301 over five years to the families who have been helped. This is £60 per year or about £1 per week. This level of help cannot stand out as a remarkably significant contribution. For families who received larger sums than this, the contribution may have been relatively more valuable, but the nature of the Fund as, for the most part, a once-for-all input of resources inevitably means that it has limitations as a source of help with the routine expenses of handicap.

Finally, in discussing the question of adequacy it is worth raising the question of take-up again. There were about 85,000 families eligible for help from the Fund. Most of the 40,000 families who are receiving the attendance allowance were eligible for help from it also. Thus, as many as 85,000 families could have applied to the Fund and certainly most of the 40,000 who get the attendance allowance could have applied. Yet only 32,000 families did so. As was argued in chapter 5, the explanation for this is very complicated. Certainly some families had not heard of the Fund or did not know enough about it. Others did not feel they needed the help the Fund offered and others did not want to ask the Fund for help. Whatever the reason, it is clearly not satisfactory if an agency can reach, even after considerable effort, only a third to a half of those who could benefit from its services. It is particularly unsatisfactory if that agency is to continue as the principal source of assistance with the expenses of looking after a child.

The managers of the Fund did and do not believe that the Fund should reach all those eligible. Their position was well put in a minute to the Management Committee from the director of the Trust in June 1976:[16]

> It has always seemed to me unlikely that more than about 50%
> of those would ever apply to the Family Fund. I have repeatedly
> written to more well to do families and sometimes to Members
> of Parliament that the help which the Fund provides is for goods

and services which the great majority of families even of quite
modest means take for granted. The ability to ensure essential
transport, the purchase of washing and drying equipment, the
cost of camping and caravan holidays, the provision of clothing
and bedding are not a difficulty for any but a relatively few
families. It has also seemed inevitable to me that the proportion
of families applying whose handicapped child was below the age
of two years would rightly be fairly small since the need for the
kind of help the Family Fund gives would not become urgent
at that stage by reason of the child's disability. Similarly it seems
to be the case that the Fund's help is less appropriate when the
child nears the age of 16. If this line of argument is sound, then
with a total approaching 35,000 applications the continuing
response will inevitably be small whilst the more intensive
publicity will draw in a larger proportion of ineligible families.

It was inevitable that given its limited resources the Fund should be
viewed in this way – as a residual service for the most hard-pressed
families. But the Fund itself has shown that the needs of families are
not residual – that they are general problems and it is not just the
hard pressed who have benefited from the help that the Fund has
given, but middle- and upper- income families as well. What are the
alternative ways of filling this gap in provision? This is the subject of
the next chapter.

# 15    The future of the Family Fund

The trustees of the Joseph Rowntree Memorial Trust accepted the administration of the Family Fund as a pioneering venture. They expected that after three years under their control, it would either be replaced by new benefits and services for handicapped children or would be taken over by government, local authorities, or some other agency. These aspirations were not unreasonable in 1972-3. The economy was expanding, albeit slowly, and inflation was in single figures; there was considerable public concern about the position of families with disabled children, new benefits were being introduced, and the social services were expanding rapidly.

However, the pioneering aspirations of the trustees have not been realised. There have been no developments in policy that have enabled the Family Fund to wither away. Few new measures for handicapped children have been enacted and the DHSS has twice been forced to ask the Trust to continue to administer the Fund. By early 1975, it was clear that there was no prospect of the DHSS's finding an alternative by the end of the initial three-year period. The general election in October 1974 had delayed the matter coming to the attention of ministers, there were no proposals for new policy initiatives for handicapped children, and the Treasury's attitude was that the Fund should come to an end. It took the view that Sir Keith Joseph had envisaged a 'two tranche' project that would be complete in itself and it believed that to establish a more permanent service raised new issues of principle. The Family Fund Management Committee agenda notes recorded (10 April 1975):

> The trustees have now agreed that they are willing, if so requested, to continue their responsibility for the administration of the Family Fund under the present agreement with DHSS up to the end of 1978. By that time the results of the research project should be available and the continuing demands on the Fund could be more clearly assessed. The trustees would be willing after the end of 1978 to continue to co-operate with DHSS in order that the present organisation for the administration of the Family Fund could transfer to whatever continuing administration the

197

government decided to establish. This arrangement would be equally applicable if the service provided by the Fund were divided between a variety of governmental and non-governmental agencies.

By the summer of 1975 the resources available to the Fund were no longer adequate to cover the number of applications that had been received and with no decision from the DHSS, the chairman of the Trust wrote to Barbara Castle, the Secretary of State for Social Services. This letter resulted in assurances that further funds would be forth-coming and the trustees agreed 'subject to a number of conditions ... to administer the Fund for a further shorter and final period'.[1]

Early in 1977, discussions again began between the DHSS and the Trust about the future of the Fund beyond the end of 1978, which was the limit of the Fund's existing commitment. A paper was discussed at a Management Committee meeting in April 1977. The DHSS member of the Management Committee[2]

> stressed that there was no possibility in the foreseeable future of further specific grants, e.g. for laundry. In the longer term the Department's view was that a general allowance to meet the special needs of handicapped children might be introduced; for the remainder of the decade the Department saw no alternative to the Family Fund.

In the light of this, the Trust again agreed to continue to administer the Fund. On this occasion it asked that six conditions should be agreed before it did so. One of these was:[3]

> decisions about the future of the Fund should not simply be set aside. Trustees would want to be assured by the Secretary of State that the matter was kept under regular and consistent review so that decisions would be made as economic circumstances allowed. The Trust neither wished permanently to assume the administration of a nationwide service, nor to see the Fund disintegrate because it became steadily more difficult to maintain what is a temporary administrative structure.

In his reply David Ennals wrote:[4]

> As you appreciate, circumstances have changed since the original agreement between the Department and the Trust. Although we are making progress we have not been able to take all the steps I would have wished to improve help to families with severely handicapped children, thus rendering the Fund's continuance

unnecessary.... I should like to assure you that we shall keep
the position of the future of the Fund under close review and
that we shall not use its existence as an excuse to delay improvements in services.

The Trust has continued to view its involvement with the Fund as a
temporary expedient and the government has promised to keep 'the
future of the Fund under close review'. What are the alternatives to
it? Three possible arrangements are considered below and in chapter 16
the option of continuing the Fund in its present form is considered.

The three choices are:

1   The Family Fund benefits could be administered by local
authority social service departments or supplementary benefits as an
extension to their discretionary powers.

2   The Family Fund benefits could be paid as an annual cash
supplement to 'qualifying families' through a new or existing division
of the social security system.

3   There could be some combination of schemes to fill the gaps
in provision.


**Arrangement 1**

*The Family Fund benefits could be administered by local authority
departments or the Supplementary Benefits Commission as an
extension of their discretionary powers*

In the light of the earlier comments in chapter 13 about overlapping,
provision to merge the operations of the Family Fund into the day-to-
day work of social services departments and/or supplementary benefits
might seem a logical solution. For example, it is clear that many of the
families who have asked for help are not known to their local social
services department. Many of these, in addition to the material problems
with which the Family Fund helps, need long-term support, guidance,
and encouragement which the Fund is not able to provide. If social
services departments were to receive applications for help, they would
be in a position to identify need and provide long-term support. Such
an arrangement would bring the Fund back into the mainstream of
social policy institutions with democratic control and public accountability and some of its administrative problems would be resolved.

However, there are a number of difficulties inherent in this proposal
relating to the powers and capacity of the existing agencies. In the case
of supplementary benefits, the 1976 Act enables the Commission to

provide grants to meet exceptional needs only to those in receipt of these benefits. Those ineligible for supplementary benefits because their resources are in excess of their requirements (under the Act), or because they are in work, can only be helped in emergencies. Even if these provisions could be altered, it is difficult to envisage the level and range of Family Fund assistance being integrated with the Commission's traditional methods of exercising discretion. The Commission's experience lies in providing small lump-sum grants as part of a minimum subsistence income and their staff might find it difficult to adapt to providing relatively larger grants to meet general expenses. The Supplementary Benefits Commission is also hard pressed to cope with the present demands on its services and is not likely to welcome additional burdens of a new service.

Social services departments do have powers to help with some of the benefits the Family Fund can give but they have no powers to provide for general transport and washing-machines and there is no tradition of using their existing powers to help with clothing/bedding and family holidays. If the Family Fund operation were to be handed over to local authorities, either new legislation would be required (at least in England, Wales, and Northern Ireland) to enable them to provide some of the things given by the Family Fund, or those items would have to be dropped from the range of benefits available.

Experience since the passage of the Chronically Sick and Disabled Persons Act 1970 has taught that there are two major difficulties in allocating services for the handicapped through the agency of local authorities. Under Sections 1 and 2 of the Act local authorities are required to inform themselves of people with handicaps in their area and to make arrangements for certain specified services to be provided in order to meet their needs. But there is great variation between authorities in the level of provision and the method of administration. In some areas these duties have been implemented with energy and enthusiasm, in others hardly at all,[5] and as has been noted in chapter 3, in the year ending April 1975 only 4,623 households containing handicapped children in England had received help with adaptations, TV, radio and other aids or telephones.[6]

This leads on to the second difficulty, already discussed in chapter 13, that the present system of financing local authorities through the block grant gives central government very little say in the allocation of resources at the local level. Even if there were procedures available to the government to ensure that resources were spent on specific kinds of provisions, it is unlikely that it would want to use them.

There is no tradition in the DHSS of giving local authorities the kind of direction that would ensure that the benefits that are provided in some areas and which have been provided by the Family Fund would be made available in every area. During the last few years the DHSS has been reluctant to issue circulars to local authorities reminding them of their obligations under existing legislation at the same time as they have been calling for no growth in existing services.[7]

There are also certain arguments in principle for separating cash assistance from social work, and British traditions have tended to try to retain a separation of functions.[8] These arguments are partly to do with reluctance, not least among the social work profession, to add control over the allocation of resources to the social work relationship, and partly with administrative problems. For most needs arising out of the care of a handicapped child, a family has to turn to services for support - to the health service for assessment, treatment and the provision of nursing aids and equipment; to the education services for the provision of schooling and educational aids and equipment; and to the social services for mobility aids and adaptations to property, for social work support, relief care, holidays and laundry service. We have found that health care and education, at least for all but pre-school children, is well developed, but the level of other kinds of support provided by services to those families is very low. In the follow-up study, only 11 per cent of families were in regular contact with their social services department (at least every four months). The failure of services to provide relief from the drudgery and expense of coping with an incontinent child has been described.[9] These delivery problems are a complicated function of lack of resources, divided administrative structures, the parents' determination to carry the burdens of care themselves, and the low priority given to child handicap in the professional perspective of field-workers. But for these reasons it seems unlikely that the improvements in material support for families with handicapped children are likely to come through improvements in services.

## Arrangement 2

*The Family Fund benefit could be paid as an annual cash supplement to 'qualifying families' through a new or existing division of the social system*

Such a benefit could take many forms. The Labour Party has proposed an allowance of £5 per week for 100,000 families[10] and the Royal

Commission on Civil Liability and Compensation for Personal Injury[11] has proposed an expenses allowance of £4 per week. An alternative would be to pay a monthly or quarterly 'bonus' type benefit separately or as a supplement to child benefits.

The experience of the Family Fund has taught that there is a value in making lump-sum payments that enable families to purchase the more expensive capital items that ease the burdens of caring for a disabled child. As Audrey Hunt remarked in relation to single-parent families:[12]

> the need is not wholly or even mainly for an income increase. The much lower level of possession of household amenities and equipment points to the need for some form of help in obtaining these things.

A standard cash benefit would be far more equitable than the help presently provided through the Family Fund. The individual assessment of the appropriateness of the request could be dispensed with and adjudication would be devoted entirely to assessing eligibility. However, standard grants would lack the flexibility that the discretionary system of the Family Fund allows. If grants worth £260 were distributed to families (considerably more than the *annual* value of grants made to each family by the Family Fund), they could be used by each family for a holiday and/or clothing and/or a washing-machine, and could assist towards the running of a car. However, they would be too small for most adaptations and too small for the purchase of a second-hand car. While most families would be better off, some families would be worse off.

The principal difficulty with new cash benefits is the cost. The Family Fund is now costing less than £2 million per annum: the Labour Party's proposal would cost £26 million. The cost of any scheme would depend on the eligibility criteria used and the level of the benefit. If the new benefit is to be an expenses allowance, then the eligibility criteria must attempt to include all those with extra expenses and to exclude all those without. This is probably not possible and criteria would have to be developed to strike an approximation. If functional impairment were to be the test, then existing Family Fund categories would need to be extended.

### Arrangement 3

*There could be some combination of these different methods*

It may be that the most satisfactory way of continuing the benefits of the Family Fund is to split the responsibility for meeting the needs identified by it between a number of different bodies. Thus, an annual capital sum could be given to each family to cover basic items; local social services and education departments, the supplementary benefits, and health authorities could have their powers extended or reinforced to give the more exceptional items; and a discretionary agency like the Family Fund could continue to exist to provide the more expensive items not covered by other agencies.

In order to see how the benefits might be split, let us explore the main needs that the Family Fund has identified.

*Transport.* The mobility allowance has been the only innovation that has taken over some of the work of the Family Fund. The Fund has a residual function to help those with mobility problems who are not eligible for the mobility allowance and who have special problems arising from visiting children in hospitals and out-patients' attendances or residential schools. If the mobility allowance were extended to include all children with mobility problems, and if hospitals became responsible for refunding fares for visits to out-patients' departments, and if the education authorities made more generous provision for visits to children in schools, then the Family Fund or its successor could dispense with help for transport altogether.

*Incontinence.* A general allowance would give families the capacity to buy their own supplies and avoid the need for area health authorities to make provision. The provision of washers and driers could continue to be a function of the Family Fund – it is a task that the Fund has performed particularly well. If the Fund were no longer to exist, the task could be performed by social services departments or the area health authorities.

*Holidays/outings.* This is a form of provision where social services departments have clear statutory responsibilities. Although some authorities are flexible and generous in their provision, most have provided very limited choice and restrict their help to the disabled person only. The Family Fund has been supplementing their provision. Local authority provision could be improved and the Family Fund could continue to supplement it, but because holidays are so much a matter of individual choice and circumstance they could be most easily catered for by providing an expenses allowance that covers the cost of holidays.

*Clothing, bedding.*   Although the Fund has been giving grants for these items, it is not appropriate for these needs to be met by a nationally organised agency; and as these costs are a recurring common expense for families with a disabled child, the expenses allowance could be expected to cover them.

*Adaptations, aids and equipment.*   Many of these items are large and cannot be expected to be met by an expenses allowance. Existing authorities already have responsibilities for the provision of most of these items and it is therefore appropriate that these needs should be met by them. However, the Family Fund has demonstrated the benefits of having a central fund to supplement provision and to even out the variations in provision between areas.

## Conclusion

With regard to the future, even if there were a general expenses allowance, an extended mobility allowance and improvements in the existing services, it would be difficult to plan comprehensive support without the Family Fund. If it did not exist, families would not be able to obtain washing equipment or have any resources for holidays aids and adaptations if they lived in areas where provision was low. One of the dilemmas presented by a highly flexible instrument such as the Family Fund is that it is most difficult to replace with institutionalised services and benefits.

# 16    Conclusion

The Family Fund was announced suddenly and established rapidly in response to a crisis over Thalidomide (chapter 2). The Joseph Rowntree Memorial Trust agreed to administer the Fund for three years in the first instance partly because it might be a 'new and flexible instrument in social policy . . . a departure in social and public administration'.[1] In the absence of measures for the Fund's replacement, the Trust has continued to administer it. It, or another non-statutory agency, could continue to administer the Fund using procedures and principles similar to those employed to date.

The principles of the present arrangements are that families apply directly and are visited by a social worker who, using guide-lines developed by the Fund, assesses eligibility and recommends the payment of a grant to cover the items requested by the family. The Fund is free from direct statutory controls and operates within the terms of broad guide-lines agreed with the Department of Health and Social Security (chapters 3 and 4).

There are a number of arguments for continuing to operate the Family Fund under the present or similar arrangement. The Family Fund has built up considerable experience in running an operation of this sort and although there have been difficulties, it now has a staff, equipment, administrative procedures, a corps of agents, and contacts with the social services. If the Joseph Rowntree Memorial Trust did not wish to continue to be responsible for the Family Fund, the organisational structure could be transferred to another agency.

The parents of handicapped children and those voluntary and statutory bodies that help them have built up a relationship with the Family Fund and an understanding of its procedures. The families who have received help appear to be satisfied with the Fund (chapter 7).

The present structure allows for each family to be assessed individually by social workers. The Fund does not have to justify the decisions it makes in particular cases to any higher authority and thus, despite the increasing use of guide-lines, it is able to respond with some flexibility to the particular needs of each family. Help can be provided in cash or in kind and the most appropriate form of help can be assessed by a social worker.

205

While the Fund does not appear to have had an impact on the emotional stress of looking after a handicapped child (chapter 8), it has gone some way towards relieving families of some of the physical burdens of care (chapter 9).

Above all, the Family Fund is a very inexpensive form of provision. It is probably the only arrangement that can provide help selectively enough to spend only £2 million a year on the families concerned. It is not unduly costly to administer (chapter 10) and it has operated without a welter of public criticism and without becoming a cause of difficulty or embarrassment for the government or the Joseph Rowntree Memorial Trust (chapter 11).

However, against these advantages should be set some of the major problems of the Family Fund that have been identified in this book.

In chapter 13 it has been argued that the Family Fund is inadequate to meet the gap in provision that it was set up to fill. Families have received quite large sums of money from the Fund but at its present level of financing and with its present procedures, it cannot sustain that level of support; alone it is not able to meet the routine extra expenses of child handicap.

In addition, only between a third and a half of those eligible for help from the Fund have been persuaded to apply (chapter 5); there is also the problem of overlap discussed in chapter 13. If the Family Fund became more widely known as a permanent source of help for families, would not the other agencies with existing responsibilities make more vigorous efforts to transfer their responsibilities than they have done to date?

Finally, there are objections to the nature of the Fund itself. It represents a kind of twentieth-century philanthropy. Although the staff do not distinguish between the deserving and the undeserving on the basis of moral worth, the workers do have to make individual decisions on the merits of each individual case – thus, one family gets a telephone and another does not. Decisions are made about who is more or less in need and because the conditions for a grant are not always clear and because judgments in individual cases vary, benefits received by families vary accordingly (chapter 12).

Parents have had no sense of entitlement to the Family Fund and very few families have expressed grievances about its discretionary decisions. However, if the Fund were to become a permanent agency, families who have been treated inequitably might more readily challenge the decisions of the Fund as unfair, arbitrary, or capricious. Whether or not families do this, can it be right that such a scheme, which is by its nature inequitable, should become the main source of help with the general costs of looking after a handicapped child?

Partly to streamline the throughput of grants, partly to reduce inconsistencies in decision-making, and partly to set limits to the range of help available, the Fund came to adopt a body of rules or guide-lines (chapters 3 and 4). These rules have inevitably limited the capacity of the Fund's staff to respond flexibly to the particular requests of each family. Some limits on the flexibility of a discretionary system are inevitable to enable it to work within budgetary constraints, but equity could only be imposed on the Fund by abandoning all the advantages of flexibility. Richard Titmuss recognised that a flexible and discretionary system was needed[2]

> in order to allow a universal rights scheme based on principles
> of equity to be as precise and inflexible as possible. These
> characteristics of precision, inflexibility and universality
> depend for their sustenance and strength on the existence of
> some element of flexible, individualised justice.

The experience of the Family Fund has emphasised that that flexible and discretionary system can only be justified as an adjunct to a system of clearly delineated rights based on principles of equity. The Family Fund has a role to play but it should be an adjunct to a general expenses allowance for families with handicapped children.

# Appendix 1: Criteria of very severe disability employed by the Family Fund
Revised - April 1976

## The Family Fund

The requirement that must be fulfilled to qualify for help from the Family Fund is that the disability must be very severe.

The following examples are given for general guidance and the circumstances of each case must be considered on its merits.

| Nature of disability | Factors which would make the disability severe |
|---|---|
| Absence or functional loss of limbs | Two or more limbs involved |
| Arthrogryposis | Severe deformity |
| Asthma | Severe involvement of lungs seriously limiting the child's activities, physical, social and educational |
| Cerebral palsy | Severe disorder of movement |
| Cystic fibrosis | Severe involvement of lungs seriously limiting the child's activities, physical, social and educational |
| Double incontinence in a child five years or over | Double incontinence, as contrasted with enuresis and encopresis, means the total absence of control of bladder and bowel through organic defect |
| Epilepsy | Frequent fits not controlled by drugs |
| Hyperkinetic syndrome | Very severe overactivity |
| Impairment of hearing | Severe impairment or complete loss |
| Impairment of vision | Severe impairment or complete loss |

| | |
|---|---|
| Infantile spinal muscular atrophy (Werdnig Hoffman disease) | Severe muscular weakness |
| Mental subnormality | IQ less than 50 (less than 35 for mongols) |
| Mongolism (Down's syndrome); (see additional note) | Additional disabilities and special problems of care |
| Multiple malformations | Severe malformations, none of which itself constituted a severe disability, might together do so |
| Muscular dystrophy | Severe disorder of movement |
| Osteogenesis imperfecta | Severe deformity |
| Spina bifida      • | Paralysis of lower limbs with incontinence of urine or faeces |

Factors to be considered in deciding if handicap is very severe:

1    Degree of disability, especially low intelligence, limitation of mobility, abnormal behaviour, impairment of vision and hearing, severe problems of communication.

2    Combined effects of disabilities occurring together.

3    Needs for night attendance, frequent visits to clinics and hospital, special diets, and modifications to home.

*Additional note re mongolism (Down's syndrome)*

The trustees, on the advice of their professional advisers, take the view that the diagnosis of mongolism should not automatically include a child in the category of 'very severely handicapped'. In order to qualify for help from the Family Fund, there will have to be a clearly recognised additional disability which is not usually present in mongolism (e.g. deafness, grossly hyperactive behaviour, or a malformation of the heart). We realise that all mongol children are difficult to manage to the extent that they require close supervision. It would help our medical advisers to come to a decision if you could say whether in your view the behaviour of this child is more disturbed than the usual pattern and, if so, give details and examples of why you take this view. Equally, it would help us if you could give details of any other additional disability which the child may have.

# Appendix 2: The prevalence of children with very severe disabilities in the UK

While there is now considerable information available on the incidence of children born with malformations, there is still very little known about the prevalence of disabilities in the living population of children. Since 1964 area medical officers have collected and returned notifications on malformed children born in their area to the Office of Population, Censuses and Surveys (OPCS).[1] These data have provided published statistics on birth incidence, enabled medical statisticians to monitor changes in incidence,[2] and are just beginning to be used together with death certificates to calculate the prevalence of certain conditions. However, a number of important handicapping conditions are not revealed at birth (muscular dystrophy, mental handicap, burns, etc.) and this method can only be used to estimate the prevalence of those conditions that are obvious at birth.

There has been no large-scale sample survey of households to obtain estimates of the prevalence of handicapped children and the General Household Survey, while containing some data on disability, does not ask specific enough questions to check for Family Fund eligibility. Concern has been expressed in Parliament at the lack of this information and there has been a demand for a national survey to establish the prevalence of handicap in children. The government has decided for the time being not to launch such an exercise. There are good reasons for not carrying out a national survey.

1 The prevalence of child handicap is less than adult handicap. If data were to be collected with a sample survey of households it has been estimated that 90,000 households would need to be screened in order to pick up a sub-sample of only 500 very severely handicapped children.[3] A sub-sample of that size would only contain small numbers of certain handicapping conditions – roughly twenty-five deaf children, twenty blind children, five autistic children, twenty muscular dystrophy children, and so on. Such small sub-groups would serve limited analytic purpose when broken down by age, sex, class, and other variables.

2 The classification of handicap in childhood presents a number of technical problems which have been discussed elsewhere.[4] Clearly a

valid and reliable scale needs to be developed for use in a national survey and no such scale exists at present.

3 There are other ways of collecting data on the prevalence and characteristics of handicapped children and these ought to be fully exploited before an expensive enterprise such as a national survey is launched. If there are still important questions that remain unanswered after this work is complete, then a sample survey could be considered.

There are, in fact, many sources of government, local authority, and survey data on the prevalence of child handicap. The attendance allowance has details of 40,000 families,[5] the Family Fund 35,000, and the DES estimate that about 150,000 are in special schools.[6] As well as keeping statistics of children at special schools, local authority social services departments are required to keep registers,[7] and a number have carried out surveys which included children under Section 1 of the Chronically Sick and Disabled Persons Act. Perhaps the most comprehensive and unexploited registers of handicapped children are those kept by community physicians (child health) and/or school medical officers. A variety of other studies of handicaps in childhood provide estimates of the prevalence of different conditions.[8]

It is probable that whatever work is done on prevalence now will be rapidly overtaken by changes in the incidence of live handicapped births. Some of the trends that are likely to affect the prevalence of child handicap over the next few years include:

1 The birth rate has fallen in recent years and may not rise again in the immediate future.[9] This may result in a fall in the number of disabled children. On the other hand, trends towards later childbirth may lead to an increased birth rate of disabled children; however, the more rapid fall in births to mothers in social classes IV and V may result in a fall in those conditions associated with low social class.[10]

2 If there are continued improvements in pre- and post-natal services, this will reduce the incidence of damage before or during childbirth but also lead to a reduction in infant mortality and the survival, *inter alia*, of damaged children.

3 Improvements in genetic counselling and family planning and abortion facilities could lead to a reduction in the occurrence and recurrence of children born with disabilities to some mothers.

4 Surgeons having become aware of the costs of human, personal, and family suffering resulting from a universal policy of management of spina bifida have begun to switch to a more selective policy and the survival rate of children with spina bifida has been declining since 1969.[11]

5    More radical changes in the birth rate of spina bifida and children with other conditions could come from the introduction of screening on a universal basis followed by amniocentesis and abortion of damaged foetuses. This technique is now a practical possibility for spina bifida.[12] About 20 per cent of very severely handicapped children applying to the Fund were spina bifida.

As part of the research on the Family Fund two original studies were carried out to enable an estimate to be made of the numbers of children meeting the Fund criteria.

## National Child Development study of the 1958 cohort: special analysis

The National Children's Bureau have already produced fairly detailed analyses of their data on handicapped children,[13] but their published data remained very difficult to analyse to produce an over-all prevalence figure. The Bureau kindly agreed to give access to a card index that contains details of all the children with some kind of impairment found in the seven- and eleven-year-old follow-up surveys of the 1958 cohort. The National Child Development study covers all children born in one week in 1958. This cohort has been followed up at regular intervals and Dr Catherine Peckham has kept this card index on the details of the 860 children having some kind of impairments.

With the help of Dr Catherine Peckham, each of these cards was scrutinised and on the basis of the description given, a decision was made about whether the condition was congenital, very severe, and whether the child was living at home or permanently in an institution. The main cause of the handicap was also recorded and whether the disability was mental, physical, or mental and physical. This procedure is open to error in those cases where there is insufficient information to make a decision with absolute certainty about whether the child is very severely disabled and whether the condition is congenital. In allocating children to different categories the Family Fund criteria was followed to the letter. Where there was insufficient information to make a decision the child was classified as not very severe. Where there was enough information but there was doubt about whether the child was severe enough to qualify for the Family Fund, the child was put into a border-line category.

There were 16,606 children in the cohort alive and contacted at seven years old. Table A2.1 shows the breakdown of these according to whether the condition was congenital or very severe under the Family Fund criteria.

*Table A2.1    1958 cohort: numbers of handicapped children*

|  | Congenital | Not congenital |
|---|---|---|
| Very severe | 114 | 19 |
| Borderline | 36 | 42 |
| Not very severe | 649 | |
| Total | 860 | |

Of those children who were very severely handicapped, six were living permanently in an institution and therefore did not satisfy the Family Fund criteria.

*Table A2.2    1958 cohort: type of impairment*

|  | No. | % |
|---|---|---|
| Severely mentally handicapped only | 15 | 11.3 |
| Physical disability only | 53 | 39.8 |
| Physical and severe mental handicap | 46 | 34.6 |
| Physical and educational handicap | 19 | 14.3 |
| Total | 133 | 100 |

Table A2.2 shows the proportion of the very severely handicapped with mental and physical impairments. Out of these, 39.8 per cent had only a physical disability and sixteen of these were the non-congenital handicapped. Before extrapolating these figures to produce a national estimate, it is worth listing the factors that operate to overestimate or underestimate the national prevalence rates from the 1958 cohort.

*Overestimate*

The register of disabled children consists of children with impairments at age seven and/or eleven and thus overrepresents conditions that develop and/or become a serious disability at those ages.

*Underestimate*

1    The register of disabled children consists of children with impairments at age seven and/or eleven. Thus children who have died or who had serious disabilities that have been cured, or where the disability occurs after eleven years old, are excluded from the analysis. These causes of underestimation may not be as serious as they sound because the vast majority of children that die do so in the first year of life.

2    There were 17,418 children in the original cohort, 16,606 were not known to have died by seven years old and of these 15,496 were surveyed. Thus, 1,110 children were not traced at seven years old and it is possible that these children are more likely to have died or be living permanently in an institution. Many of the missing handicapped children not traced at seven later turned up in the eleven-year-old follow-up and are therefore included in the register. However, there will still be a number of children not traced at seven or eleven who had handicaps.

3    Since 1958, the number of children born with an impairment and surviving is likely to have increased.

On balance, the 1958 cohort is likely to provide an underestimate – but not a gross one – of the true prevalence.

Out of 16,606 traced at eleven years old, 110 children were very severely congenitally handicapped and living at home. This is a national rate of 6.6 per 1,000 children. We can be 95 per cent confident that the true prevalence for the UK lies between 76,000 and 110,000. Out of 16,606 traced at eleven years old, seventeen children were very severely non-congenitally handicapped or 1.01 per 1,000 children. We can be 95 per cent confident that the true prevalence for the UK lies between 8,000 and 21,000. Out of 16,606 traced at eleven years old, 127 children were very severely handicapped or 7.65 per 1,000 children. We can be 95 per cent confident that the true prevalence for the UK lies between 89,000 and 126,000.

### The York register

The procedure for this attempt to obtain a prevalence rate was rather different. With the co-operation of the York county borough medical officer of health and the director of social services, a register of all children living in York with serious handicapping conditions and known to their departments was compiled. This list, together with the names of those children who had applied to the Family Fund and who did not appear on the list, was submitted to Dr Walter Henderson, the former consultant paediatrician for York, and medical adviser to the Family Fund – and therefore thoroughly conversant with their criteria. He consulted the hospital records for each child and gave a decision about whether the disability was very severe and whether it was congenital. Using this procedure it was not only possible to produce a prevalence rate of severe handicap in York but also to examine the comprehensiveness of departmental registers.

Before extrapolating these findings to produce a national estimate, it is worth listing the factors that appear to overestimate and under-estimate national prevalence rates from the York data. York may not be typical of the country as a whole. There is no way of telling how untypical it is but families with handicapped children from the rural hinterland of York (particularly families with deaf children) may come to live in York to be nearer the better facilities provided in York than by neighbouring authorities.

*Overestimate*

Some of the children identified as very severe may, if more recent infor-mation had been available to Dr Henderson than that provided in hospital records, be classified as not very severe. Three children classified by him as very severe were rejected by the Family Fund as not very severe.

*Underestimate*

1   The York register may not be a complete record of all handi-capped children. There were twenty-eight families who had applied to the Family Fund but who were not on the lists. Most of these were either not very severe or had been born after the list was drawn up. There were only three cases of families applying to the Fund where there was no reasonable explanation for them not being on the lists. But because three children were not on the register and very severely handicapped, an allowance has been made in the prevalence estimates below for six additional very severely disabled children (on the basis that only half those not on the register have applied to the Fund).

2   Some of the children identified as not very severe may, if more recent information had been available to Dr Henderson than that provided by hospital records, be classified as very severe. Eight of the children accepted by the Family Fund had been classified by Dr Hender-son as not very severe or doubtful. Five of these children were mongols and were classified by Dr Henderson as not very severe at the time when the Family Fund was still working out its criteria.

It is now possible to produce an estimate of the numbers of children in York who are very severely handicapped.

One hundred and thirty-nine were children classified as very severe and by April 1976, sixty-six (47.5 per cent) of these children had applied to the Family Fund (see Table A2.3). In addition, a further nineteen had applied for the other categories.

*Table A2.3    York register of handicapped children*

|                | Applied | Not applied | Total |
|----------------|---------|-------------|-------|
| Very severe    | 66      | 73          | 139   |
| Not very severe | 15     | 112         | 127   |
| Doubtful       | 4       | 11          | 15    |
| Don't know     | 28      | 0           | 28    |
| Total          | 113     | 196         | 309   |

*Table A2.4    Very severely handicapped children in York*

| | |
|---|---|
| From the register | 139 |
| Not on the register | 6 |
| Accepted by the Family Fund but not classified as very severe by Dr Henderson, less three classified as very severe but not accepted by Family Fund | 5 |
| Total | 150 |

Out of 24,630 children under sixteen in York, 150 were very severely handicapped (see Table A2.4). This is a national rate of 6.1 per 1,000 children. We can be 95 per cent confident that the prevalence for the UK lies between 74,000 and 102,000.

*Table A2.5    All very severely handicapped*

|                              | Rate per 1,000 | Low range | High range |
|------------------------------|----------------|-----------|------------|
| National Childrens' Bureau   | 7.6            | 89,000    | 126,000    |
| York                         | 6.1            | 72,000    | 100,000    |
| Pooled                       | 6.7            | 83,000    | 106,000    |

Where there is a 95 per cent probability that the individual proportions have come from the same populations, it is possible to narrow the confidence limits by pooling the sample estimates. This has been done in Table A2.5. We end up with an estimate that there are between 83,000 and 106,000 children under sixteen eligible for help from the Family Fund.

This estimate obviously leaves a lot to be desired, based as it is on two samples that may not be representative of the population as a whole; nevertheless, it is better than no estimate at all. To produce an estimate with narrower confidence limits from a random sample of the population would require an initial sample of at least 40,000 households.

**Bristol data**

Since completing this work, it has been possible to compare applicants from Bristol with a list of very severely handicapped children drawn up by Diana Pomeroy from local records. Pomeroy, who was working with the Department of Child Health at Bristol University on a study of the housing problems of families with handicapped children, produced a list containing the names of 288 children born between 1 April 1959 and 30 April 1969, including six families with two children. Of the 282 families on her list, we found that 126, or 44.7 per cent, had applied to the Family Fund.

Her list excluded children with cystic fibrosis, sensory handicaps, and hole in the heart, and these handicaps make up 9.1 per cent of all Family Fund applications. Fifty-two families had applied to the Family Fund who were not on her list, including seven in excluded categories. If these forty-five children are 44.7 per cent of all those in the age range not on her lists, then the total in her age range not on her list would be 101.

Hence the number of Bristol families with handicapped children in the age range but excluding cystic fibrosis, etc. is 383. This suggests that there are 607 children under sixteen and 668 children with the cystic fibrosis categories included in Bristol. This gives a prevalence rate for Bristol of 6.7 per 1,000 – which is identical to the pooled estimate of families with very severely disabled children given in Table A2.5.

# Notes

## Introduction

1  *House of Commons Debates*, vol. 847, col. 498.

## Chapter 1   Methods

1  For definitions of evaluative research see E. Suchman, 'Principles and Practice of Evaluative Research', in J. Doby (ed.), *An Introduction to Sociological Research*, Appleton-Century-Crofts, New York, 1967; R. Weber and N. Polansky, 'Evaluation', in N. Polansky (ed.), *Social Work Research*, University of Chicago, 1975.
2  R. Lees, *Research Strategies for Social Welfare*, Routledge & Kegan Paul, London, 1975.
3  A.H. Halsey (ed.), *Educational Priority*, HMSO, London, 1972.
4  A.L. Cochrane, *Effectiveness and Efficiency*, Nuffield Provincial Hospitals Trust, Oxford, 1972.
5  Halsey, op. cit.; E.M. Goldberg, *Helping the Aged*, Allen & Unwin, London, 1970.
6  F.G. Caro, 'Issues in the Evaluation of Social Programmes', *Review of Educational Research*, vol. 41, no. 2.
7  G. Smith, 'Action Research: Experimental Social Administration', in R. Lees and G. Smith (eds), *Action Research in Community Development*, Routledge & Kegan Paul, London, 1975.
8  J.R. Bradshaw and D. Lawton, 'Some Characteristics of Children with Severe Disabilities', *Journal of Biosocial Science*, vol. 10, 1978, pp. 107–20.
9  S.M. Baldwin, 'Families with Handicapped Children', in K. Jones and S.M. Baldwin (eds), *The Year Book of Social Policy in Britain 1975*, Routledge & Kegan Paul, London, 1976.
10  J.R. Bradshaw, C. Glendinning and S. Hatch, 'Voluntary Organisations for Handicapped Children and their Families: The Meaning of Membership', *Child Care, Health and Development*, vol. 3, no. 4, 1977.

## Chapter 2   The origins of the Family Fund

1  P. Hall, H. Land, R. Parker and A. Webb, *Change, Choice and Conflict in Social Policy*, Heinemann, London, 1975.
2  From a letter from Sir Keith Joseph to the author, 14 March 1974.
3  Sir Keith Joseph, House of Commons Debate, *Hansard*, vol. 847, col. 476.

4  *Report of the Committee on Local Authority and Allied Personal Social Services* (Seebohm Report), Cmnd 3703, HMSO, London, 1968.

5  *Better Services for the Mentally Handicapped*, Cmnd 4683, HMSO, London, 1971.

6  A. Harris, *Handicapped and Impaired in Great Britain*, Office of Population Census and Surveys, HMSO, London, 1971.

7  J. Buckle, *Work and Housing of Impaired Persons in Great Britain*, OPCS, HMSO, London, 1971; A. Harris, *Income and Entitlement to Supplementary Benefits of Impaired People in Great Britain*, OPCS, HMSO, London, 1972.

8  Carnegie UK Trust, *Handicapped Children and their Families*, Constable, London, 1964; J. Tizard and J. Grad, *The Mentally Handicapped and their Families*, Oxford University Press, 1961; S. Hewitt, *The Family and the Handicapped Child*, Allen & Unwin, London, 1970.

9  E. Younghusband, D. Birchall, R. Davie and M.L. Kellmer Pringle (eds), *Living with Handicap*, NCB, London, 1970.

10  Ibid., pp. 46 and 47.

11  It is interesting that since 1973 many books and pamphlets have been published exploring the burdens of families caring for handicapped children. Among these are: L. Burton, *The Family Life of Sick Children*, Routledge & Kegan Paul, London, 1975; M. Voysey, *A Constant Burden*, Routledge & Kegan Paul, London, 1975; J. Copeland, *For the Love of Ann*, Arrow, London, 1973; C. Hannam, *Parents and Mentally Handicapped Children*, Penguin, Harmondsworth, 1975; J. and E. Wilks, *Bernard: Bringing up our Mongol Son*, Routledge & Kegan Paul, London, 1974; S. Kew, *Handicap and Family Crisis*, Pitman, London, 1975; L. Cooper and R. Henderson (eds), *Something Wrong*, Arrow, London, 1973; J. Loring and G. Burn, *Integration of Handicapped Children in Society*, Routledge & Kegan Paul, London, 1975.

12  T. Lynes, 'Creating a National Disability Income', *New Society*, April 1973.

13  *Creating a National Disability Income*, DIG, London, 1972.

14  *Social Security Provision for Chronically Sick and Disabled People*, HC 276, HMSO, London, 1974.

15  *Royal Commission on Civil Liability and Compensation for Personal Injury* (Pearson Report), Cmnd 7054, HMSO, London, 1978.

16  *Law Commission Report on Injuries to Unborn Children*, Cmnd 5709, HMSO, London, 1974.

17  Congenital Diseases (Civil Liability) Act 1976.

18  *Sunday Times*, 29 October 1972.

19  *House of Commons Debates*, vol. 846, col. 770.

20  *House of Commons Debates*, vol. 846, col. 772.

21  *Sunday Times*, 19 November 1972.

22  *Sunday Times*, 25 November 1972.

23  *House of Commons Debates*, vol. 847, col. 431.

24  *House of Commons Debates*, vol. 847, cols 444–5.
25  *House of Commons Debates*, vol. 847, col. 446.
26  *House of Commons Debates*, vol. 847, col. 447.
27  *House of Commons Debates*, vol. 847, cols 498–9.
28  *The Times*, 1 December 1972.
29  *Guardian*, 2 December 1972.
30  *Sunday Times*, 3 December 1972.
31  T.D. Mason, *Thalidomide: My Fight*, Allen & Unwin, London, 1976.
32  *House of Commons Debates*, vol. 847, col. 499.
33  *House of Commons Debates*, vol. 847, col. 447.
34  Mason, op. cit.
35  *House of Commons Debates*, vol. 847, col. 439.
36  *House of Commons Debates*, vol. 847, col. 438.
37  Hall *et al.*, op. cit., ch. 15.
38  G. Myrdal, *Beyond the Welfare State*, Duckworth, London, 1960, p. 13. Quoted in Hall *et al.*, op. cit., p. 492.
39  *Minds Matter*, Annual Conference Report, NAMH, London, 1971, p. 39. Quoted in Hall *et al.*, op. cit., p. 493.
40  Hall *et al.*, op. cit., p. 500.

**Chapter 3    Organising the Family Fund**

1  C.C. Hood and J.R. Bradshaw, 'Implications of an Unorthodox Agency,' *Public Administration*, vol. 55, Winter 1977, pp. 447–64.
2  Joseph Rowntree Memorial Trust and the Family Fund, Report to the DHSS, 8 August 1974.
3  Management Committee Minutes, 29 November 1973.
4  Management Committee Minutes, February 1974.
5  A form of intensive and often costly private treatment for mentally handicapped children run by an organisation based in Philadelphia, US.
6  L. Waddilove, A Report to the DHSS on the Family Fund, August 1974.
7  Family Fund Note to the Management Committee, June 1974.
8  Letter from L. Waddilove to the trustees of the Joseph Rowntree Memorial Trust, August 1975.
9  P. Blau and W.R. Scott, *Formal Organisations*, Routledge & Kegan Paul, London, 1977, p. 244.
10  K. Jones, J. Brown and J.R. Bradshaw, *Issues in Social Policy*, Routledge & Kegan Paul, London, 1979.
11  M.J. Hill, *The Sociology of Public Administration*, Weidenfeld & Nicolson, London, 1972, p. 62.
12  R.M. Titmuss, 'Welfare Rights, Law and Discretion', *Political Quarterly*, vol. 42, no. 2, 1971.
13  D. Donnison, 'Against Discretion', *New Society*, 15 April 1977.
14  D. Donnison, 'How Much Discretion', *Supplementary Benefits Commission Notes and News*, 7 April 1977.

## Chapter 4 The work of the Family Fund

1 J.R. Bradshaw, *Incontinence: A Burden for Families with Handicapped Children*, Disabled Living Foundation, London, 1978.
2 Family Fund, Notes of Guidance to Social Workers.
3 Family Fund, Guide-lines on telephones.
4 Letter to the Joseph Rowntree Memorial Trust from the DHSS, dated 21 December 1972.
5 Ibid.
6 Notes of meeting between the Joseph Rowntree Memorial Trust and the DHSS, 6 December 1972.
7 Letter to the Joseph Rowntree Memorial Trust from the DHSS, dated 21 December 1972.
8 Notes of Guidance for the Panel, 11 April 1973.
9 Report of Panel, 23 May 1973.
10 Family Fund, Information for social workers' representatives, para. 9.
11 Letter of agreement to the Joseph Rowntree Memorial Trust from the DHSS, dated 21 December 1972.
12 Information for social workers' representatives, para. 11.
13 *House of Commons Debates*, vol. 847, col. 446.
14 *House of Commons Debates*, vol. 847, col. 498.
15 *House of Commons Debates*, vol. 847, col. 446.
16 Letter to the Joseph Rowntree Memorial Trust from DHSS, dated 21 December 1972.
17 This scale is described in J.R. Bradshaw, 'Examining Benefits for Families with Handicapped Children', in DHSS (eds), *Social Security Research*, HMSO, London, 1977.
18 Family Fund, Possible Areas of Budgetary Control, 16 September 1975.

## Chapter 5 Take-up of the Family Fund

1 P. Townsend, 'The Scope and Limitations of Means Tested Social Services in Britain', in *Sociology and Social Policy*, Penguin, Harmondsworth, 1976; R. Lister, *Take-up of Means Tested Benefits*, Child Poverty Action Group, London, 1976; National Consumer Council, *Means Tested Benefits*, NCC, London, 1976.
2 Though the new benefits for the disabled have been described as being allocated on the basis of a physiological and psychological means test. (H. Bolderson, 'Compensation for Disability', *Journal of Social Policy*, vol. 3, no. 3, 1974, pp. 193–211.)
3 *Hansard*, Written Answers, 21 March 1977, col. 410.
4 F. Field, *Unequal Britain*, Arrow, London, 1976.
5 J.R. Bradshaw, 'Examining Benefits for Families with Handicapped Children', in DHSS (eds), *Social Security Research*, HMSO, London, 1977.
6 I. Leck, *British Medical Bulletin*, vol. 30, 1974, pp. 158–63.

7    J.R. Bradshaw and D. Lawton, 'Some Characteristics of Children with Severe Disabilities', *Journal of Biosocial Science*, vol. 10, 1978, pp. 107–20.
8    A. Harris, *Handicapped and Impaired in Great Britain*, OPCS, HMSO, London, 1971; D. Evans, 'The Severely Disabled at Home', *Health Trends*, vol. 6, 1974.
9    V. Imber, 'A Multivariate Classification of the English Local Authorities with Responsibility for the Personal Social Services', *DHSS Statistics and Research Series 16*, HMSO, London, 1977.
10   Chartered Institute of Public Finance and Accountancy, *Personal Social Services Statistics 1974/75*, CIPFA, London 1976; and DHSS, *Personal Social Services Statistics : Aids to Households, Year Ending 31 March 1975*, DHSS, London, 1976.
11   Diana Pomeroy and her colleagues at the Department of Child Health, University of Bristol, were kind enough to provide these data.
12   See for instance P. Taylor Gooby, 'Rent Benefits and Tenants' Attitudes', *Journal of Social Policy*, vol. 5, no. 1, 1976, pp. 33–48.
13   The Advisory Committee on Rent Rebates and Allowances, *Report Number 2*, HMSO, London, 1977, pp. 32 and 33.

## Chapter 6    The publicity programme and source of referrals to the Fund

1    An outline plan for publicity, Forman House, 8 August 1973.
2    Contact Report, 8 October 1973.
3    Forman House Report, February 1974.
4    Contact Report, 21 May 1974.
5    *House of Commons Debates*, vol. 882, cols 1519–26.

## Chapter 7    The consumer's view of the Fund

1    In this chapter I have drawn heavily on the work of my colleagues: Sally Baldwin and Caroline Glendinning who interviewed in depth seventeen families helped by the Fund.

## Chapter 8    Relief of stress

1    DHSS circular, LASSL, 8/73.
2    This four-part model was developed from ideas in S. Harrison, *Families in Stress*, Royal College of Nursing, London, 1977.
3    *House of Commons Debates*, vol. 847, col. 498.
4    J.R. Bradshaw, 'The Financial Needs of Disabled Children', *Disability Alliance*, London, 1975; S. Baldwin, 'Counting the Cost', *Disability Alliance*, London, 1977.
5    M. Rutter, J. Tizard and K. Whitmore, *Education, Health and Behaviour*, Longman, London, 1970.
6    B. Tew and K. Lawrence, 'Some Sources of Stress Found in Mothers of Spina Bifida Children', *British Journal of Private and Social Medicine*, vol. 291, no. 1, 1975.

7  S. Dorner, 'The Relationship of Physical Handicap to Stress in Families with an Adolescent with Spina Bifida', *Dev. Med. and Child Neur.*, vol. 17, 1975, pp. 765–6.

8  Rutter *et al.*, op. cit.

9  M. Rutter, P. Graham and B. Yule, *A Neuropsychiatric Study in Childhood*, Heinemann, London, 1970.

10  M. Rutter, B. Yule, D. Quinton, O. Towland, W. Yule and M. Berger, 'Attainment and Adjustment in Two Geographical Areas', *British Journal of Psychiatry*, vol. 126, 1975, pp. 520–33.

11  Personal communication from Department of Child Health Research Unit, University of Bristol.

12  S. Dorner, Personal communication, 1977.

13  Tew and Lawrence, op. cit.

14  W. Jaehnig, 'Mentally Handicapped Children and Their Families', University of Essex, 1974.

15  Dorner, 'The Relationship of Physical Handicap to Stress in Families with an Adolescent with Spina Bifida'.

16  Tew and Lawrence, op. cit.

17  J.R. Bradshaw and D. Lawton, 'Tracing the Causes of Stress in Families with Handicapped Children', *British Journal of Social Work*, vol. 8, no. 2, 1978.

## Chapter 9    The relief of burden

1  A study of the work of the Fund in relation to incontinence has been published separately in J.R. Bradshaw, *Incontinence: A Burden for Families with Handicapped Children*, Disabled Living Foundation, London, 1978.

2  The mobility allowance has been the subject of a study by K. Cooke, *A Study of Child Beneficiaries of the Mobility Allowance*, Social Policy Research Unit Working Paper, University of York, 1979.

3  DHSS circular, 'Travelling Expenses and Transport for Hospital Patients and Visits', HM(73)20, HMSO, London, 1973.

4  The Report of the Committee on the Welfare of Children in Hospital (Platt Report), HMSO, London, 1959.

5  See National Association for the Welfare of Children in Hospital, The Fares Enquiry, 1972.

6  'Visiting Arrangements for Children in Residential Schools', Department of Education and Science Administrative memorandum (6/66), HMSO, London, 1966.

7  *Hansard*, vol. 919, cols 1000–2, 22 November 1976.

8  See CPAG Evidence to the Royal Commission on the Distribution of Income and Wealth, 1977.

9  Margaret Wynn, *Family Policy*, Michael Joseph, London, 1971.

10  Ministry of Education Report of the Working Party on Educational Maintenance Allowances (Weaver), HMSO, London, 1959.

11  *Supplementary Benefits Commission Annual Report 1976*, Cmnd 6910, HMSO, London, 1977.

12  Supplementary Benefits Commission, *Exceptional Needs Payments*, HMSO, London, 1973; DHSS, *Families Receiving Supplementary Benefits*, HMSO, London, 1972.
13  See D. Bull (ed.), *School Clothing in Bristol,* CPAG, London, 1973.
14  Minutes of the Family Fund Management Committee, 29 November 1973.
15  Paper to the DHSS on the administration of the Fund, August 1974.
16  Possible areas of budgetary control, undated.


## Chapter 10   Cost effectiveness

1  *Supplementary Benefits Commission Annual Report, 1976,* Cmnd 6910, HMSO, London, 1977, para. 2.9.
2  Ibid., Table 2.1.
3  Ibid., paras 7.31 and 7.32.
4  Ibid., para. 1.37.
5  These data were obtained directly from the Attendance Allowance Board.


## Chapter 11   Implicit aims

1  *House of Commons Debates*, vol. 882, cols 1519–26.
2  See also C.C. Hood and J.R. Bradshaw, 'The Family Fund: Implications of an Unorthodox Agency', *Public Administration,* Winter 1977.
3  G.W. Keeton, *The Modern Law of Charities*, Pitman, London, 1962.
4  *House of Commons Debates*, vol. 854, col. 36; vol. 855, col. 179; vol. 861, col. 29; vol. 866, cols 196–201; vol. 867, col. 248; vol. 880, col. 217; vol. 896, col. 551 and cols 607–9; vol. 897, cols 729–30 and col. 771; vol. 906, col. 181, cols 194–6 and col. 657; vol. 909, col. 64; vol. 910, col. 83; vol. 913, col. 640; vol. 914, cols 1969–82 (debate).
5  The Congenital Disabilities Civil Liability Bill, *House of Commons Debates*, vol. 904, cols 1589–1648.
6  Mr Alfred Morris in *House of Commons Debates*, vol. 939, col. 326.


## Chapter 12   Equity and the Family Fund

1  Albert Weale, *Equality and Social Policy*, Routledge & Kegan Paul, London, 1977.
2  K. Jones, J. Brown and J.R. Bradshaw, *Issues in Social Policy*, Routledge & Kegan Paul, London, 1978.
3  J. Heywood and B. Allen, *Financial Help in Social Work*, Manchester University Press, 1971; R.M. Titmuss, 'Welfare Rights, Law and Discretion', *Political Quarterly*, vol. 42, no. 2, 1971.
4  Titmuss, op. cit.

5  *House of Commons Debates*, vol. 276. British Social Security
   Problem for the Handicapped, *Social Security Provision for
   Chronically Sick and Disabled People*, HC 276, HMSO, London,
   1974.
6  W. Jaehnig, 'Mentally Handicapped Children and their Families',
   University of Essex, 1974.
7  For a discussion of this scale see J.R. Bradshaw, 'Examining
   Benefits for Families with Handicapped Children', in DHSS (eds),
   *Social Security Research*, HMSO, London, 1977.
8  J.R. Bradshaw and D. Lawton, 'Some Characteristics of Children
   with Severe Disabilities', *Journal of Biosocial Science*, vol. 10,
   1978, pp. 107–20.
9  J.A. Sonquist and J.N. Morgan, 'The Detection of Interaction
   Effects', Monograph 35, Survey Research Centre, *Institute for
   Social Research*, The University of Michigan, 1964. This package
   was obtained from Michigan especially for this analysis. Dorothy
   Lawton carried out the computer runs.
10 Family Fund, Notes of Guidance to Social Workers.

## Chapter 13   The boundary problem

1  *House of Commons Debates*, vol. 847, col. 446.
2  Letter from DHSS to the Joseph Rowntree Memorial Trust,
   dated 21 December 1972.
3  DHSS circular, LASSL, 8/73.
4  Management Committee Minutes, 24 June 1974.
5  Report to DHSS, 8 August 1974, pp. 14–15.
6  *House of Commons Debates*, vol. 897, col. 218.
7  Agenda Notes for Management Committee, 26 September 1975.
8  Note of a Family Fund staff meeting, 17 March 1975.
9  *Supplementary Benefit Commission Annual Report*, Cmnd 6910,
   HMSO, London, 1977.
10 National Fund for Research into Crippling Diseases, *The
   Implementation of the Chronically Sick and Disabled Persons
   Act*, Action Research monograph, London, 1973.
11 DHSS circular, 12/70.
12 DHSS Local Authority Circular (74) (36) *Rate Fund Expenditure
   and Rate Calls in 1975/76*, 23 December 1974.
13 Plank Report, Report of the working party of DHSS statistics on
   the Personal Social Services. David Plank (ed.), *Social Services
   Research Group*, July 1975.
14 Chartered Institution of Public Finance and Accountancy, *Personal
   Social Services Statistics 1974/75*, CIPFA, London, 1976.

## Chapter 14   Adequacy of the Family Fund

1  This appraisal has been published as J.R. Bradshaw, C. Glendinning
   and S. Baldwin, 'Services that Miss Their Mark and Leave Families
   in Need', *Health and Social Services Journal*, April 1977, pp. 664–5.

2   *Fit for the Future*, The Report of the Committee on Child Health
    Services (Court Report), Cmnd 6684, HMSO, London, 1977.
3   Central Council for Education and Training in Social Work, Paper
    5, *Social Work : People with handicaps need better trained
    workers*, August 1974.
4   The only discussion of the case for improved cash benefits for
    families with disabled children has been J.R. Bradshaw, 'The
    Financial Needs of Disabled Children', *Disability Alliance*,
    London, 1975. This discussion is a development of the ideas in
    that paper.
5   'Social Security Provision for Chronically Sick and Disabled
    People', *House of Commons Paper 276*, 1974.
6   Ibid., para. 16.
7   Ibid., para. 6.
8   Ibid.
9   Bradshaw, op. cit; S.M. Baldwin, 'Counting the Cost', *Disability
    Alliance*, London, 1977; J.R. Bradshaw, 'Examining Benefits for
    Families with Handicapped Children', in DHSS (eds), *Social
    Security Research*, HMSO, London, 1977.
10  Baldwin, op. cit.
11  *House of Commons Paper 276*, op. cit.
12  Ibid., para. 37.
13  S.M. Baldwin, 'Families with Handicapped Children', in K. Jones
    and S.M. Baldwin (eds), *The Year Book of Social Policy in Britain
    1975*, Routledge & Kegan Paul, London, 1976.
14  *Disability Alliance*, 'Poverty and Disability', July 1975.
15  Susy Large, 'Mobility for Physically Disabled', in K. Jones (ed.),
    *The Year Book of Social Policy in Britain 1976*, Routledge &
    Kegan Paul, London, 1977.
16  Management Committee Minutes, June 1976.

## Chapter 15   The future of the Family Fund

1   Agenda notes, Management Committee, 3 February 1976.
2   Minutes, Management Committee, 28 April 1977.
3   Lord Seebohm to David Ennals, 13 July 1977.
4   David Ennals to Lord Seebohm, 3 August 1977.
5   Fund for Research into Crippling Diseases, *The Implementation
    of the Chronically Sick and Disabled Persons Act*, Action Research
    monograph, London, 1973.
6   *Local Authority Social Services Departments Aids to Households*,
    DHSS Statistics and Research Division, 1975.
7   *Rate Fund Expenditure and Rate Calls in 1975-76*, Joint Circular
    171/74 (Department of the Environment), December 1974.
8   See G. Hoshino, 'Separating Maintenance from Social Service',
    *Public Welfare*, Spring 1972, pp. 54-61; G. Hoshino, 'Money and
    Morality', *Social Work*, vol. 16, no. 2, April 1971, pp. 16-24.
9   J.R. Bradshaw, *Incontinence : A Burden for Families with Handi-
    capped Children*, Disabled Living Foundation, London, 1978.

10   The Labour Party, *Programme for Britain*, London, 1976.
11   Royal Commission on Civil Liability and Compensation for
     Personal Injury (Pearson Report), Cmnd 7054, HMSO, London,
     1978.
12   Audrey Hunt, *Families and Their Needs*, SS 466, HMSO, London,
     1973.


**Chapter 16   Conclusion**

1   Lewis Waddilove, paper to the Family Fund Management
    Committee, August 1974.
2   R.M. Titmuss, 'Welfare Rights, Law and Discretion', *Political
    Quarterly*, vol. 42, no. 2, 1971, p. 131.


**Appendix 2   The prevalence of children with very severe disabilities
               in the UK**

1   J.A.C. Weatherall and J.C. Haskey, 'Surveillance of Malformations',
    *British Medical Bulletin*, vol. 32, no. 1, 1976.
2   J.A.C. Weatherall, *Studies in Medical and Population Subjects*,
    no. 31, OPCS, 1976.
3   J.R. Bradshaw, 'The Financial Needs of Disabled Children',
    *Disability Alliance*, London, 1975.
4   J.R. Bradshaw, 'Examining Benefits for Families with Handicapped
    Children', in DHSS (eds), *Social Security Research*, HMSO, London
    1977.
5   D. Evans, 'The Severely Disabled at Home', *Health Trends*, vol. 6,
    1974.
6   *Social Trends no. 6*, HMSO, London, 1975.
7   S.S. Hilton, V. Imber and H.A. Mitchell, 'Personal Social Services
    Statistics', Royal Statistical Society Paper, 1974.
8   J.R. Bradshaw, 'Financial Needs of Disabled Children,' op. cit.
9   Central Policy Review Staff, *Population and the Social Services*,
    HMSO, London, 1977.
10  C. Pearce and M. Britton, 'The Decline in Births : Some Socio-
    economic Aspects', *Population Trends 7*, OPCS, HMSO, London,
    1977.
11  J.A.C. Weatherall and G.C. White, 'A Study of Survival of Children
    with Spina Bifida', in *Child Health – a Collection of Studies*, OPCS,
    1976.
12  'UK Collaborative Study on Alpha-fetoprotein in Relation to
    Neural-tube Defects', *Lancet*, 1977, i. 1323.
13  R. Davies, N. Butler and H. Goldstein, *From Birth to Seven*,
    Longman, London, 1972; R. Frew and C. Peckham, 'Mental
    Retardation: A National Study', *British Hospital Journal and
    Social Services Review*, 16 September 1972.

# Index

229

# Routledge Social Science Series

Routledge & Kegan Paul    London, Henley and Boston

39 Store Street, London WC1E 7DD
Broadway House, Newtown Road,
Henley-on-Thames, Oxon RG9 1EN
9 Park Street, Boston, Mass. 02108

# Contents

*Authors wishing to submit manuscripts for any series in
this catalogue should send them to the Social Science Editor,
Routledge & Kegan Paul Ltd, 39 Store Street,
London WC1E 7DD*

●*Books so marked are available in paperback*
*All books are in Metric Demy 8vo format (216 × 138mm approx.)*

# International Library of Sociology

*General Editor*   John Rex

## GENERAL SOCIOLOGY

**Barnsley, J. H.** The Social Reality of Ethics. *464 pp.*
**Brown, Robert.** Explanation in Social Science. *208 pp.*
●   Rules and Laws in Sociology. *192 pp.*
**Bruford, W. H.** Chekhov and His Russia. *A Sociological Study. 244 pp.*
**Burton, F.** and **Carlen, P.** Official Discourse. *On Discourse Analysis, Government Publications, Ideology. About 140 pp.*
**Cain, Maureen E.** Society and the Policeman's Role. *326 pp.*
●**Fletcher, Colin.** Beneath the Surface. *An Account of Three Styles of Sociological Research. 221 pp.*
**Gibson, Quentin.** The Logic of Social Enquiry. *240 pp.*
**Glucksmann, M.** Structuralist Analysis in Contemporary Social Thought. *212 pp.*
**Gurvitch, Georges.** Sociology of Law. *Foreword by Roscoe Pound. 264 pp.*
**Hinkle, R.** Founding Theory of American Sociology 1883-1915. *About 350 pp.*
**Homans, George C.** Sentiments and Activities. *336 pp.*
**Johnson, Harry M.** Sociology: *a Systematic Introduction. Foreword by Robert K. Merton. 710 pp.*
● **Keat, Russell** and **Urry, John.** Social Theory as Science. *278 pp.*
**Mannheim, Karl.** Essays on Sociology and Social Psychology. *Edited by Paul Keckskemeti. With Editorial Note by Adolph Lowe. 344 pp.*
**Martindale, Don.** The Nature and Types of Sociological Theory. *292 pp.*
● **Maus, Heinz.** A Short History of Sociology. *234 pp.*
**Myrdal, Gunnar.** Value in Social Theory: *A Collection of Essays on Methodology. Edited by Paul Streeten. 332 pp.*
**Ogburn, William F.** and **Nimkoff, Meyer F.** A Handbook of Sociology. *Preface by Karl Mannheim. 656 pp. 46 figures. 35 tables.*
**Parsons, Talcott,** and **Smelser, Neil J.** Economy and Society: *A Study in the Integration of Economic and Social Theory. 362 pp.*
**Podgórecki, Adam.** Practical Social Sciences. *About 200 pp.*
**Raffel, S.** Matters of Fact. *A Sociological Inquiry. 152 pp.*
● **Rex, John.** (Ed.) Approaches to Sociology. *Contributions by Peter Abell,* Sociology and the Demystification of the Modern World. *282 pp.*
● **Rex, John** (Ed.) Approaches to Sociology. *Contributions by Peter Abell, Frank Bechhofer, Basil Bernstein, Ronald Fletcher, David Frisby, Miriam Glucksmann, Peter Lassman, Herminio Martins, John Rex, Roland Robertson, John Westergaard and Jock Young. 302 pp.*
**Rigby, A.** Alternative Realities. *352 pp.*
**Roche, M.** Phenomenology, Language and the Social Sciences. *374 pp.*
**Sahay, A.** Sociological Analysis. *220 pp.*

**Strasser, Hermann.** The Normative Structure of Sociology. *Conservative and Emancipatory Themes in Social Thought. About 340 pp.*
**Strong, P.** Ceremonial Order of the Clinic. *About 250 pp.*
**Urry, John.** Reference Groups and the Theory of Revolution. *244 pp.*
**Weinberg, E.** Development of Sociology in the Soviet Union. *173 pp.*

## FOREIGN CLASSICS OF SOCIOLOGY

● **Gerth, H. H.** and **Mills, C. Wright.** From Max Weber: *Essays in Sociology. 502 pp.*
● **Tönnies, Ferdinand.** Community and Association. *(Gemeinschaft and Gesellschaft.) Translated and Supplemented by Charles P. Loomis. Foreword by Pitirim A. Sorokin. 334 pp.*

## SOCIAL STRUCTURE

**Andreski, Stanislav.** Military Organization and Society. *Foreword by Professor A. R. Radcliffe-Brown. 226 pp. 1 folder.*
**Carlton, Eric.** Ideology and Social Order. *Foreword by Professor Philip Abrahams. About 320 pp.*
**Coontz, Sydney H.** Population Theories and the Economic Interpretation. *202 pp.*
**Coser, Lewis.** The Functions of Social Conflict. *204 pp.*
**Dickie-Clark, H. F.** Marginal Situation: *A Sociological Study of a Coloured Group. 240 pp. 11 tables.*
**Giner, S.** and **Archer, M. S.** (Eds.). Contemporary Europe. *Social Structures and Cultural Patterns. 336 pp.*
● **Glaser, Barney** and **Strauss, Anselm L.** Status Passage. *A Formal Theory. 212 pp.*
**Glass, D. V.** (Ed.) Social Mobility in Britain. *Contributions by J. Berent, T. Bottomore, R. C. Chambers, J. Floud, D. V. Glass, J. R. Hall, H. T. Himmelweit, R. K. Kelsall, F. M. Martin, C. A. Moser, R. Mukherjee, and W. Ziegel. 420 pp.*
**Kelsall, R. K.** Higher Civil Servants in Britain: *From 1870 to the Present Day. 268 pp. 31 tables.*
● **Lawton, Denis.** Social Class, Language and Education. *192 pp.*
**McLeish, John.** The Theory of Social Change: *Four Views Considered. 128 pp.*
● **Marsh, David C.** The Changing Social Structure of England and Wales, 1871-1961. *Revised edition. 288 pp.*
**Menzies, Ken.** Talcott Parsons and the Social Image of Man. *About 208 pp.*
● **Mouzelis, Nicos.** Organization and Bureaucracy. *An Analysis of Modern Theories. 240 pp.*
**Ossowski, Stanislaw.** Class Structure in the Social Consciousness. *210 pp.*
● **Podgórecki, Adam.** Law and Society. *302 pp.*
**Renner, Karl.** Institutions of Private Law and Their Social Functions. *Edited, with an Introduction and Notes, by O. Kahn-Freud. Translated by Agnes Schwarzschild. 316 pp.*

**Rex, J.** and **Tomlinson, S.** Colonial Immigrants in a British City. *A Class Analysis. 368 pp.*

**Smooha, S.** Israel: Pluralism and Conflict. *472 pp.*

**Wesolowski, W.** Class, Strata and Power. *Trans. and with Introduction by G. Kolankiewicz. 160 pp.*

**Zureik, E.** Palestinians in Israel. *A Study in Internal Colonialism. 264 pp.*

## SOCIOLOGY AND POLITICS

**Acton, T. A.** Gypsy Politics and Social Change. *316 pp.*

**Burton, F.** Politics of Legitimacy. *Struggles in a Belfast Community. 250 pp.*

**Etzioni-Halevy, E.** Political Manipulation and Administrative Power. *A Comparative Study. About 200 pp.*

● **Hechter, Michael.** Internal Colonialism. *The Celtic Fringe in British National Development, 1536–1966. 380 pp.*

**Kornhauser, William.** The Politics of Mass Society. *272 pp. 20 tables.*

**Korpi, W.** The Working Class in Welfare Capitalism. *Work, Unions and Politics in Sweden. 472 pp.*

**Kroes, R.** Soldiers and Students. *A Study of Right- and Left-wing Students. 174 pp.*

**Martin, Roderick.** Sociology of Power. *About 272 pp.*

**Myrdal, Gunnar.** The Political Element in the Development of Economic Theory. *Translated from the German by Paul Streeten. 282 pp.*

**Wong, S.-L.** Sociology and Socialism in Contemporary China. *160 pp.*

**Wootton, Graham.** Workers, Unions and the State. *188 pp.*

## CRIMINOLOGY

**Ancel, Marc.** Social Defence: *A Modern Approach to Criminal Problems. Foreword by Leon Radzinowicz. 240 pp.*

**Athens, L.** Violent Criminal Acts and Actors. *About 150 pp.*

**Cain, Maureen E.** Society and the Policeman's Role. *326 pp.*

**Cloward, Richard A.** and **Ohlin, Lloyd E.** Delinquency and Opportunity: *A Theory of Delinquent Gangs. 248 pp.*

**Downes, David M.** The Delinquent Solution. *A Study in Subcultural Theory. 296 pp.*

**Friedlander, Kate.** The Psycho-Analytical Approach to Juvenile Delinquency: *Theory, Case Studies, Treatment. 320 pp.*

**Gleuck, Sheldon** and **Eleanor.** Family Environment and Delinquency. *With the statistical assistance of Rose W. Kneznek. 340 pp.*

**Lopez-Rey, Manuel.** Crime. *An Analytical Appraisal. 288 pp.*

**Mannheim, Hermann.** Comparative Criminology: *a Text Book. Two volumes. 442 pp. and 380 pp.*

**Morris, Terence.** The Criminal Area: *A Study in Social Ecology. Foreword by Hermann Mannheim. 232 pp. 25 tables. 4 maps.*

**Podgorecki, A.** and **Łos, M.** Multidimensional Sociology. *About 380 pp.*

**Rock, Paul.** Making People Pay. *338 pp.*

● **Taylor, Ian, Walton, Paul,** and **Young, Jock.** The New Criminology. *For a Social Theory of Deviance. 325 pp.*

● **Taylor, Ian, Walton, Paul** and **Young, Jock.** (Eds) Critical Criminology. *268 pp.*

## SOCIAL PSYCHOLOGY

**Bagley, Christopher.** The Social Psychology of the Epileptic Child. *320 pp.*

**Brittan, Arthur.** Meanings and Situations. *224 pp.*

**Carroll, J.** Break-Out from the Crystal Palace. *200 pp.*

● **Fleming, C. M.** Adolescence: Its Social Psychology. *With an Introduction to recent findings from the fields of Anthropology, Physiology, Medicine, Psychometrics and Sociometry. 288 pp.*

●       The Social Psychology of Education: *An Introduction and Guide to Its Study. 136 pp.*

**Linton, Ralph.** The Cultural Background of Personality. *132 pp.*

● **Mayo, Elton.** The Social Problems of an Industrial Civilization. *With an Appendix on the Political Problem. 180 pp.*

**Ottaway, A. K. C.** Learning Through Group Experience. *176 pp.*

**Plummer, Ken.** Sexual Stigma. *An Interactionist Account. 254 pp.*

● **Rose, Arnold M.** (Ed.) Human Behaviour and Social Processes: *an Interactionist Approach. Contributions by Arnold M. Rose, Ralph H. Turner, Anselm Strauss, Everett C. Hughes, E. Franklin Frazier, Howard S. Becker et al. 696 pp.*

**Smelser, Neil J.** Theory of Collective Behaviour. *448 pp.*

**Stephenson, Geoffrey M.** The Development of Conscience. *128 pp.*

**Young, Kimball.** Handbook of Social Psychology. *658 pp. 16 figures. 10 tables.*

## SOCIOLOGY OF THE FAMILY

**Bell, Colin R.** Middle Class Families: *Social and Geographical Mobility. 224 pp.*

**Burton, Lindy.** Vulnerable Children. *272 pp.*

**Gavron, Hannah.** The Captive Wife: *Conflicts of Household Mothers. 190 pp.*

**George, Victor** and **Wilding, Paul.** Motherless Families. *248 pp.*

**Klein, Josephine.** Samples from English Cultures.
    1. Three Preliminary Studies and Aspects of Adult Life in England. *447 pp.*
    2. Child-Rearing Practices and Index. *247 pp.*

**Klein, Viola.** The Feminine Character. *History of an Ideology. 244 pp.*

**McWhinnie, Alexina M.** Adopted Children. *How They Grow Up. 304 pp.*

● **Morgan, D. H. J.** Social Theory and the Family. *About 320 pp.*

● **Myrdal, Alva** and **Klein, Viola.** Women's Two Roles: *Home and Work. 238 pp. 27 tables.*

**Parsons, Talcott** and **Bales, Robert F.** Family: Socialization and Interaction Process. *In collaboration with James Olds, Morris Zelditch
and Philip E. Slater. 456 pp. 50 figures and tables.*

## SOCIAL SERVICES

**Bastide, Roger.** The Sociology of Mental Disorder. *Translated from the
French by Jean McNeil. 260 pp.*

**Carlebach, Julius.** Caring For Children in Trouble. *266 pp.*

**George, Victor.** Foster Care. *Theory and Practice. 234 pp.*
Social Security: *Beveridge and After. 258 pp.*

**George, V.** and **Wilding, P.** Motherless Families. *248 pp.*

● **Goetschius, George W.** Working with Community Groups. *256 pp.*

**Goetschius, George W.** and **Tash, Joan.** Working with Unattached
Youth. *416 pp.*

**Heywood, Jean S.** Children in Care. *The Development of the Service for
the Deprived Child. Third revised edition. 284 pp.*

**King, Roy D., Ranes, Norma V.** and **Tizard, Jack.** Patterns of Residential Care. *356 pp.*

**Leigh, John.** Young People and Leisure. *256 pp.*

● **Mays, John.** (Ed.) Penelope Hall's Social Services of England and Wales.
*About 324 pp.*

**Morris, Mary.** Voluntary Work and the Welfare State. *300 pp.*

**Nokes, P. L.** The Professional Task in Welfare Practice. *152 pp.*

**Timms, Noel.** Psychiatric Social Work in Great Britain (1939-1962).
*280 pp.*

● Social Casework: *Principles and Practice. 256 pp.*

## SOCIOLOGY OF EDUCATION

**Banks, Olive.** Parity and Prestige in English Secondary Education: a
Study in Educational Sociology. *272 pp.*

● **Blyth, W. A. L.** English Primary Education. *A Sociological Description.*
2. Background. *168 pp.*

**Collier, K. G.** The Social Purposes of Education: *Personal and Social
Values in Education. 268 pp.*

**Evans, K. M.** Sociometry and Education. *158 pp.*

● **Ford, Julienne.** Social Class and the Comprehensive School. *192 pp.*

**Foster, P. J.** Education and Social Change in Ghana. *336 pp. 3 maps.*

**Fraser, W. R.** Education and Society in Modern France. *150 pp.*

**Grace, Gerald R.** Role Conflict and the Teacher. *150 pp.*

**Hans, Nicholas.** New Trends in Education in the Eighteenth Century.
*278 pp. 19 tables.*

● Comparative Education: *A Study of Educational Factors and Traditions. 360 pp.*

● **Hargreaves, David.** Interpersonal Relations and Education. *432 pp.*

● Social Relations in a Secondary School. *240 pp.*

School Organization and Pupil Involvement. *A Study of Secondary
Schools.*

● **Mannheim, Karl** and **Stewart, W.A.C.** An Introduction to the Sociology of Education. *206 pp.*

● **Musgrove, F.** Youth and the Social Order. *176 pp.*

● **Ottaway, A. K. C.** Education and Society: An Introduction to the Sociology of Education. *With an Introduction by W. O. Lester Smith. 212 pp.*

**Peers, Robert.** Adult Education: *A Comparative Study. Revised edition. 398 pp.*

**Stratta, Erica.** The Education of Borstal Boys. *A Study of their Educational Experiences prior to, and during, Borstal Training. 256 pp.*

● **Taylor, P. H., Reid, W. A.** and **Holley, B. J.** The English Sixth Form. *A Case Study in Curriculum Research. 198 pp.*

## SOCIOLOGY OF CULTURE

**Eppel, E. M.** and **M.** Adolescents and Morality: *A Study of some Moral Values and Dilemmas of Working Adolescents in the Context of a changing Climate of Opinion. Foreword by W. J. H. Sprott. 268 pp. 39 tables.*

● **Fromm, Erich.** The Fear of Freedom. *286 pp.*

● The Sane Society. *400 pp.*

**Johnson, L.** The Cultural Critics. *From Matthew Arnold to Raymond Williams. 233 pp.*

**Mannheim, Karl.** Essays on the Sociology of Culture. *Edited by Ernst Mannheim in co-operation with Paul Kecskemeti. Editorial Note by Adolph Lowe. 280 pp.*

**Zijderfeld, A. C.** On Clichés. *The Supersedure of Meaning by Function in Modernity. About 132 pp.*

## SOCIOLOGY OF RELIGION

**Argyle, Michael** and **Beit-Hallahmi, Benjamin.** The Social Psychology of Religion. *About 256 pp.*

**Glasner, Peter E.** The Sociology of Secularisation. *A Critique of a Concept. About 180 pp.*

**Hall, J. R.** The Ways Out. *Utopian Communal Groups in an Age of Babylon. 280 pp.*

**Ranson, S., Hinings, B.** and **Bryman, A.** Clergy, Ministers and Priests. *216 pp.*

**Stark, Werner.** The Sociology of Religion. *A Study of Christendom.*
Volume II. *Sectarian Religion. 368 pp.*
Volume III. *The Universal Church. 464 pp.*
Volume IV. *Types of Religious Man. 352 pp.*
Volume V. *Types of Religious Culture. 464 pp.*

**Turner, B. S.** Weber and Islam. *216 pp.*

**Watt, W. Montgomery.** Islam and the Integration of Society. *320 pp.*

## SOCIOLOGY OF ART AND LITERATURE

**Jarvie, Ian C.** Towards a Sociology of the Cinema. *A Comparative Essay on the Structure and Functioning of a Major Entertainment Industry.* *405 pp.*

**Rust, Frances S.** Dance in Society. *An Analysis of the Relationships between the Social Dance and Society in England from the Middle Ages to the Present Day. 256 pp. 8 pp. of plates.*

**Schücking, L. L.** The Sociology of Literary Taste. *112 pp.*

**Wolff, Janet.** Hermeneutic Philosophy and the Sociology of Art. *150 pp.*

## SOCIOLOGY OF KNOWLEDGE

**Diesing, P.** Patterns of Discovery in the Social Sciences. *262 pp.*

● **Douglas, J. D.** (Ed.) Understanding Everyday Life. *370 pp.*

**Glasner, B.** Essential Interactionism. *About 220 pp.*

● **Hamilton, P.** Knowledge and Social Structure. *174 pp.*

**Jarvie, I. C.** Concepts and Society. *232 pp.*

**Mannheim, Karl.** Essays on the Sociology of Knowledge. *Edited by Paul Kecskemeti. Editorial Note by Adolph Lowe. 353 pp.*

**Remmling, Gunter W.** The Sociology of Karl Mannheim. *With a Bibliographical Guide to the Sociology of Knowledge, Ideological Analysis, and Social Planning. 255 pp.*

**Remmling, Gunter W.** (Ed.) Towards the Sociology of Knowledge. *Origin and Development of a Sociological Thought Style. 463 pp.*

## URBAN SOCIOLOGY

**Aldridge, M.** The British New Towns. *A Programme Without a Policy. About 250 pp.*

**Ashworth, William.** The Genesis of Modern British Town Planning: *A Study in Economic and Social History of the Nineteenth and Twentieth Centuries. 288 pp.*

**Brittan, A.** The Privatised World. *196 pp.*

**Cullingworth, J. B.** Housing Needs and Planning Policy: *A Restatement of the Problems of Housing Need and 'Overspill' in England and Wales. 232 pp. 44 tables. 8 maps.*

**Dickinson, Robert E.** City and Region: *A Geographical Interpretation. 608 pp. 125 figures.*

The West European City: *A Geographical Interpretation. 600 pp. 129 maps. 29 plates.*

**Humphreys, Alexander J.** New Dubliners: *Urbanization and the Irish Family. Foreword by George C. Homans. 304 pp.*

**Jackson, Brian.** Working Class Community: *Some General Notions raised by a Series of Studies in Northern England. 192 pp.*

● **Mann, P. H.** An Approach to Urban Sociology. *240 pp.*

**Mellor, J. R.** Urban Sociology in an Urbanized Society. *326 pp.*

**Morris, R. N.** and **Mogey, J.** The Sociology of Housing. *Studies at Berinsfield. 232 pp. 4 pp. plates.*

**Rosser, C.** and **Harris, C.** The Family and Social Change. *A Study of Family and Kinship in a South Wales Town. 352 pp. 8 maps.*

● **Stacey, Margaret, Batsone, Eric, Bell, Colin** and **Thurcott, Anne.** Power, Persistence and Change. *A Second Study of Banbury. 196 pp.*

## RURAL SOCIOLOGY

**Mayer, Adrian C.** Peasants in the Pacific. *A Study of Fiji Indian Rural Society. 248 pp. 20 plates.*

**Williams, W. M.** The Sociology of an English Village: *Gosforth. 272 pp. 12 figures. 13 tables.*

## SOCIOLOGY OF INDUSTRY AND DISTRIBUTION

**Dunkerley, David.** The Foreman. *Aspects of Task and Structure. 192 pp.*

**Eldridge, J. E. T.** Industrial Disputes. *Essays in the Sociology of Industrial Relations. 288 pp.*

**Hollowell, Peter G.** The Lorry Driver. *272 pp.*

● **Oxaal, I., Barnett, T.** and **Booth, D.** (Eds) Beyond the Sociology of Development. *Economy and Society in Latin America and Africa. 295 pp.*

**Smelser, Neil J.** Social Change in the Industrial Revolution: *An Application of Theory to the Lancashire Cotton Industry, 1770–1840. 468 pp. 12 figures. 14 tables.*

**Watson, T. J.** The Personnel Managers. *A Study in the Sociology of Work and Employment. 262 pp.*

## ANTHROPOLOGY

**Brandel-Syrier, Mia.** Reeftown Elite. *A Study of Social Mobility in a Modern African Community on the Reef. 376 pp.*

**Dickie-Clark, H. F.** The Marginal Situation. *A Sociological Study of a Coloured Group. 236 pp.*

**Dube, S. C.** Indian Village. *Foreword by Morris Edward Opler. 276 pp. 4 plates.*

India's Changing Villages: *Human Factors in Community Development. 260 pp. 8 plates. 1 map.*

**Firth, Raymond.** Malay Fishermen. *Their Peasant Economy. 420 pp. 17 pp. plates.*

**Gulliver, P. H.** Social Control in an African Society: a Study of the Arusha, Agricultural Masai of Northern Tanganyika. *320 pp. 8 plates. 10 figures.*

Family Herds. *288 pp.*

**Jarvie, Ian C.** The Revolution in Anthropology. *268 pp.*

**Little, Kenneth L.** Mende of Sierra Leone. *308 pp. and folder.*

Negroes in Britain. *With a New Introduction and Contemporary Study by Leonard Bloom. 320 pp.*

**Madan, G. R.** Western Sociologists on Indian Society. *Marx, Spencer, Weber, Durkheim, Pareto. 384 pp.*

**Mayer, A. C.** Peasants in the Pacific. *A Study of Fiji Indian Rural Society. 248 pp.*

**Meer, Fatima.** Race and Suicide in South Africa. *325 pp.*

**Smith, Raymond T.** The Negro Family in British Guiana: *Family Structure and Social Status in the Villages. With a Foreword by Meyer Fortes. 314 pp. 8 plates. 1 figure. 4 maps.*

## SOCIOLOGY AND PHILOSOPHY

**Barnsley, John H.** The Social Reality of Ethics. *A Comparative Analysis of Moral Codes. 448 pp.*

**Diesing, Paul.** Patterns of Discovery in the Social Sciences. *362 pp.*

● **Douglas, Jack D.** (Ed.) Understanding Everyday Life. *Toward the Reconstruction of Sociological Knowledge. Contributions by Alan F. Blum, Aaron W. Cicourel, Norman K. Denzin, Jack D. Douglas, John Heeren, Peter McHugh, Peter K. Manning, Melvin Power, Matthew Speier, Roy Turner, D. Lawrence Wieder, Thomas P. Wilson and Don H. Zimmerman. 370 pp.*

**Gorman, Robert A.** The Dual Vision. *Alfred Schutz and the Myth of Phenomenological Social Science. About 300 pp.*

**Jarvie, Ian C.** Concepts and Society. *216 pp.*

**Kilminster, R.** Praxis and Method. *A Sociological Dialogue with Lukács, Gramsci and the early Frankfurt School. About 304 pp.*

● **Pelz, Werner.** The Scope of Understanding in Sociology. *Towards a More Radical Reorientation in the Social Humanistic Sciences. 283 pp.*

**Roche, Maurice.** Phenomenology, Language and the Social Sciences. *371 pp.*

**Sahay, Arun.** Sociological Analysis. *212 pp.*

**Slater, P.** Origin and Significance of the Frankfurt School. *A Marxist Perspective. About 192 pp.*

**Spurling, L.** Phenomenology and the Social World. *The Philosophy of Merleau-Ponty and its Relation to the Social Sciences. 222 pp.*

**Wilson, H. T.** The American Ideology. *Science, Technology and Organization as Modes of Rationality. 368 pp.*

# International Library of Anthropology

*General Editor* Adam Kuper

**Ahmed, A. S.** Millenium and Charisma Among Pathans. *A Critical Essay in Social Anthropology. 192 pp.*
  Pukhtun Economy and Society. *About 360 pp.*

**Brown, Paula.** The Chimbu. *A Study of Change in the New Guinea Highlands. 151 pp.*

**Foner, N.** Jamaica Farewell. *200 pp.*

**Gudeman, Stephen.** Relationships, Residence and the Individual. *A Rural Panamanian Community. 288 pp. 11 plates, 5 figures, 2 maps, 10 tables.*

The Demise of a Rural Economy. *From Subsistence to Capitalism in a Latin American Village. 160 pp.*

**Hamnett, Ian.** Chieftainship and Legitimacy. *An Anthropological Study of Executive Law in Lesotho. 163 pp.*

**Hanson, F. Allan.** Meaning in Culture. *127 pp.*

**Humphreys, S. C.** Anthropology and the Greeks. *288 pp.*

**Karp, I.** Fields of Change Among the Iteso of Kenya. *140 pp.*

**Lloyd, P. C.** Power and Independence. *Urban Africans' Perception of Social Inequality. 264 pp.*

**Parry, J. P.** Caste and Kinship in Kangra. *352 pp. Illustrated.*

**Pettigrew, Joyce.** Robber Noblemen. *A Study of the Political System of the Sikh Jats. 284 pp.*

**Street, Brian V.** The Savage in Literature. *Representations of 'Primitive' Society in English Fiction, 1858–1920. 207 pp.*

**Van Den Berghe, Pierre L.** Power and Privilege at an African University. *278 pp.*


# International Library of Social Policy

*General Editor* Kathleen Jones

**Bayley, M.** Mental Handicap and Community Care. *426 pp.*

**Bottoms, A. E.** and **McClean, J. D.** Defendants in the Criminal Process. *284 pp.*

**Butler, J. R.** Family Doctors and Public Policy. *208 pp.*

**Davies, Martin.** Prisoners of Society. *Attitudes and Aftercare. 204 pp.*

**Gittus, Elizabeth.** Flats, Families and the Under-Fives. *285 pp.*

**Holman, Robert.** Trading in Children. *A Study of Private Fostering. 355 pp.*

**Jeffs, A.** Young People and the Youth Service. *About 180 pp.*

**Jones, Howard,** and **Cornes, Paul.** Open Prisons. *288 pp.*

**Jones, Kathleen.** History of the Mental Health Service. *428 pp.*

**Jones, Kathleen,** with **Brown, John, Cunningham, W. J., Roberts, Julian** and **Williams, Peter.** Opening the Door. *A Study of New Policies for the Mentally Handicapped. 278 pp.*

**Karn, Valerie.** Retiring to the Seaside. *About 280 pp. 2 maps. Numerous tables.*

**King, R. D.** and **Elliot, K. W.** Albany: Birth of a Prison—End of an Era. *394 pp.*

**Thomas, J. E.** The English Prison Officer since 1850: *A Study in Conflict.*
*258 pp.*
**Walton, R. G.** Women in Social Work. *303 pp.*
● **Woodward, J.** To Do the Sick No Harm. *A Study of the British Voluntary Hospital System to 1875. 234 pp.*

# International Library of Welfare and Philosophy

*General Editors* Noel Timms and David Watson

● **McDermott, F. E.** (Ed.) Self-Determination in Social Work. *A Collection of Essays on Self-determination and Related Concepts by Philosophers and Social Work Theorists. Contributors: F. B. Biestek, S. Bernstein, A. Keith-Lucas, D. Sayer, H. H. Perelman, C. Whittington, R. F. Stalley, F. E. McDermott, I. Berlin, H. J. McCloskey, H. L. A. Hart, J. Wilson, A. I. Melden, S. I. Benn. 254 pp.*
● **Plant, Raymond.** Community and Ideology. *104 pp.*
**Ragg, Nicholas M.** People Not Cases. *A Philosophical Approach to Social Work. About 250 pp.*
● **Timms, Noel** and **Watson, David.** (Eds) Talking About Welfare. *Readings in Philosophy and Social Policy. Contributors: T. H. Marshall, R. B. Brandt, G. H. von Wright, K. Nielsen, M. Cranston, R. M. Titmuss, R. S. Downie, E. Telfer, D. Donnison, J. Benson, P. Leonard, A. Keith-Lucas, D. Walsh, I. T. Ramsey. 320 pp.*
● (Eds). Philosophy in Social Work. *250 pp.*
● **Weale, A.** Equality and Social Policy. *164 pp.*

# Primary Socialization, Language and Education

*General Editor* Basil Bernstein

**Adlam, Diana S.,** with the assistance of Geoffrey Turner and Lesley Lineker. Code in Context. *About 272 pp.*
**Bernstein, Basil.** Class, Codes and Control. *3 volumes.*
● 1. *Theoretical Studies Towards a Sociology of Language. 254 pp.*
2. *Applied Studies Towards a Sociology of Language. 377 pp.*
● 3. *Towards a Theory of Educational Transmission. 167 pp.*
**Brandis, W.** and **Bernstein, B.** Selection and Control. *176 pp.*

**Brandis, Walter** and **Henderson, Dorothy.** Social Class, Language and Communication. *288 pp.*

**Cook-Gumperz, Jenny.** Social Control and Socialization. *A Study of Class Differences in the Language of Maternal Control. 290 pp.*

● **Gahagan, D. M** and **G. A.** Talk Reform. *Exploration in Language for Infant School Children. 160 pp.*

**Hawkins, P. R.** Social Class, the Nominal Group and Verbal Strategies. *About 220 pp.*

**Robinson, W. P.** and **Rackstraw, Susan D. A.** A Question of Answers. *2 volumes. 192 pp. and 180 pp.*

**Turner, Geoffrey J.** and **Mohan, Bernard A.** A Linguistic Description and Computer Programme for Children's Speech. *208 pp.*

# Reports of the Institute of Community Studies

**Baker, J.** The Neighbourhood Advice Centre. A Community Project in Camden. *320 pp.*

● **Cartwright, Ann.** Patients and their Doctors. *A Study of General Practice. 304 pp.*

**Dench, Geoff.** Maltese in London. *A Case-study in the Erosion of Ethnic Consciousness. 302 pp.*

**Jackson, Brian** and **Marsden, Dennis.** Education and the Working Class: *Some General Themes raised by a Study of 88 Working-class Children in a Northern Industrial City. 268 pp. 2 folders.*

**Marris, Peter.** The Experience of Higher Education. *232 pp. 27 tables.*

● Loss and Change. *192 pp.*

**Marris, Peter** and **Rein, Martin.** Dilemmas of Social Reform. *Poverty and Community Action in the United States. 256 pp.*

**Marris, Peter** and **Somerset, Anthony.** African Businessmen. *A Study of Entrepreneurship and Development in Keyna. 256 pp.*

**Mills, Richard.** Young Outsiders: *a Study in Alternative Communities. 216 pp.*

**Runciman, W. G.** Relative Deprivation and Social Justice. *A Study of Attitudes to Social Inequality in Twentieth-Century England. 352 pp.*

**Willmott, Peter.** Adolescent Boys in East London. *230 pp.*

**Willmott, Peter** and **Young, Michael.** Family and Class in a London Suburb. *202 pp. 47 tables.*

**Young, Michael** and **McGeeney, Patrick.** Learning Begins at Home. *A Study of a Junior School and its Parents. 128 pp.*

**Young, Michael** and **Willmott, Peter.** Family and Kinship in East London. *Foreword by Richard M. Titmuss. 252 pp. 39 tables.*

The Symmetrical Family. *410 pp.*

# Reports of the Institute for Social Studies in Medical Care

**Cartwright, Ann, Hockey, Lisbeth** and **Anderson, John J.** Life Before Death. *310 pp.*

**Dunnell, Karen** and **Cartwright, Ann.** Medicine Takers, Prescribers and Hoarders. *190 pp.*

**Farrell, C.** My Mother Said. . . . *A Study of the Way Young People Learned About Sex and Birth Control. 200 pp.*

# Medicine, Illness and Society

*General Editor* W. M. Williams

**Hall, David J.** Social Relations & Innovation. *Changing the State of Play in Hospitals. 232 pp.*

**Hall, David J.,** and **Stacey, M.** (Eds) Beyond Separation. *234 pp.*

**Robinson, David.** The Process of Becoming Ill. *142 pp.*

**Stacey, Margaret** *et al.* Hospitals, Children and Their Families. *The Report of a Pilot Study. 202 pp.*

**Stimson G. V.** and **Webb, B.** Going to See the Doctor. *The Consultation Process in General Practice. 155 pp.*

# Monographs in Social Theory

*General Editor* Arthur Brittan

● **Barnes, B.** Scientific Knowledge and Sociological Theory. *192 pp.*

**Bauman, Zygmunt.** Culture as Praxis. *204 pp.*

● **Dixon, Keith.** Sociological Theory. *Pretence and Possibility. 142 pp.*

**Meltzer, B. N., Petras, J. W.** and **Reynolds, L. T.** Symbolic Interactionism. *Genesis, Varieties and Criticisms. 144 pp.*

● **Smith, Anthony D.** The Concept of Social Change. *A Critique of the Functionalist Theory of Social Change. 208 pp.*

# Routledge Social Science Journals

**The British Journal of Sociology.** *Editor – Angus Stewart; Associate Editor – Leslie Sklair. Vol. 1, No. 1 – March 1950 and Quarterly. Roy. 8vo. All back issues available. An international journal publishing original papers in the field of sociology and related areas.*

**Community Work.** *Edited by David Jones and Marjorie Mayo. 1973. Published annually.*

**Economy and Society.** *Vol. 1, No. 1. February 1972 and Quarterly. Metric Roy. 8vo. A journal for all social scientists covering sociology, philosophy, anthropology, economics and history. All back numbers available.*

**Ethnic and Racial Studies.** *Editor – John Stone. Vol. 1 – 1978. Published quarterly.*

**Religion. Journal of Religion and Religions.** *Chairman of Editorial Board, Ninian Smart. Vol. 1, No. 1, Spring 1971. A journal with an inter-disciplinary approach to the study of the phenomena of religion. All back numbers available.*

**Sociology of Health and Illness.** *A Journal of Medical Sociology. Editor – Alan Davies; Associate Editor – Ray Jobling. Vol. 1, Spring 1979. Published 3 times per annum.*

**Year Book of Social Policy in Britain, The.** *Edited by Kathleen Jones. 1971. Published annually.*

# Social and Psychological Aspects of Medical Practice

*Editor*   Trevor Silverstone

**Lader, Malcolm.** Psychophysiology of Mental Illness. *280 pp.*

● **Silverstone, Trevor** and **Turner, Paul.** Drug Treatment in Psychiatry. *Revised edition. 256 pp.*

**Whiteley, J. S.** and **Gordon, J.** Group Approaches in Psychiatry. *256 pp.*

Printed in Great Britain by
Lowe & Brydone Printers Limited, Thetford, Norfolk